THE
VICTORIAN SAGE

Studies in Argument

BY

JOHN HOLLOWAY

The Norton Library

W · W · NORTON & COMPANY · INC ·
NEW YORK

FIRST PUBLISHED IN THE NORTON LIBRARY 1965

Published simultaneously in Canada by
George J. McLeod Limited, Toronto

W. W. Norton & Company, Inc. is also the publisher of *The Norton Anthology of English Literature*, edited by M. H. Abrams, Robert M. Adams, David Daiches, E. Talbot Donaldson, George H. Ford, Samuel Holt Monk, and Hallett Smith; *The American Tradition in Literature*, edited by Sculley Bradley, Richmond Croom Beatty, and E. Hudson Long; *World Masterpieces*, edited by Maynard Mack, Kenneth Douglas, Howard E. Hugo, Bernard M. W. Knox, John C. McGalliard, P. M. Pasinetti, and René Wellek; *The Norton Reader*, edited by Arthur M. Eastman, Caesar R. Blake, Hubert M. English, Jr., Alan B. Howes, Robert T. Lenaghan, Leo F. McNamara, and James Rosier; and the NORTON CRITICAL EDITIONS, in hardcover and paperbound: authoritative texts, together with the leading critical interpretations, of major works of British, American, and Continental literature.

ISBN 0 393 00264 0

PRINTED IN THE UNITED STATES OF AMERICA

4 5 6 7 8 9 0

PREFACE

MY initial obligation is to the late Warden Sumner, of All Souls College, without whose interest and encouragement (which I valued very greatly) this book might not have been begun; and to the College itself, for accepting the book as a research project in 1948. I should also like to thank Mr. Rohan Butler and Mr. F. W. Bateson for reading and commenting upon parts of the manuscript, and Mr. A. L. Rowse and Mr. J. B. Bamborough for other help. I am indebted also to the Bodleian Library, the Cambridge University Library, the Aberdeen University Library, and particularly, for their special help to a new-comer, the National Library of Scotland. My chief debt in both the planning and preparation of the book is to my wife.

J. H.

CONTENTS

CHAPTER I

THE VICTORIAN SAGE: HIS MESSAGE AND METHODS

PERHAPS it is right to say at the outset that this introductory chapter is no formality, and the reader who wishes to understand the later chapters fully needs to read this one with some care. This is because the rest of the book discusses authors who were engaged in a quite distinctive activity, and a distinctive method is going to be used here in studying them. On both points some explanation is needed. Consider first what Carlyle, Newman, George Eliot and the rest were doing: all of them sought (among other things) to express notions about the world, man's situation in it, and how he should live. Their work reflects an outlook on life, an outlook which for most or perhaps all of them was partly philosophical and partly moral. It is true, of course, that giving expression to this outlook was by no means the only thing they attempted to do: Carlyle and Arnold had more specific social or political interests, Newman's chief concern was doctrinal or ecclesiastical, Disraeli and George Eliot and Hardy were novelists with many of the special and partly independent purposes of the novelist. Nearly all, moreover, had literary gifts which can largely be enjoyed and partly be appreciated without regard to their 'teaching'. These facts need to be recognized at once. But interest of a general or speculative kind in what the world is like, where man stands in it, and how he should live is perhaps the chief thing they have in common; and this is where the present enquiry starts.

All these writers belong to the middle or later part of the nineteenth century; and this is a period which appears now to have won a steadily increasing interest and sympathy. The fashion for thinking that in Victorian culture there was nothing of any value, nothing which does not warrant supercilious exposure, is happily passing. We are coming to see that for all their blindness and taboos, and for all their wildness and crudity too, the Victorians made a praiseworthy and fascinatingly interesting attempt to retain and reorganize and even deepen their culture, despite changes in knowledge, technique and society which really set them an impossibly difficult task. It was these changes that made one after another of the more gifted and thoughtful members of that society decide that traditional outlooks and the traditional *credos* were outmoded; that they must make a new start, come to terms afresh with fundamentals. Perhaps our increased respect for and interest in them today comes from a sense that their problems, both social and speculative, remain largely unsolved.

No one, of course, is suggesting that Victorian 'prophetic' literature is an all-sufficing treasury of forgotten wisdom. But by now we can see that the Victorian prophets deserve not embarrassed disregard but respect and thoughtful attention. For their own time they performed an activity which has an enduring place in human life: the activity, we might call it, of the sage. If we find them insufficient guides for the present time, that is as it should be. They are sufficiently remote for us not now to labour their errors and inconsistencies, but to set instead about an objective understanding of what they did. If any reader desires a miscellany of tit-bits from the author's own outlook, presented under the guise of a book about Victorian literature, he had better look elsewhere, and will easily find more than he wants. But these back-seat-driver homilies belong to the pre-history of criticism.

This book, then, aims, to begin with, simply at a fuller and realler understanding of what these authors wrote. But it also has a purpose not so much second to this understanding as the twin of it: for a further insight into their writings unavoidably brings with it fuller knowledge of what it really is to give expression to notions about the world, man's place in it, and how he should live; and conversely, before we can begin to get this fuller insight

in individual cases, we are virtually obliged to equip ourselves with some idea of what it is that any sage is doing,
and how he can hope to do it. The activity of the sage, a
distinctive activity, a unique use of words, presents difficulties and problems. That his earnestness and oracular pose
are (or recently were) unfashionable is unimportant. What
matters is rather that it is not altogether clear how these
prophetic utterances are legitimate in any way at all; and
the crucial thing is that seeing how they can be legitimate
leads to seeing what is trivial and what is central in the
sage's whole mode of utterance, and this is obviously an
essential first step in making real progress with Carlyle or
Arnold or any other sage in particular.

Perhaps this is most clearly seen if one disregards the
novelists, whose very inclusion in the book will need some
justification later, and thinks of Carlyle. One of the things
that most disturbs a modern reader of his work is constant
dogmatism. Through Carlyle's prose the nerve of proof —
in the readily understood and familiar sense of straightforward argument — simply cannot be traced; and the
succession of arbitrary and unproved assertions tends to
forfeit our attention. Yet this is only a subordinate
difficulty, because although proof is clearly missing, it is
by no means clear what would supply this lack, as it is by
no means clear what needs proof. The general principles
which would summarize Carlyle's 'system' are broad
sweeping gestures, hints thrown out, suggestions which
leave us quite uncertain about their detailed import. And
what is clearly true of his work is also true of the others:
there is a question always of what we are committed to in
agreeing, for example, with Newman that the universe is
one great system, with Carlyle that it is *not* a universe of
matter, with George Eliot that 'things hang together', or
with Hardy that 'neither Chance nor Purpose governs the
Universe, but Necessity'. What is true of their speculative
principles, moreover, is about equally true of their moral
ones. This point is totally unrelated to the claims of some
modern philosophers that assertions like these are 'metaphysical' or meaningless; it is a quite straightforward

point — a point that suggests itself to the general reader — that while these assertions mean a great deal, they are at the same time somehow indefinite or cryptic. Everything depends on their interpretation in detail; and they do not interpret themselves. Thus, though the sage may indeed provide us with real knowledge, there is a difficulty not only about its proof, but also — and a more central one — about its exact meaning.

But the sages themselves throw light here, and their own statements do something to resolve the difficulties. They all knew that what they had to offer was special in kind; and they take trouble to show how it is confirmed and given meaning in its own way, or how, to grasp it properly, the reader requires a special insight or sense. It is interesting to trace, at a rather earlier time, this pre-occupation with how a 'philosophy of life' is understood and confirmed in Coleridge's prose. 'I assume a something, the proof of which no man can *give* to another, yet every man can *find* for himself. If any man assert, that he *can* not find it, I am *bound* to disbelieve him! I cannot do otherwise without unsettling the very foundations of my own moral Nature.'[1] Coleridge might almost be called the founder in modern England of this kind of thought, and his influence on both Newman and Carlyle was very great. Carlyle takes this attitude further. He emphasizes that he has answers to ultimate questions; that his answers offer themselves to imagination rather than logic; that they are not recondite, for everyone can read them in his own heart, from 'a felt indubitable certainty of Experience'; [2] and finally that failure to do so is a kind of blindness and a kind of viciousness. This is how he brings home that what he calls 'Life-Philosophy' has its own mode of confirmation. He is aware, too, that a difficulty remains to be overcome about its meaning. 'To *know*; to get into the truth of anything, is ever a mystic act, — of which the best logics can but babble on the surface.'[3] Hence he constantly

---

[1] *Aids to Reflection* (Preliminary to the Aphorisms on Spiritual Religion, para. 7).

[2] *Sartor Resartus*, p. 133 (for editions of Carlyle, etc., see Appendix).

[3] *Heroes and Hero-Worship*, p. 47.

invites the reader to meditate humbly and carefully on some assertion that he admits is essentially simple. The kind of understanding that he has at heart is a kind which merely supervenes upon dutiful attentiveness.

Newman's discussion of this sort of knowledge was so full that it must be left until last. But the other writers in the list give a picture much like Carlyle's, though usually more sketchily. Disraeli often conveys a sense of the matter through the characters of his heroes: they are concerned about ultimate questions; they learn by a kind of trustful meditation that supplements reason with imagination; and the understanding to which they finally come is something concrete and particular, which abstract formulae cannot express. Utilitarian abstractions are his constant butt, and his remark, 'the fallacy of the great Utilitarian scheme consists in confounding wisdom with knowledge' [1] indicates just the distinction all these writers were trying to draw. Arnold says less than the others, but even he mentions the essential simplicity of the knowledge that matters to him, and how it is something which cannot be learnt off like an abstract formula, but must come gradually alive in our minds, through a right disposition chiefly. George Eliot says enough to show that her idea of what a 'solution' to 'life' was like, and how it could be known, closely followed Carlyle's. The contrast she draws between 'feeling the truth of a commonplace' and merely 'knowing' is worth a mention in passing. [2]

Perhaps Hardy's insistence that the more general meaning of what he wrote did not really stand or fall by logical consistency was self-defence, and not entirely relevant here. But an interesting passage in *The Return of the Native* shows him fully conscious that there is something special about the proof and the meaning of what Disraeli calls 'wisdom'. Shortly after Clym Yeobright's return in this novel to the village of his childhood, he and his mother argue about what is meant by 'doing well'. Clearly, this is just the sort of point upon which the sage, in his rôle as

---

[1] *Vindication of the English Constitution* (see *Whigs and Whiggism*, p. 146).
[2] *Middlemarch*, p. 307.

moralist, has something to say. Hardy writes that Clym found he could not prove his point by 'a logic that, even under favouring circumstances, is almost too coarse a vehicle for the subtlety of the argument'.[1] But he is able to convey a sense of his outlook by more intangible methods. Because Clym had inherited some of his view from his mother he 'could not fail to awaken a reciprocity in her through her feelings, if not by arguments'; [2] and later on Hardy supplements this: 'he had despaired of reaching her by argument, and it was almost a discovery to him that he could reach her by a magnetism which was as superior to words as words are to yells'.[3] The disparagement of logic as not subtle enough, the emphasis on feelings and on reawakening dormant understanding to a new life, the use of a word like 'magnetism', and the suggestion that this is proof of a higher kind, are all typical of the sage's notion of his own insights and how to communicate them.

These writers, then, thought along rather similar lines of a knowledge — a 'wisdom' — which had to be both acquired and confirmed in a distinctive manner. A fairly clear and comprehensive idea of it emerges from all their remarks taken together. But Newman almost spares us the trouble of constructing such an idea, because he wrote a whole book to discuss and identify it, and to distinguish it from its correlates. *The Grammar of Assent* systematically studies the various forms taken by conviction, and the various mental processes which may generate it; and it undertakes this survey for the ultimate purpose of establishing and justifying exactly that kind of knowledge with which we are concerned, and of which Newman saw religious belief as the crucial example. 'I do not want to be converted' — or to convert — 'by a smart syllogism: if I am asked to convert others by it, I say plainly that I do not care to overcome their reason without touching their hearts'.[4] Indeed, Newman believed that conversion by a smart syllogism was impossible as well as inappropriate. No merely logical arguments existed for the general

---

[1] *Op. cit.* pp. 207-8.   [2] *Ibid.* pp. 207-8.
[3] *Ibid.* p. 223.   [4] *Op. cit.* p. 425.

principles of religious or Christian doctrine. Instead, he thought, various arguments for limited truths accumulate one by one, until at last the enquirer simply finds his mind, under their legitimate influence, converging irresistibly on a whole philosophical or religious or moral outlook.

It is for this reason that, in *The Grammar of Assent*, Newman contrasts the credence given to a proposition in logic, science or mathematics, and to a proposition of practical concern in human life. To the former kind he gave the name 'notional assent': it is assent to a general, abstract proposition, lacking the indefinite richness of experience because somehow held away from it; but possessing, instead, a clear and definite minimum of meaning. 'Our notions of things are never simply commensurate with the things themselves; they are aspects of them, more or less exact, and sometimes a mistake *ab initio*.'[1] Assent like this does not give full and certain knowledge; it is too much and too deliberately restricted. It yields various degrees of belief, which Newman calls Profession, Credence, Opinion, Presumption or Speculation; and in all of them there is something of a mechanical acceptance, of a taking for granted. The mental activity which contrasts with these Newman calls Real Assent. This kind of Assent is directed towards assertions based on the whole trend of our experience; and because of this foundation, their meaning is too rich to be sharply limited, always liable to be unfolded further, and likely to vary from one person to another in exact content. It is a meaning which arises for the individual out of his own history, and exists for him in vivid particular images that bring his belief to life,[2] and naturally lead him in the end to some active and practical step like joining a church, for example.

Logical inference, in Newman's opinion, was quasi-mechanical calculating; it could not lead to Real Assent. 'Inference requires no apprehension of the things inferred . . . is necessarily concerned with surfaces and aspects . . .

---

[1] *Ibid.* p. 49.
[2] Cf. Carlyle, 'The Concrete, in which lies always the Perennial' (*Cromwell's Letters and Speeches*, ii, p. 228).

it does not reach as far as facts . . . it is employed upon formulas.'[1] Such inference gives birth only to abstractions. For real assent, the formal arguments of logic must be supplemented by something richer, more varied, more personal; something irreducible to any mechanism or pattern. Certainly we may begin, in our proof, with mechanical logic, 'but we are obliged to supplement it by the more subtle and elastic logic of thought; for forms by themselves prove nothing'.[2] No one can make argument in words give the grounds of Real Assent. 'The reasons of . . . conviction are too delicate, too intricate; nay, they are in part invisible; invisible, except to those who from circumstances have an intellectual perception of what does not appear to the many. They are personal to the individual.'[3] In particular, Newman believed this of the argument for Catholicism. It strikes only minds in a natural and healthy condition; and 'such minds it addresses both through the intellect and through the imagination; creating a certitude of its truth by arguments too various for enumeration, too personal and deep for words, too powerful and concurrent for refutation. Nor need reason come first and faith second (though this is the logical order), but *one and the same teaching is in different aspects both object and proof, and elicits one complex act both of inference and of assent.*' [4]

This last quotation is particularly important, because it shows how closely Newman related the sage's difficulty in expressing his insight with his difficulty in confirming it. In the end the two are one. Exposition, as it develops, actually becomes proof; and it is easy to see how naturally this may be said of a knowledge that is somehow both elusive and simple, that cannot even be formulated unless by a well-ordered and healthy mind, and that ultimately is known by a special sense, an intuition. All in all, this is a kind of thinking which at present seems steadily to be gaining interest and prestige — so much so, in fact, that modern admirers tend at times to exalt it indiscriminately,

---

[1] *The Grammar of Assent*, p. 90. [2] *Ibid*. p. 359.
[3] *Ibid*. p. 329. [4] *Ibid*. pp. 490-91 (my italics).

without considering whether (as with the narrower thinking of logic) there may be an invalid form of it as well as a valid.[1] 'The whole man moves' is Newman's well-known phrase; and he did not fail himself to notice that a whole man might sometimes move awry, though he gives this very little attention — to my mind, revealingly little. But hardly anyone has considered whether in this organic thinking, as it might be called, there can be fallacies as well as valid operations; and it cannot be considered until something else is done first. This is, to discover in detail what the methods are whereby the sage gives expression to his outlook; what techniques can really contribute something to this joint process of proof and exposition; exactly where, in his writing, we may trace what re-creates for the reader the sage's somehow esoteric insight. Here again may be seen the twin purposes of the present book. Empirically studying what sages have written, and finding where their strength has lain, will probably give much more and much truer information than any inventing of theory; but on the other hand it would be useful to form some preliminary idea of where to look, in writing of this kind, and what to look for, even if our chief interest is in some particular writer.

Three points seem to be helpful in attempting to sketch out this preliminary idea, this line of guidance. The first is that all of these authors insist on how acquiring wisdom is somehow an opening of the eyes, making us see in our experience what we failed to see before. This unanimity suggests that conviction comes here essentially from modifying the reader's perceptiveness, from stimulating him to notice something to which he was previously blind. This new perception, moreover, is usually allied to ordinary perception by the senses. It is not of some quite new reality; it is seeing old things in a new way. Wisdom in

[1] See, for example, G. H. Bantock, 'Newman and Education', *Cambridge Journal*, July 1951, especially pp. 664-6. Oddly enough, almost the opposite conclusion — that there is no real knowledge but scientific knowledge — was enunciated with about equal confidence in another Journal at the very same time. See A. Gerard, 'Coleridge, Keats, and the Modern Mind', *Essays in Criticism*, July 1951, pp. 259-60.

the sage's sense, that is, may not be wholly about experience, but it does find an adequate sanction in experience. The second of the three points is that when the outlooks of most of these sages appear in the bald epitomes of literary histories, they lose their last vestige of interest. They provoke only bored surprise that anyone could have insisted so eagerly on half-incomprehensible dogmas or trite commonplaces. This suggests that what gave their views life and meaning lay in the actual words of the original, in the sage's own use of language, not in what can survive summarizings of their 'content'. The third point is that to work by quickening the reader to a new capacity for experience is to work in the mode of the artist in words. Conrad's account of his own purpose is relevant here: 'before all, to make you *see*. That, and no more, and it is everything. If I succeed, you shall find there . . . all you demand — and, perhaps, also that glimpse of the truth for which you have forgotten to ask.' [1] Other ways of formulating what distinguishes the literary artist carry the same suggestion. He too is what he is by virtue of an appeal to imagination as well as intelligence, and by virtue of a wide and subtle control over the reader's whole experience. And this suggests in its turn that properly studying the work of these authors in their capacity as sages must — though perhaps to a varying degree — bring us near to their proper study as writers of literature.

The method used in this book arises from these points. To recapitulate for a moment, the sage has a special problem in expounding or in proving what he wants to say. He does not and probably cannot rely on logical and formal argument alone or even much at all. His main task is to quicken his reader's perceptiveness; and he does this by making a far wider appeal than the exclusively rational appeal. He draws upon resources cognate, at least, with those of the artist in words. He gives expression to his outlook imaginatively. What he has to say is not a matter just of 'content' or narrow paraphrasable meaning, but is transfused by the whole texture of his writing as it

[1] Preface to *The Nigger of the Narcissus* (Uniform Edition, p. x).

constitutes an experience for the reader. The lesson in method which these points convey is simple: and the chapters which follow examine how, in a series of particular cases, the parts of this texture contribute to the impression mediated by the whole.

A very important point is that we are not studying techniques of *persuasion*; not at least in one common sense of that phrase. Many (by no means all) of the techniques and methods comprising rhetoric, as it used to be called, did not relate specially to the conclusions they recommended. They increased the listener's or reader's credulity in a quite general way, and served one conclusion no better and no worse than they did others. But the methods traced here persuade because they clarify, and clarify because they are organic to a view presented not by one thread of logical argument alone, but by the whole weave of a book. Some of them used to be studied in the science of rhetoric, and some did not. Ideally, to marshal the details of the matter one must draw on what both the philosopher and the literary critic know about language; and to grasp the integration of these details in complete books one must have a critic's sense of how the parts of a book unite in what is not a logical unity. And just as good criticism never comes from working mechanically through a list of relevant factors (one knows the fatuity of that tag-criticism which reports successively on 'characterization', 'music', 'emotion', and the rest), so there is no closed list of what we shall need to give attention to here. The sage has no standard bag of tools, there is no recipe for mediating world views. Any detail of real life may seem to open our eyes and show us everything henceforth in a new light, and anything or everything in an imaginatively conceived prophetic book may bring home the living quality of the writer's insight.

Logical scrutiny of a writer's work means that we bring to it certain demands of consistency, rigour or completeness from outside, and judge it against an established standard. Here the method is the reverse, and comes much nearer to that of a critic, because the first step must be response,

response to what (despite all his faults) the sage is conveying by his whole work; and it is this work itself, not any preconceived theory, which must be left to suggest what elements contribute to the effect. Each writer, even each book, may require a quite fresh start; and nothing can determine whether it does or does not, except what scrutiny proves it to be like.

The next few paragraphs do not infringe this caution, although they put forward a few of the factors which have proved important in studying particular authors. They certainly do not outline a theory which the rest of the book merely applies. Their correct place would perhaps be at the end, because they briefly extract a few of the findings of the subsequent chapters; but it may help the reader to put them first so that they make a chart for the detailed discussions, and one can see beforehand how it is natural and to be expected that the various methods of exposition which the enquiry discovers, in fact can operate together. What follows here, then, is no more than a cursory survey for which the rest of the book contains the evidence.

One thing which this enquiry will make very clear indeed is that the novelist is every bit as well equipped as the discursive essayist to mediate a view of life. This hardly needs any proof, though the chapter on Carlyle's historical works will do something to show how a view of things which we already know from directly polemical books may be conveyed in a narrative form. But the importance of the novel in this field really follows directly from something mentioned above, that the prophet's sense of things is more readily expressed concretely and not abstractly. 'There is nothing like positive instances to illustrate general propositions of this kind and to make them believed', says Matthew Arnold.[1] The writings of Newman, Carlyle and Arnold himself abound with real or invented examples that illustrate and indeed largely replace general propositions. All that happens when we turn to the novel is that we find illustrative incidents in a story instead of illustrative examples in an argument.

[1] *Discourses in America* (*Works*, vol. iv, p. 298).

Indeed, novelists have here one advantage. A character may be an example of some general principle quite as easily as an incident. This suggestive use of character is used more or less elaborately by all the three novelists considered here, and also, most elaborately of all perhaps, by Carlyle in his history. Indeed, in this way it is so powerful a means of expression that both Carlyle and Arnold use it very often in prose argument, and so once or twice does Newman : they develop the personalities of real or imaginary people with much of the sustained care of a novelist. About both incident and character there is another important point. Essentially they are in no way small-scale or transient modes of expression, mere details of an author's work. There is only a difference of degree between a brief incident and the plot of a whole novel, or between a 'character' as a brief comprehensive description of someone, and as a personality developed throughout a book. And these larger effects are not to be found in the novels alone. Newman's *Apologia*, Carlyle's *Sartor Resartus* or *French Revolution*, Arnold's *Friendship's Garland*, are all polemical, but a personality or a situation (real or imagined) make them up entirely.

Incidents narrated in a book seem to have a good deal in common with something else which is prominent in the sage's means of expression : his use, for several different purposes, of figurative language. In George Eliot the point is brought sharply and unexpectedly home : exactly the same situation is described twice in her work, once at length as a major incident in a novel, once briefly as a simile in a moralizing comment. Whether simile or metaphor, figurative language plays a most significant part in books of the kind we are concerned with. That the figure or 'trope' is a half-covert but powerful form of argument has of course been known for a long time. Recent scholarship has stressed how it was a commonplace of critical and rhetorical theory in the time of Shakespeare ; and Coleridge, in a sense an intellectual parent of all these writers, stressed it explicitly too by contrasting metaphors and analogies. '*Analogies* are used in aid of *Conviction* :

Metaphors, as means of *illustration*.'[1]   It will be clear later
that this is only a simple first account of something quite
complex. Moreover, besides the help that metaphors and
the rest can give to argument — or to exposition — at the
very point of their appearance, they also operate more
generally. Addison says that 'a noble metaphor . . .
casts a kind of Glory round it, and darts a lustre through a
whole sentence'; [2] in fact, it may radiate other things than
lustre, and much more widely than this. Carlyle jots
down : 'Prodigious influence of metaphors ! Never saw
into it till lately.' [3] Above all, figurative language is largely
what sustains the outlook of a book through its entire
length, and throughout those parts of it which seem at a
glance to contribute nothing to the whole. It is therefore
especially important, for a piecemeal accumulation of
details is of very little value unless informed by some
larger sense of a single total impression, and it is towards
this, obviously, that anyone relying on language as something in which to create art must continually strive.

We must return for a moment to the significance which
a character can have in a novel. He may not simply be an
example, by his behaviour, of something that the author
believes to be either typical or valuable ; to think only of
this is too simple. Characters, because they can talk, can
be authorities, more or less good or bad, for the points of
view adopted or rejected by their creator ; and more than
this, they are not ventriloquist's mouthpieces only, but
people whom we get to know well and whose whole situation we are likely to live through sympathetically. They
make up the different and perhaps opposing forces of the
novel, and the author's viewpoint may emerge in its fullness
more through the tangle of their discussions and arguments
than from the unqualified pronouncements of characters
that are entirely 'good'. The novelists are not alone in
feeling the value of this mode of expression, and both
Carlyle and Arnold, in their polemical books, are elaborately
ingenious in inventing people to speak for or against them,

[1] *Aids to Reflection*, Aphorism 104, para. 5.
[2] *Spectator*, No. 421.   [3] *Two Notebooks*, p. 142.

or to argue with each other. What is particularly interesting is that, in Arnold at least, the part played by these fictitious authorities in some books is taken by real authorities in others. Genuine quotation in support of one's view, that is, and these methods of dramatizing it, have not a little in common.

These points, however, direct attention to something else. In proportion as the novelist relies on speaking through character and dialogue, he absents and effaces himself; and the same technique has the same effect in a polemical essay. Here, perhaps, the author can never quite disappear, but if the reader always retains some impression of him, it is an impression which can be modified very greatly by how much the writer depends upon direct assertion and how much on indirect (like using real or fictitious authorities), by many things which control what is best called the *tone* of his work, by the quality of his style, by the kind of argument that he most often or most willingly uses, and by whatever he may do directly to control the reader's notion of his personality. These also are factors which must be given attention if we are to see in full what conveys the sage's view of things; and they are important for another reason. They not only create an impression of the author, but in large part, and largely through this, they create the pervasive quality of the book. Once again, therefore, they are important, because they modify the experience of reading it, and it is on his book as an experience taking account of one's whole personality that the sage largely relies.

Arnold brings these points out in a comment on Emerson, who would certainly have been included among these writers had space allowed. 'Yes, truly his insight is admirable; his truth is precious. Yet the secret of his effect is not . . . in *these*; it is in his temper. It is in the hopeful, serene, beautiful temper wherewith these, in Emerson, are indissolubly joined; in which they work, and have their being.' [1]   It is interesting to find Arnold so stressing in another's writings what will prove central in

[1] *Discourses in America* (*Works*, vol. iv, p. 375).

his own; and in the same essay, writing this time of Newman, he clinches the point. It was, he says, the direct impact of Newman's presence and voice as he stood before one in the pulpit that made him irresistible; and part of the present enquiry will be to trace how writers like Newman (and Arnold too) can so bring themselves before the reader that he can hardly resist their arguments.

One other aspect of these writers' work has to be given a good deal of attention, and this is the way that some of them control the senses of the words they use. The theory of meaning has been expanded by now to formidable dimensions, but the importance of this control for the present enquiry can perhaps be put quite simply. 'He who wants to persuade', wrote Conrad, 'should put his trust not in the right argument, but in the right word'; [1] and controlling and modifying the senses of one's words is in part like a dexterous use of example in illustration, or even like inventing examples when no convenient ones exist. To state a generalization in one set of terms rather than another powerfully redirects the reader's attention; it is not at all unlike supplying him with a whole new range of fact — and this is sometimes in itself difficult enough. Other things, of course, are important too. Using verbal arguments instead of accumulating particulars of evidence profoundly changes the tone, and therefore the whole imaginative quality of the work and the reader's concept of the author. What distinguishes the sage, as we saw, in that he seems to have glimpsed something not conspicuous to the common eye. This is what he has in common with the mystic, and Arnold is revealing something of his own resources as sage when he writes 'nothing is so natural to the mystic as rich single words such as faith, light, love, to sum up and take for granted, without specially enumerating them, all good moral principles and habits'. [2] The rich single word is a mode of expression peculiarly apt for the distinctive task which the sage is attempting — as we saw, a task often of

[1] *A Personal Record*, p. 13 (Uniform Edition).
[2] *St. Paul and Protestantism* (*Works*, vol. ix, p. 33).

awakening or reawakening something, not of transmitting information. Verbal argument does not always mechanically bring with it the same effect: in Newman and Carlyle, for example, it has quite contrasting influences. But at least in these two writers its place cannot possibly be ignored; and there is something of it in George Eliot, who wrote 'we learn *words* by rote, but not their meanings; *that* must be paid for with our life-blood, and printed in the subtler fibres of our nerves'.[1] Here a link with what the sage typically says of his knowledge cannot be mistaken.

Clearly, when the senses of words are to a greater or lesser extent under the writer's control, two rather different things may happen: it becomes possible either to say what is true in a form which at first sight appears untrue, or what is important in a form which at first appears self-evident and trivial. Both these modes of assertion are prominent in Carlyle, and the second at least is quite prominent in Arnold. It is easy to see the attraction that they are likely to have for anyone attempting to perform the sage's task; for the important truth which the common eye has missed is exactly the kind of truth which the significant paradox or the thought-provoking truism seems to express. But there is a good deal to be learnt of how a sage is likely to prepare his reader for the paradox or the truism, what genuine work these modes of expression can do, and how their use may contribute in one way or another to the whole effect. In the end we may also discover something about paradoxes and truisms from the authors who rarely use them; for it is a likely guess that they must be getting the same result by some other means, and we may be able to distinguish what this is.

From these remarks one general point becomes very clear: the quotations above from authors studied later in the book show that often they were fully conscious of the means of expression which we have been surveying, and indeed were particularly interested in them. Sometimes their comments are remarkably acute, and several further examples of this will be mentioned later in the book.

[1] *The Lifted Veil* (see *Silas Marner*, etc., p. 290).

Yet all the same, the enquiry is concerned first of all not with the authors' conscious intentions, but with what they actually produced — whether they fully thought out how and where it would take effect on the reader or not. That is to say, this is an enquiry about the nature and organization of certain books, and only about their authors because it is about them.

Since this (I take it) is what is also true of ordinary criticism, when it is performing its essential function, something should perhaps be said of what this enquiry has to do with literary criticism of the more usual kind. As the argument proceeds, it will become more and more clear that the two are closely related : criticism is concerned with the methods and materials of an imaginative integration, and so is this enquiry. To be sure, its materials are not the familiar stock-in-trade of critics, exactly because the problem does lie in tracing how this distinctive kind of writing comes to possess a non-logical unity and compulsion like that of art in words. But understanding these things is necessary before they can be assessed critically, and their unfamiliarity betrays itself in the fact that when writing of the three novelists studied here, critics have tended to extrude their 'philosophy' from consideration, and that sometimes they have simply been unable to come to grips at all with Newman, Carlyle or Arnold. Their comments have often had that peripheral quality — praise for a purple patch or 'style', something about consistency, a telling thrust about how the author has betrayed his own psychology — which puts it beyond question that they have brought to one kind of artefact the questions that are proper for another. Since the very raw materials for understanding the synthesis of a work expressing a 'view of life' are still not fully familiar, though, the chief emphasis in this present book is on marshalling and understanding the evidence to which criticism of the sage's literary achievement must have regard, rather than on pronouncing in each case exactly how successful the final result appears to me to be.

But, from time to time, marshalling the evidence has

plainly suggested a judgement or conclusion; and this book may encourage readers to find new values in some of the authors it examines. It suggests, for example, that Carlyle's wild imagery and distorted meanings are less irresponsible than they seem at first reading; and it makes clearer, perhaps, the speed and integration of *The French Revolution*, and the organization as well as the comprehensiveness of *Frederick the Great* — which is unexpected enough, in all conscience. It does something to show how there is a gap between *Daniel Deronda* and George Eliot's other works, how Arnold's so-called 'complacency' is a figment of cursory reading, how little *Jude the Obscure* has in common with the novels with which Hardy classed it, how what is frivolous in Disraeli or bizarre in Hardy has a serious point, how Hardy's scheme of things has a massive consistency and a richness of detail often quite ignored. And in smaller matters it does something to show the exact kind of contribution which this or that detail may make, *if it is successful*, to the whole book. But the qualification stressed by these italics cannot be overstressed. Literary analysis in general, and the method of this book in particular, can show the kind of relevance that a detail may have, if it has any; but it can never really settle whether the handling of this detail succeeds or fails, and by how much. This is ultimately a matter for each reader's response (the responses of some readers proving of general interest, and of others not). The present analysis may considerably modify a reader's reactions to the works it examines, by helping him towards a more systematic and more comprehensive picture of what is being done in them. But its purpose is, within this particular field, to provide and elucidate the subject-matter for responses, not to control them.

In conclusion I had better say something of the arrangement of the book and of how various kinds of reader might best read it. None of the following chapters assumes any pre-existing knowledge of that 'something about language' which makes some people so enthusiastic, and others so bored; and the analyses avoid technical terms, and are relatively easy to follow by anyone likely to read this book anyhow. On the other hand the extreme subtlety of some of Newman's work, and the complexity (not to say riotous confusion) of some of Carlyle's, necessarily mean that Chapters I and V require fairly close reading; and those whose chief interest is in the least discursive kinds of literature may prefer to begin with Disraeli or Hardy, or Carlyle's historical writings. As for the novelists, the chapter on George Eliot sets out in an orderly way some of the recurrently important features in the work of the explicit sage-novelist; I have tried to avoid repeating this catalogue in discussing the other two novelists, and besides this the 'content' of Hardy's and Disraeli's outlook needed in part to be expounded straightforwardly, because surprisingly enough this seems not to have been done really fully before. The book is also written so as, I hope, to minimize a reader's disadvantage if he happens not to have read a particular work or to recall a particular part of it, and not maximize that disadvantage — something by no means unknown, though presumably never intended. Finally, it should be mentioned that this book makes no reference to the poetical works of any of the authors it studies, and also none to those of Newman's prose works which clearly belong to his Anglican period. Occasionally, too, isolated minor points have been left out, on the ground that quite enough minor points had been let in. Since these restrictions have been imposed for brevity's sake, I hope that the reader will see them in a kindly light.

A NOTE ON THE FOOTNOTES

In the chapters which follow, all references to the works of authors under immediate discussion are printed in a shortened form, consisting usually of the initial letters of the words of the title, followed by the page number. Full details of these abbreviations and of the editions referred to will be found in the Appendix.

CHAPTER II

CARLYLE

(i) 'Life-Philosophy' Knowledge

IN aim if not in method Carlyle is typical of the writers
studied in this book. He wants to state, and to clinch,
the basic tenets of a 'Life-Philosophy',[1] of something
that will veritably transform men's outlook. 'We shall
awaken; and find ourselves in a world greatly widened.'[2]
'Pray that your eyes be opened that you may see what is
before them! The whole world is built, as it were, on
Light and Glory.'[3] He is writing for 'these mean days
that have no sacred word';[4] he envies the preacher his
pulpit, and he does so because he feels that his own message
has an almost sacred quality.[5] 'What am I? What *is*
this unfathomable Thing I live in, which men name
Universe? What is Life; what is Death? What am I to
believe? What am I to do?'[6] Carlyle puts these questions into the mouth of the Young Mahomet; he means
to answer them himself.

Insight into 'the sacred mystery of the Universe'[7] is
not, in Carlyle's view, hard to get. It is the '"*open*
secret*"*, — open to all';[8] and it is open to all because
everyone has the conclusive evidence for it of introspec-
tion. 'Men at one time read it in their Bible. . . . And
if no man could now see it by any Bible, there is written
in the heart of every man an authentic copy of it direct

---

[1] SR. 51.   [2] CL. iii. 302.   [3] TN. 136.   [4] CL. iii. 316.
[5] 'What an advantage has the pulpit! . . . how infinitely harder when
you have . . . to create . . . the symbols and the mood of mind . . . nevertheless,
in all cases where man addresses man . . . there is a sacredness, could we
but find it.' TN. 215.
[6] HH. 45.   [7] *E.g.* HH. 67.   [8] HH. 67.

from Heaven itself: there, if he have learnt to decipher Heaven's writing . . . every born man may still find some copy of it.'[1] In his later books Carlyle tends to call this power of knowledge 'conscience';[2] in the earlier ones Goethe's influence is more prominent, and he discredits clear utterance, rigid argument, and 'mere logic'[3] instead. It is at this time that he writes 'not our Logical, Mensurative faculty, but our Imaginative one is King over us . . .'.[4] But to call this power of knowledge Imagination or Conscience is hardly important, so long as it is steadily contrasted with the knowledge that comes from strict logic and abstract argument.

But this account is an exaggeration. Insight did not come, in Carlyle's opinion, quite so easily. The secret, though 'open to all' was 'seen by almost none'. A man must be of 'loyal heart',[5] as he says; and even if he is, 'to *know*; to get into the truth of anything, is ever a mystic act',[6] bringing not any facile through-and-through comprehension, but an imperfect glimpse of some basic puzzling truth. 'Believe it thou must; understand it thou canst not.'[7] Moreover, there must be an initial leap. The effort precedes the insight. Knowledge of God comes from confident belief in him; and if we want to discover what our duties are, we must first actually set our hand to the duty which seems to be the nearest.[8] Whether we are willing to pay this price is no trivial matter. In the search for ultimate truth, the Imagination is one of only two things: 'Priest and Prophet to lead us heavenward; or Magician and Wizard to lead us hellward'.[9] But if it is allowed to operate correctly it will transform our lives, for the state of illumination, of truly understanding the fundamentals about man and the world, is to ordinary life as waking is to sleeping,[10] or open to closed eyes; and indeed, these contrasts are among Carlyle's favourites.

[1] LDP. 67.   [2] LDP. 119.
[3] HH. 51. Cf. PP. 137, 'opaque Practicality, with no logic utterance . . . has in him what transcends all logic-utterance'.
[4] SR. 150.   [5] *Portraits of John Knox*, 138.   [6] HH. 47.
[7] SR. 177.   [8] SR. 133.   [9] SR. 150.
[10] CL. iii. 356.

(ii) *The live Cosmos*

The philosophy of Carlyle is simple, and it hardly changes all through his life. It is a revolt; or rather, a counter-revolution. In a word, it is *anti-mechanism*. Its main tenets are:

(1) the universe is fundamentally not an inert automatism, but the expression or indeed incarnation of a cosmic spiritual life;

(2) every single thing in the universe manifests this life, or at least could do so;

(3) between the things that do and those that do not there is no intermediate position, but a gap that is infinite;

(4) the principle of cosmic life is progressively eliminating from the universe everything alien to it; and man's duty is to further this process, even at the cost of his own happiness.

Such is Carlyle's outlook in brief — regardless of the apparent inconsistencies latent in it at certain points. Its sources do not matter, except that one of them provided him with an invaluable means of expressing this outlook in a really vivid and telling way, expounding what he had to say and simultaneously making it convincing. The doctrine of self-renunciation may recall Carlyle's admiration for Goethe, and the belief that what the senses show of the world is not reality but only appearance recalls Fichte and the German Idealists; but judged as a whole, Carlyle's view of life is enormously indebted to Scottish Calvinism. The omnipotence and omnipresence of God, a universe governed everywhere by relentless necessity, a final division between elect and damned, renunciation of temporal pleasures, and the delusiveness (in a non-philosophical sense) of the shows of the world are Calvin's tenets; and of course they were largely accepted in the England of Carlyle's time, so far as this was nonconformist or evangelical, and have indeed some measure of affinity with Christianity of any and every kind. It was therefore a powerful weapon for Carlyle, to write in a language which

is influenced through and through by that of the Authorized Version.[1] This revived a whole world of associations
that were deeply rooted in his readers' minds. Even if
they had become dissatisfied (as Carlyle was himself)[2]
with orthodox Church Christianity, Biblical language
might still mean a great deal to them, and its use by Carlyle
could attach his outlook to an elaborately developed world
view with which his readers would be deeply familiar, and
for which they would probably have a deep though perhaps
a qualified sympathy. Actually, by using this Biblical
language and at the same time often sharply criticizing
conventional religion, Carlyle gets the best of both worlds.

The following extract from *Sartor Resartus*,[3] purporting
to be the opinions of the mythical Professor Teufelsdröckh,
is typical of Carlyle's wildest rhetoric. It will be seen that
the specific parallels given from the Authorized Version by
no means exhaust the echoes of Biblical style or thought :

There is in man a Higher than Love of Happiness : he can do without
'Behold, a greater than Solomon is here' (Matt. 12. 42)

Happiness, and instead thereof find Blessedness! Was it not
'thou shalt . . . find the knowledge of.God' (Prov. 2. 5)
'that we may . . . find grace' (Heb. 4. 16)

to preach-forth this same Higher that Sages and Martyrs, the Poet
'to preach   Jesus Christ' (Acts 5. 42)

and the Priest, in all times, have spoken and suffered;
'I will bless the Lord at all   'If I yet preach circumcision, why do
times' (Psa. 34. 1)   I yet suffer persecution ?' (Gal. 5. 11)

bearing testimony, through life and through death, of the Godlike
'bare record . . . of the testimony of Jesus' (Rev. 1. 2 ; cf. John 8. 17-18).

that is in Man, and how in the Godlike only has he Strength and
'he knew what was in man'   'in the Lord have I righteousness and
(John 2. 25)

Freedom? Which God-inspired Doctrine art thou also honoured to be
strength' (Isa. 45. 24)

---

[1] See PP. 7 : 'Can it be needful now . . . after eighteen centuries of
Christian preaching for one thing, to remind thee of such a fact'; and
LDP. 279 : 'I have to speak in crude language . . . and if thou find no truth
under this but the phantom of an extinct Hebrew one, I at present cannot
help it'.
[2] See SR. 157 : 'For the last three centuries, and especially the last three-
quarters of a century . . . Religion . . . has been smote at . . . needfully and
needlessly ; till now it is quite rent into shreds'.   [3] SR. 131.

taught; O Heavens! and broken with
'I am broken with their whorish heart' (Ezek. 6. 9)
                                 'in heaviness through

manifold merciful Afflictions, even till thou become contrite, and
manifold temptations (I Peter 1. 6)
'thy manifold mercies' (Neh. 9. 19) 'even until now' (Gen. 46. 34)
'his merciful kindness is great' (Psa. 117. 2)
'your manifold transgressions' (Amos 5. 12)

learn it! O, thank thy Destiny for these; thankfully bear what
yet remain: thou hadst need of them; the Self in thee needed to be
               'what things ye have need of' (Matt. 6. 8)

annihilated. By benignant fever-paroxysms is Life rooting out the
deep-seated chronic Disease, and triumphs over Death. On the
          'Death is swallowed up in victory' (I Cor. 15. 54)
                                (cf. Isa. 25. 8)

roaring billows of Time, thou art not engulfed, but borne aloft
       'the righteous runneth . . . and is set on high' (Prov. 18. 10)

into the azure of Eternity. Love not Pleasure; Love God. This is
     'Lovers of pleasures more than lovers of God'
                                  (II Tim. 3. 4)

the Everlasting Yea, wherein all contradiction is solved: wherein
whoso walks and works, it is well with him.
'whether they will walk   'when it shall be well with thee'
in my law' (Exod. 16. 4)   (Gen. 40. 14)
'whosoever doeth work therein' (Exod. 35. 2)
'ye shall . . . keep mine ordinances, to walk therein' (Lev. 18. 3)

    And again: small is it that thou canst trample the Earth with its
'Seemeth it a small thing unto   'the young lion and the dragon
you' (Ezek. 34. 18) (cf. Isa. 7. 13)   'lest they trample them under
injuries under thy feet, as old Greek Zeno trained thee: thou canst
shalt thou trample under feet' (Psa. 91. 13)
their feet' (Matt. 7. 6)
love the Earth while it injures thee, and even because it injures thee:
for this a Greater than Zeno was needed, and he too was sent.
'a greater than Solomon' (Matt. 12. 42) 'them which are sent' (Matt. 23. 37)
              'a messenger was sent' (Ezek. 23. 40)

Knowest thou that 'Worship of Sorrow'? The Temple thereof, founded
'Knowest thou not that I have a   'the foundation of the Lord's temple
power to crucify thee?' (John 19. 10)   was laid' (Hag. 2. 18)
        'A man of Sorrows' (Isa. 53. 3)

some eighteen centuries ago, now lies in ruins, overgrown with jungle,
the habitation of doleful creatures: nevertheless, venture forward;
'an habitation of dragons' (Isa. 34. 13)
'their houses . . . full of doleful creatures' (Isa. 13. 21)
in a low crypt, arched out of falling fragments, thou findest the

Altar still there, and its sacred Lamp perennially burning.
'the fire shall be ever burning upon the altar' (Lev. 6. 13)
'the salvation . . . as a lamp that burneth' (Isa. 62. 1)
'to cause the lamp to burn always' (Exod. 27. 20).

Readers of Goethe or of the German Romantic philosophers will notice other influences at work in this curious stylistic medley. But these are not relevant to the present issue, which is how the texture of Carlyle's writing very often draws unconsciously on the associations and on the whole cosmic outlook of the Bible; and in doing so, of course, it encourages belief in the first of the guiding principles mentioned above, that the universe is not a mechanism but expresses a principle of cosmic life.

But it is important to remember what this principle meant, and upon what part of that meaning Carlyle wanted to insist. The universe was not a mechanism, but it was still governed by law. 'I, too, must believe . . . that God . . . does indeed never change; that Nature . . . does move by the most unalterable rules.' [1] But they were rules of a distinctive kind, and Carlyle goes on, 'What are the Laws of Nature? To me perhaps the rising of one from the dead were no violation of these Laws, but a confirmation; were some far deeper Law, now first penetrated into, and by Spiritual Force, even as the rest have all been, brought to bear on us with its Material Force.' 'Even as the rest have all been'; this is the crucial phrase. Carlyle wrote for those all too ready, perhaps, to believe that the rules of Nature were unalterable; for him it was of more significance to show that these laws expressed a 'Spiritual Force'.

At the expense, it must be admitted, of leaving little or no impression of system, there is much in Carlyle's language to suggest this life in the universe. It is possible to distinguish three devices whereby he seeks this effect, and two of these can be discussed quite briefly. First, at the simplest level, is his style: a wild, passionate energy runs through it, disorderly and even chaotic, but leaving an indelible impression of life, force, vitality. The main

[1] SR. 173.

units of sense and still more of the phrases are brief; punctuation is heavy, expression marks are used in lavish profusion. On the other hand there is little of sustained or close-knit argument demanding concentrated, dispassionate study; the reader is hurried, as if by an all-pervading and irresistible violence, from one problem to another.

Second comes another device, which might be called the dramatization of discussions. Carlyle does not always speak in his own person; his discussion is enlivened by a variety of characters, most fictitious and some not, who interrupt the author, confirm his outlook, defend their own, contradict him, and illustrate the points of view that he wishes to commend or condemn. *Sartor Resartus* is entirely based on this technique: Carlyle merely introduces and comments on the manuscripts of a mythical German Professor Teufelsdröckh, who appears as the real author of the Clothes-Philosophy. Teufelsdröckh comes again in *Past and Present*, this time with 'Sauerteig' (of the Pig-Philosophy), and the 'Houndsditch Indicator'. The same device is employed in the Introduction to *Cromwell's Letters and Speeches*, where the second speaker, 'my impatient friend', is anonymous although clearly he is a mouthpiece for Carlyle;[1] and a variety of unidentified speakers, together with 'Sauerteig', 'Crabbe' of the 'Intermittent Reflector', the 'Department of Woods and Forests', 'John Bull', 'Ben Brace', 'Gathercoal' and the egregious M'Crowdy, all do something to diversify the pages of *Latter-Day Pamphlets*. This method tends to be naïve and crude, though not without effect. It seems to have grown on Carlyle until he used it for its own sake, but its intrinsic tendency to make the style more varied, violent, surprising, and forceful is indisputable, especially since Carlyle often employed his mythical personages to deliver the wildest passages of rhetoric.

[1] It might well be argued that the whole latter part of the book, where Carlyle prints speeches by Cromwell with constant interpolations by himself, employs the same technique, as Cromwell's words are utilized for general speculative and moralizing purposes. A modern reader is likely to find it vulgar.

The third feature is Carlyle's use of figurative language. It is probably the most influential of all. In different ways, figurative language operates through both its content and its organization. The importance of its content is easily seen. Time and again Carlyle's images are of some power or force or energy, disorderly perhaps, but passionate, violent, irrepressible. First, the image of fire runs like a bright thread through everything he wrote. Its contribution in this respect is self-evident. 'As I rode through the Schwarzwald, I said to myself: That little fire which glows starlike across the dark-growing moor, where the sooty smith bends over his anvil . . . is it a detached, separated speck, cut-off from the whole Universe? Thou fool, that smithy-fire was (primarily) kindled at the sun . . . it is a little . . . nervous centre, in the great vital system of Immensity'; [1] 'that fire-development of the Universal Spiritual Electricity . . . Love'; [2] 'the Great Man was always as lightning out of Heaven; the rest of men waited for him like fuel, and then they too would flame'; [3] 'the blessed glow of Labour . . . is it not as purifying fire?'; [4] 'that autograph Letter, it was once all luminous as a burning beacon, every word of it a live coal . . . it was once a piece of the general fire and light of Human Life'; [5] 'the age of Miracles had come back! "Behold the World-Phoenix, in fire-consummation and fire-creation."' [6] Fire — and light too — becomes almost the permanent context of Carlyle's argument, appearing in the least expected and most trivial places. In *Cromwell*, for example, he even speaks of 'editing' documents 'by fire', when he simply means destroying those that are useless. [7]

Two other kinds of image acquire this contextual function in varying degrees: those of moving water and of animal life. Sometimes these are fused with images of fire or light; 'the inner fountains of life may again begin, like eternal Light-fountains'; [8] 'this Planet, I find, is but an inconsiderable sand-grain in the continents of Being . . .

---

[1] SR. 49.   [2] SR. 93.   [3] HH. 63.   [4] PP. 166.   [5] CL. i. 68.
[6] FR. i. 185.   Cf. SR. 165, 'the World-Phoenix is burning herself . . . so slowly'.
[7] *E.g.* CL. i. 113 and iii. 173.   [8] PP. 20.

that eternal Light-Sea and Flame-Sea'.[1] But images of
water are frequent alone: 'the roaring Billows of Time'; [2]
'a life-purpose . . . like an ever-deepening river . . . it runs
and flows'; [3] 'the undiscovered Sea of Time'; [4] 'the
Scotch people . . . look into a sea of troubles, shoreless,
starless, on which there seems no navigation possible'.[5]
The different uses to which Carlyle puts the images of
stream and *ocean* are not relevant at present; both suggest
a world that is all power and life, whether clear and purpose-
ful like a stream, or turbulent and confused like a stormy
sea.

Perhaps Carlyle's animal imagery also contributes
something, by its astonishing frequency and variety. His
work is a veritable verbal menagerie: within a mere sixty
pages of *Latter-Day Pamphlets*, for example,[6] the ape,
wolf, ox, dog, pig, ass, hyena, dragon, serpent, sparrow,
python, buzzard, eagle, owl, mouse, horse, mole, rat,
beaver, spider, wren and canary all make their appearance
in metaphorical uses, many of them several times over.[7]
Elsewhere, there are Kilkenny cats, beetles, lions, crows,
bees, beagles, boa-constrictors, ostriches, cormorants,
camels, lynxes, krakens, hydras, centaurs, chimeras, megatherions, and a multitude of anonymous monsters. The
ass chews a thistle, the boa-constrictor wrestles with the
lion, the Kilkenny cats are at their legendary occupation,
the owl screeches, the apes gibber and chatter. Whether
his images enlighten us about the good things in the world
or the bad, this effect is equally present: everything seems
busy with a restless, overwhelming life.[8]

The impression is accentuated: images that do not
suggest life and energy by themselves can do so through
their sequence. This is conspicuous in the chapter on

[1] PP. 190.   [2] SR. 131.   [3] PP. 167.
[4] LDP. 15.   [5] CL. ii. 81.   [6] PP. 49-105.
[7] The list does not include 'red-herring', which has associations in the
context with the fish when dead, nor 'fox' and 'partridge' which occur
several times but in a literal use — though this is not without its contribution.
[8] Cf. PP. 148, where the unfortunate English nation is likened to a bird
with nowhere to land 'hovering on the wing'; 'dolefully shrieking'; and
'burying itself . . . in the waste unfirmamented seas'.

'Natural Supernaturalism' of *Sartor Resartus*.[1] Here Carlyle's purpose is exactly that now under discussion — to convince his readers that the universe pulsates with life. We are dealing here with a mixture, in fact, of metaphors or comparisons, and simple vivid images : but what they contribute to the book lies partly in what supervenes upon them because they all come so close together. It is their extraordinary sequence which hurries the reader first to the day on which the world was created, then to 'Sirius and the Pleiades', then under the sea, then to the planets in their courses, then from the laws of Nature as 'celestial hieroglyphics' to the laws of Nature as an 'inexhaustible Domestic-Cookery Book', then to the inside of the human body, then to the surface of the earth, the 'habitable flowery Earth-rind', then back to the Creation and forward to the Cataclysm, then to 'stretch forth my hand and clutch the Sun', then down into Hell, at least by implication ('Orpheus' and 'a huge Troglodyte Chasm') and up to Heaven, and at last (should we have retained breath enough to follow so far) 'like some wild-flaming, wild-thundering train of Heaven's Artillery, does this mysterious MANKIND thunder and flame, in long-drawn, quick-succeeding grandeur, through the unknown Deep . . . like a God-created, fire-breathing Spirit-host, we emerge from the Inane; haste stormfully across the astonished Earth; then plunge again into the Inane. Earth's mountains are levelled, and her seas filled up, in our passage.'[2] That seems almost to happen in this passage too. It is the astonished reader who is made to hasten stormfully throughout the Cosmos, and by a well-known process of association to transfer the violence of his journey to the Cosmos through which in imagination he journeys.

(iii) *The Ocean rolling round the Islet*

So much for how Carlyle gives expression to the first principle, that the world is filled with cosmic life. The second was that this spiritual life might be manifested by

---

[1] Book III, chapter 8.   [2] SR. 180.

everything in the universe, however apparently humble it may be. Vivifying this doctrine was a very important part of Carlyle's purpose. Ultimately, like every other writer of his kind, he wants to make the reader see familiar things in a new way, to dwell on and emphasize aspects of them that were overlooked or neglected before. Things are more than the casual eye takes in: the lowest resembles and indeed is in continuity with the highest. Explicit statements of the view are frequent enough in Carlyle. But hints and reminders and particular illustrations pervade his work like an atmosphere, and Carlyle thereby achieves a twin purpose: he spreads the character of those things agreed to be noble or exalted to everything in the universe, and thus he emphatically reinforces our impression that this universe is a giant system moving according to a single pattern.

It is fanciful, perhaps, but not unilluminating, to compare this technique with the form of a *passacaglia* in music. Sooner or later one hears the theme unadorned; but in various modified forms it runs without interruption, the unadorned version audible below. Carlyle approximates to the plain statement in, for example, the words he gives King William Rufus in an attack upon the rigidities of medieval Catholicism: 'Behold . . . the world is *wider* than any of us think . . . there are . . . immeasurable Sacrednesses in this that you call . . . Secularity'.[1] The variations are numerous: 'Sooty Manchester, — it too is built on the infinite Abysses; overspanned by the skyey Firmaments . . . every whit as wonderful . . . as the oldest Salem or Prophetic City'.[2] 'The Present Time, youngest-born of Eternity, child and heir of all the Past Times with their good and evil.' [3] In these the intention and the effect are clear. Greater interest attaches to passages which at first sight seem like nothing more than idyllic descriptive interludes. For example, from *Cromwell's Letters and Speeches*, 'Oliver farmed part or whole of these . . . lands

---

[1] PP. 209; cf. TN.; 'the whole world is built, as it were, on Light and Glory' (quoted on p. 21 above).
[2] PP. 192.   [3] LDP. 3.

. . . past which the river Ouse slumberously rolls . . . his
cattle grazed here, his ploughs tilled here' — so far the
passage is plain description; but Carlyle continues 'the
heavenly skies and infernal abysses overarched and under-
arched him here'; [1] or from the description of the monas-
tery of Edmundsbury in *Past and Present*: 'These old
St. Edmundsbury walls . . . For twenty generations . . .
bells tolled to prayers; and men, of many humours, various
thoughts, chanted vespers, matins; — and round the little
islet of their life rolled for ever (as round ours still rolls,
though we are blind and deaf) the illimitable Ocean,
tinting all things with *its* eternal hues and reflexes'.[2]

Often, in Carlyle, the lightest touches remind the reader
that the world is wider than it seems. For example, he is
fond of imagery of green landscapes; and it does not come
without its influence. 'The green foliage and blossoming
fruit-trees of Today . . . the leafy blossoming Present
Time'; [3] 'Man's life . . . no idle promenade through
fragrant orange-groves and green flowery spaces'; [4] 'Work
is Worship . . . *its* Cathedral . . . coped with the star-
galaxies; paved with the green mosaic of land and ocean'; [5]
'Chaos is dark . . . let light be, and there is instead a green
and flowery world'; [6] 'Wisdom . . . rests there, as on its
dark foundations does a habitable flowery Earth-rind.'[7]
Thus a thought of the whole earth and of all the living
things that spread over it is worked more intimately still
into the texture of the argument. Ultimately, these
passages set every immediate and restricted topic in a
wider context, in the context of the whole earth, or indeed
the whole universe; and they modify the reader's attitude
until he tends to think of any small thing as like the grandest
and most beautiful and most alive things he knows, and
as influenced by them through a direct and genuine
continuity. Carlyle's argument is a foreground that is
developed against a background; and by sustaining an
ever-present sense that this background is grand and awe-
inspiring, he is able, without explicit reference, to diffuse

[1] CL. i. 79.   [2] PP. 41.   [3] CL. i. 8.
[4] PP. 245.   [5] PP. 196.   [6] PP. 250.   [7] SR. 176.

our attitude towards it until we have the same attitude
towards his immediate subject.

Carlyle's intention in this respect is most clearly seen
in his use of the word 'miracle'. He wishes to say that
every existing thing is miraculous; this indeed is almost
his central tenet. 'Daily life is girt with Wonder, and
based on Wonder, and thy very blankets and breeches are
Miracles.'[1] What we have been exploring is a device
which makes us see things under the influence of those
other more portentous things that they are girt with.

(iv) *Shams and Diabolisms*

Between the second and the third of Carlyle's central
tenets there is perhaps a latent contradiction, for the
second explains how everything reflects the cosmic life,
and the third how some things in the universe most
emphatically lack it. Our problem, however, is not
whether he solves this contradiction in logical terms, but
how the two parts of it are developed and amplified and
made emotionally convincing. And certainly, in pursuing
this problem, we discover two contrasting techniques:
for the second tenet was conveyed to the reader by devices
that hinted at unsuspected affinities, while the third is
constantly reinforced through expressions which crystallize a single, pervasive, fundamental dichotomy in the
world.

Consider first the plain statement of this dichotomy,
and then the indirect devices that keep the reader attuned
to it. Carlyle praises Dante, for example, because he 'felt
Good and Evil to be the two polar elements of this Creation,
on which it all turns; that these two differ not by *prefer-
ability* of one to the other, but by incompatibility absolute
and infinite; that the one is excellent and high as light and
Heaven, the other hideous, black as Gehenna and the Pit
of Hell'.[2] Absolute contrasts of this kind attract Carlyle:

---

[1] SR. 183. Cf. TN. 151, 'What is a Miracle? Can there be a thing
more miraculous than any other thing?'

[2] HH. 80; cf. HH. 165; 'Nature . . . if not divine, then diabolic'.

Revenge is a divine feeling, *but its excess is diabolic*; [1] historical periods differ not merely greatly, *but infinitely*.[2] All good, and all bad things are assimilated: 'at bottom the Great Man, as he comes from the hand of Nature, is ever the same kind of thing',[3] while 'independence, in all kinds, is rebellion',[4] and untruths are all the Devil's.[5]

This contrast runs sharply through Carlyle's work, because the vocabulary he uses for comment and evaluation tends always to draw upon it. The first quotation from *Heroes and Hero-Worship* above did so by comparing the good to Heaven and Light, the bad to Hell and darkness. The other quotations illustrate Carlyle's use of the contrast between what is divine and what is diabolic, but the contrast between light and dark is perhaps more prominent still. Cromwell's work was for 'the Protestant world of struggling light against the Papist world of potent darkness'.[6] Elsewhere, Cromwell is as a 'luminous body . . . crossing a dark Country, a dark Century'; [7] and — a hint of the same — the intellect of the Younger Vane is 'atrabiliar'.[8] Carlyle rings many changes, but the guiding principle is simply that there are contrasting extremes and nothing whatever between them. Occasionally he cannot avoid speaking of something good but imperfect; even so he retains the contrast as sharply as he can by employing the usual metaphor in a modified way: perfect religion is like light, imperfect religion (at least in some cases) like 'red smoky scorching fire'. It can be purified into light, and 'Is not Light grander than Fire? It is *the same element* in a state of purity.'[9] Thus it is that Carlyle manages to say something of intermediates within a vocabulary that draws the advantages of precluding them.

But the contrast is equally fundamental if made between *true* light and *false* or factitious light. The contrast between the 'true' and the 'sham' in Carlyle is worked out for light in expressions like 'a poor paper-lantern with

[1] LDP. 68.   [2] CL. i. 73.   [3] HH. 35.
[4] SR. 158.   [5] JS. 82.   [6] CL. iii. 65-6.
[7] CL. ii. 194.   [8] CL. ii. 228.
[9] PP. 203 (my italics); cf. PP. 166, where 'the blessed glow of labour' (operating presumably one stage below) transmutes 'smoke' into 'flame'.

a candle-end in it',[1] and in the attack on those who believe
that 'Heroism means gas-lighted Histrionism; that seen
with "clear eyes" (as they call Valet-eyes), no man is a
Hero'.[2] This quotation introduces two new methods
employed by Carlyle to emphasize his basic contrast.
The 'seeing eye' is a frequent alternative for light: 'Thor
red-bearded, with his blue sun-eyes',[3] and then the contrast
is made, for example, in passages like this about Mirabeau:
'he has an *eye*, he is a reality; while others are formulas
and eye-*glasses*'[4] (alternatives elsewhere to the eye-glass
are glass-eyes[5] and spectacles[6]). In view of this, the
expressions above, 'gas-lighted Histrionism' and 'Valet-
eyes', are exactly comparable in Carlyle's vocabulary, and
they introduce, as two further illustrations of the ultimate
contrast, the contrast of real life with acting, and that of
master with servant. The first takes many different
forms: 'Well may the buckram masks start together,
terror-struck . . . let whosoever is but buckram and a
phantasm look to it';[7] 'considering the Treaty mainly
as a piece of Dramaturgy, which must . . . leave a good
impression on the Public'.[8] The contrast between master
and servant is conspicuous in Carlyle's frequent tirades
against flunkies and valets and 'Valetism, the *reverse* of
Heroism';[9] 'England will . . . learn to reverence its
Heroes and distinguish them from its Sham-heroes and
Valets and gas-lighted Histrios'.[10]

Another slash at actors introduces a fresh contrast.
Government, says Carlyle, in *Latter-Day Pamphlets*, is
'really a heroic work, and cannot be done by histrios, and

[1] CL. i. 359. Cf. PP. 198, 'paper-lanterns and tumultuous brayings',
and SR. 48, 'the hand-lamp of . . . Attorney-logic'.
[2] PP. 125.
[3] PP. 232. Cf. PP. 42. 'Readers who please to go along with us . . .
shall wander . . . as in wintry twilight . . . but . . . some real human figure
is seen moving . . . and we look into a pair of eyes deep as our own, *imaging*
our own, but all unconscious of us.'
[4] FR. i. 189.   [5] LDP. 95.
[6] CL. iii. 260. Cf. PP. 205, the Methodist minister 'droning through
his old nose-spectacles', and LDP. 86, 'your appointed workers have been
reduced to work as moles; and it is one vast boring and counter-boring, on
the part of eyeless persons'.
[7] FR. i. 181.   [8] CL. i. 333.   [9] PP. 125.   [10] PP. 186.

dexterous talkers having the honour to be'; [1] and many times the contrast of good with bad is likened to that of deed with mere word. 'Not a better Talking-Apparatus . . . but an infinitely better Acting-Apparatus' [2] (that is, Doing-Apparatus) is wanted. This explains the innumerable attacks on 'cant' and 'jargon'; and the tirades against quacks too, for a quack is one who talks of his healing powers but cannot do anything — this is brought out in the words 'Sir Jabesh Windbag . . . or what other Cagliostro'.[3] The attacks on 'dilettantes' serve the same purpose — 'unserious Dilettantism . . . grinning with inarticulate incredulous incredible jargon about all things'.[4]

The next comparison represents good by the human, and bad by the animal. The type appears in the 'dusky potent insatiable animalism' [5] of a 'Chartist Notability' (the word 'dusky' hints, of course, at the analogy with darkness). It is best illustrated in the analogy between cynics and 'Apes . . . *gibbering and chattering* very genuine nonsense . . . they sit . . . with their wizened *smoke*-dried visages . . . looking out through those *blinking smoke-bleared eyes* of theirs, into the wonderfulest universal *smoky Twilight* and undecipherable disordered Dusk of Things'.[6] In this passage of intricate rhetoric, the cynic is belittled first by the analogy with the sub-human, and then through the hints of idle chatter, smoke, defective eyes, and darkness. All these metaphors have their established and characteristic function in Carlyle, and here their fusion and interaction is plain.

(v) *The Growth of Metaphor*

Figurative language in Carlyle is so elaborate that a question arises which is really prior to that of its use; for his work displays not merely its use, but its creation. The valet, the eye-glass, the smoke, the buckram mask — these

---

[1] LDP. 82.   [2] LDP. 81-2.   [3] PP. 188.
[4] PP. 143.   [5] LDP. 47.
[6] PP. 129 (my italics). The dog, the beaver ('beaver-sciences') and above all the fox (the 'vulpine intellect') are other metaphors within this range.

metaphors are scarcely intelligible unless sooner or later they are 'cashed', and their significance explained. They are 'technical-term' metaphors, effective through other metaphors used prior to them and effective of themselves. But once a connection is made between metaphors that need an introduction and those that need none, the former can vary and amplify the latter. Carlyle uses this method elaborately. He develops a figurative language that becomes more and more esoteric; and the developments do not occur in isolation, but interconnect and sometimes fuse.

Since, of necessity, this has already been a good deal illustrated, it will be enough here to give two examples which display the whole process of image-creation. Consider first how the metaphor of darkness is elaborated. Carlyle asserts that the surviving materials for a life of Cromwell are the 'dreariest continent of shot-rubbish the eye ever saw . . . in *lurid twilight* . . . peopled only by *somnabulant* Pedants . . . and doleful creatures . . . by *Nightmares*, pasteboard Norroys, griffins, wiverns and chimeras dire'.[1] The sleep-metaphor, as an adjunct to darkness, reappears: 'Such darkness, thick sluggish clouds of cowardice . . . thickening as if towards the eternal sleep'.[2] What of the griffins and wiverns? They echo another extension of the darkness-metaphor, to be seen in the 'thousand-fold wrestle with pythons and mud-demons . . . enormous Megatherions, as were ever born of mud, loom huge and hideous out of the twilight Future' of *Latter-Day Pamphlets*.[3] In this work the same figure is plentiful: 'British industrial existence . . . one huge poison-swamp of reeking pestilence . . . communicating with the Nether Deeps . . . that putrefying well of abominations . . . the universal Stygian quagmire of British industrial life'.[4] These passages, besides utilizing the idea that darkness gives rise to monsters, also fuse the metaphor of darkness with that of the swamp, contrast to the fresh flowing stream of healthy life. Later in the same work comes 'a dim

---

[1] CL. i. 5 (my italics). [2] JS. 82.
[3] LDP. 19. [4] LDP. 24.

horn-eyed owl-population'.[1]   The owl, with these same
associations, appears often enough: 'a too miserable
screech-owl phantasm of talk and struggle'[2] (here 'screech-
owl' is reminiscent of 'darkness' and also 'jargon'); 'the
human Owl, living in his perennial London fog, in his
Twilight of all imaginable corrupt exhalations'.[3]   Already,
in an earlier passage, we have been given a hint as to what
these exhalations may include: 'accumulated owl-drop-
pings and foul guano-mountains',[4] which once more fuses
the darkness and the swamp.   Sleep, the owl and the
swamp, reappear in *Latter-Day Pamphlets*: 'twenty-seven
millions of my fellow-countrymen, sunk deep in Lethean
sleep, with mere owl-dreams of Political Economy . . . in
this pacific thrice-infernal slush-element'.[5]   Thus it becomes clear that the metaphor of darkness is used to *coin*
metaphors of sleep, monsters, the owl and the muddy
swamp; and through the guano and the mud, owl and
swamp share more of each other's qualities than a joint
affinity with darkness, and jointly contrast with Carlyle's
image of flowing water with its characteristic meaning.

The concept of 'silence' also illustrates how Carlyle
develops and utilizes a whole interconnected vocabulary
of figurative expressions.   In one way or another, it serves
to amplify each of the three basic tenets discussed so far.
It expresses, first, the belief that the universe possesses a
mysterious life: 'It is fit that we *say* nothing, that we
think only in silence; for what words are there! The
Age of Miracles past?   The Age of Miracles is forever
here!—'.[6]   Second, it reminds us that the universe is vast
in space; and by doing so is a symbol that everything,
however trivial apparently, has really something of the
greatness of those spaces: 'The SILENCE of deep Eternities,
of Worlds from beyond the morning-stars, does it not

---

[1] LDP. 72. 'Horn-eyed' probably revives the sleep metaphor. Carlyle
mentions the 'miraculous Horn-gate' in CL. ii. 247.
[2] PP. 141.   [3] CL. ii. 274.
[4] CL. ii. 236. Cf. CL. ii. 278, 'the obscene droppings of an extensive
Owl-population, the accumulated *guano* of Human Stupor in the course of
ages'.
[5] LDP. 122.   [6] HH. 105.

speak to thee ? . . . the Stars in their never-resting courses, all Space and all Time, proclaim it to thee in continual silent admonition'.[1] Sometimes these two ideas are fused : 'The divine Skies all silent'.[2] Third, silence is an antithesis of speech, and serves in the rich vocabulary that contrasts the sham and the true : 'Silence . . . here and there . . . how eloquent in answer to . . . jargon'.[3]

This concept re-occurs in expressions like 'it is an authentic, altogether quiet fact',[4] or 'poor Manchester operatives . . . they put their huge inarticulate question "What do you mean to do with us ?"'[5] or 'England in her own big dumb heart'.[6] That these are sympathetic descriptions would not be altogether clear, did not Carlyle prepare us for them elsewhere. But the most interesting extension from the concept of silence is Carlyle's occasional use of the word 'open'. Sometimes he links this with silence directly — 'while the world lay yet silent, and the heart true and open' ;[7] and sometimes there is an indirect link, through the word 'secret' : 'SILENCE and SECRECY ! Altars might still be raised to them' ;[8] and 'the open secret'.[9] Then the concept 'open' is used for all the three tasks which 'silence' proved to carry out : reminding us, that is, of the world's mysterious life, of its vast extent in space, and of the contrast between real and sham. It recalls (1) the mysterious life of the world in such a phrase as 'the sacred mystery of the universe ; what Goethe calls "the open secret"'. But (2) the secret is open because the mystic force shows itself everywhere throughout the world. 'That divine mystery', Carlyle continues, 'which lies everywhere in all Beings . . . of which all Appearance, from the starry sky to the grass of the field, but especially the Appearance of Man and his work, is but the *vesture*, the embodiment that renders it visible.'[10] Finally (3), the *opened* heart is something true and real, not a sham : 'Wholly a blessed time : when jargon might abate, and

[1] PP. 170.   [2] PP. 198.   [3] PP. 20.   [4] PP. 16.   [5] PP. 14.
[6] LDP. 27.   [7] PP. 196.   [8] SR. 148.   [9] HH. 67.
[10] *Loc. cit.* In this passage Carlyle makes his concept of the mystery clearer by saying specifically that, if we overlook it, the universe becomes *inert*.

here and there some genuine speech begin. When to the noble opened heart . . . the difference between . . . true and false, between work and sham-work, between speech and jargon, was once more . . . infinite.'[1]

These then, are some of the methods whereby Carlyle preserves, throughout the whole texture of his work, an ultimate and absolute contrast between what in his view is good and what bad. They are methods embedded so deeply and intimately in his language that, so far at least as they are successful, they permanently sustain the attitude that Carlyle desires in the reader. The general effect of this basic contrast is plain enough: it makes Carlyle's philosophy simple, and makes it emphatic. Palliation disappears. The normal judgement to pass on anything is one of outright commendation or censure; qualified judgements, if any, preserve abstract accuracy, but tend to evoke the same attitudes as they would if unqualified.

This irreducible distinction is worked into the texture of Carlyle's argument in another way. Like Newman, Carlyle believes the universe to be a system; but what makes it a system for him must largely be explained through this contrast, since he sees the system of the world as two great movements that spread the good in the world everywhere and annihilate the bad. Thus the third tenet is what gives content to the fourth. Destiny is 'Didactic Destiny'[2] and the universe is 'a Temple and Hall of Doom';[3] what destiny teaches being that 'a divine message, or eternal regulation of the Universe there verily is, in regard to every conceivable procedure and affair of man: faithfully following this, said procedure or affair will prosper, and have the whole Universe to second it, and carry it, across the fluctuating contradictions, towards a victorious goal; not following this; mistaking this, disregarding this, destruction and wreck are certain for every affair'.[4] Certainly, this has its optimistic side. There is an 'inevitable necessity . . . in the nature of things'[5] for human progress; 'a man is right and invincible . . . while

<hr>

[1] PP. 21.   [2] PP. 31.   [3] LDP. 16.
[4] LDP. 16.   [5] HH. 97.

he joins himself to the great deep Law of the World'.[1]
But there is a pessimistic side too : 'no world, or thing here
below, ever fell into misery, without having first fallen into
folly, into sin against the Supreme Ruler of it, by adopting
as a law of conduct what was not a law, but the reverse of
one'.[2] In one direction or the other, however, the event
must turn: 'the Highest did of a surety dwell in this
Nation . . . leading . . . this Nation heavenward . . . or
else the terrible *inverse*'.[3] Vice and Virtue have, one
as much as the other, their ultimate, uncompromising
rewards.

(vi) *The Control of Meaning*

So far we have been concerned with how Carlyle's distinctive tenets are lent support by his style, his imagery, and
his diction. The next problem — and it is a particularly
important one in his case — is to see how some of his
arguments and assertions are less factual than verbal.

Arguments and assertions cannot ever, perhaps, become
verbal, unless they contain vague expressions. Newman's
verbal discussions will prove to consist largely of refusing
to employ words in loose or unusual senses, and insisting
upon their normal, or some other rather strict sense. His
discussions claim to revert to exact standard usage. This
meticulous, perhaps rather pedestrian approach made little
appeal to Carlyle; and his verbal arguments justify the use
of words in new, surprising, paradoxical or unexpectedly
pregnant senses. The number, the variety of these arguments is amazing. In order to say what he wished to say,
Carlyle had to remould and modify a quite appreciable
part of the language. On a scale not fully recognized, he
created language.

---

[1] HH. 47. Carlyle's thought is sometimes misunderstood at this point.
He believed that success was not the *criterion* of virtue, but its infallible
ultimate sequel. Cf. JS. 161, '"Might and Right", the identity of these two,
if a man will understand this God's-Universe, and that only he who con-
forms to the law of *it* can in the long run have any "might"'. The *commands*
of morality are not equivalent to, but exactly paralleled by, *general truths*
about what ultimately happens.

[2] LDP. 44.   [3] LDP. 278.

Therefore, before we see how he used language, we must see how he made it. But the two processes, though distinguishable in theory, can scarcely be isolated in practice. Carlyle's figurative language has already raised a problem: just as esoteric metaphors are used in a context which clarifies their meaning, and yet at the same time are really describing something, so individual words often acquire their new senses exactly through their appearance in new metaphors. If we attempt to trace the stages by which Carlyle transformed language, we often find a range of sentences from those whose sole purpose is to modify the sense of an expression, to those that take a modified sense for granted and merely employ it. The task of analysis is easier, though, if we consider these two extremes. Creating and exploiting new senses may not be rigidly separable, but the two processes can be observed in their turn.

The earliest stage in coining a sense is apparently to suggest that the real meaning of a word is not properly known. Thus 'Hast thou ever meditated on that word, Tradition?' [1] or '"Cheap and nasty"; there is a pregnancy in that poor vulgar proverb, which I wish we better saw and valued'; [2] or 'the Poet . . . communicates . . . a certain character of "infinitude", to whatsoever he delineates. This, though not very precise, yet on so vague a matter is worth remembering: if well meditated some meaning will gradually be found in it.' [3] Next, a hint is given of the kinds of sense that may have escaped us: 'Is not the poorest nature *a mystery* . . . is he not an individual? And who shall explain all the significance of that one word?' [4] 'This *momentous* and now almost forgotten truth, *Man is still Man*' [5] — the enquiry, that is, has for goal the momentous and mysterious. Next a sense is more or less explicitly given, but some qualifying phrase is employed to make it acceptable in spite of its strangeness. 'To know a thing, what we can call knowing, a man must first *love* the thing, sympathize with it: that is, be *virtuously* related to

---

[1] SR. 167.   [2] Niagara (ME. iii. 614).   [3] HH. 69.
[4] TN. 125.   [5] TN. 159.

it.'[1] 'Let Oliver take comfort in his . . . melancholies. The quantity of sorrow he has, does it not mean withal the quantity of *sympathy* he has, the quantity of faculty and victory he shall yet have ?'; [2] 'the very editor . . . had, if reading mean understanding, never *read* them'; [3] ' "Reign of God" . . . giving place to modern Reign of the No-God, whom men name Devil'; [4] 'all real "Art" is definable as Fact, or say as the disimprisoned "Soul of Fact"'; [5] '*virtue to produce belief*, which is the highest and in reality the only literary success'; [6] 'You are of the nature of *slaves* — or if you prefer the word, of *nomadic, and now even vagrant and vagabond, servants that can find no master on those terms*; which seems to me a much uglier word.' [7]

Some phrase or another, or perhaps only a word in italics, has occurred in all these cases to indicate a novel sense; and often the novel sense is introduced not at once, but in two stages, of which the first is nearer to normal usage than the second.[8] The examples above deserve careful attention, because they also show how giving novel senses to words can make them terms of more emphatic praise or blame. This is explicit in the last two examples, but easily seen in the others and extremely important. Two further points are significant. First, a word may only be given a novel sense ('know', 'sorrow', 'read' and the rest) if its own sense is vague in part, and the senses of some other words are precise in part. Thus in their contexts, 'love', 'sympathize', 'virtuously', 'victory', 'understand' and the others do what is required of them because their meaning is definite and is not in question. Second, this process is entirely different from 'defining one's terms'. Carlyle does not wish to be thought of as explicitly allotting

---

[1] HH. 88. This is an interesting specimen, the italics serving both to emphasize the terms, and (especially with 'virtuously') to admit novel senses; moreover, it is conspicuous that while italics are supported by two qualifying phrases for 'love', they can be used unweakened for 'virtuously', once we have been introduced by the first part of the sentence to their use as admitting novelty.

[2] CL. i. 46.   [3] CL. i. 67.   [4] CL. i. 3.
[5] Niagara (ME. iii. 608).   [6] CL. i. 9.   [7] LDP. 36.
[8] The last three examples quoted illustrate this, though in the first and last of them the more unusual sense is given first.

his own senses to these words, but as discovering what really they mean already, what their existing present use both depends upon, and perhaps conceals. But that the senses of the words are not being simply discovered, but really being changed, is clear from such phrases as 'does it not mean withal', or 'whom men name'; yet these occur indifferently with 'of the nature of' and 'in reality', which proves that Carlyle is claiming to discover the true meaning, not to prescribe his own.

Sometimes Carlyle unfolds the full meaning of a term as he sees it in a long and elaborate discussion. Thus in two chapters of *Past and Present* he expands the concept of *work*.[1] Elaborating the meaning and applying it go on together, but the varieties of amplification are easy to trace. Near the beginning comes the simple call to reflection: 'It has been written, "an endless significance lies in Work"'. Then he begins to add new ideas to the meaning: 'there is a perennial nobleness, and even sacredness, in Work'. 'Work is of a religious nature: — work is of a *brave* nature; which it is the aim of all religion to be.' 'Religion' is already a powerful and definite term of praise; and next, religious authority is invoked to the same end — 'we do entirely agree with those old monks, *Laborare est Orare*. In a thousand senses, from one end of it to the other, true Work *is* Worship.'

Another important stage in the expansion is: 'Work . . . is in communication with Nature'. At first, illustrations of this point are literal: 'foul jungles are cleared away, fair seed-fields rise instead'; 'true hand-labour . . . wide as the Earth . . . sweat of the brow'. Then metaphors follow: as some raise fair seedfields from jungles, so Christopher Wren raised a cathedral from London's ashes; the sweat of hand-labour leads us to sweat of the brain and heart, to Kepler, Newton, poets, martyrs, finally to 'that "Agony of bloody sweat" which all men have called divine'. And now the two parts of the elaboration can be seen working together, for this last point seems naturally to confirm that

[1] PP. Book III, chapters 11-12 (pp. 165-76). All the subsequent quotations illustrating this point come from these two chapters.

'properly speaking, all true Work is Religion'. There are other metaphors. To have 'found' one's work is to have a life purpose, to follow it as it runs like a clear stream 'through the sour mud-swamp of one's existence'; and this leads naturally through 'all work of man is as the swimmer's: a waste ocean threatens to drown him; if he front it not bravely', to literal examples again, Columbus and the Vikings. Finally there is amplification by contrast. The religion of the 'idle man' is that 'beggary or thievery' may suffice; work without religion is 'eye-service, greedy grasping of wages . . . manufacture of semblances . . . lath-and-plaster . . . stuffed hair-and-leather . . . Galvanism' — and throughout the whole passage, of course, in both expansion and contrast, the metaphors are Carlyle's own distinctive metaphors, and mean what he has made them mean.

One can distinguish here five activities: 'scene-setting', or the suggestion that a hidden meaning awaits discovery, if only we will meditate; verbal paradox (qualified conspicuously or inconspicuously so as to make it plausible); illustration; elaboration by metaphor; and expansion through contrast. Now, having seen the new sense of 'work' perfected, we can trace the uses to which it is put. First, Carlyle discredits abstract theoretical enquiry: since work communicates with Nature, the knowledge that 'will hold good in working' is to be valued, other knowledge on the whole not. Second, because work is divine, our well-being must be in it alone; and since 'all works . . . are a making of Madness sane; — truly enough a religious operation', we must struggle unremittingly against disorder, chaos and abuse. Third, we must not complain of a life of toil in the plain sense of physical labour, for if we call it labour at all, we must do so on Carlyle's terms, and then it is noble and divinely ordained. Even industrial manufacture is divine — 'Labour is not a devil, even while encased in Mammonism; Labour is ever an imprisoned God, writhing unconsciously or consciously to escape out of Mammonism' — and the industrialist, or 'Master-Worker' is thus intrinsically a power for good.

Next, the word 'wages' is given an expanded sense through the expanded sense of 'work'. If work is really sacred, religious, divine, 'the "wages" of every noble Work do . . . lie in Heaven'. Undeniably, the worker must be paid what enables him to go on working; but there cannot be, in money, wages exactly proportionate to work done — indeed, 'money-wage' is a contradiction. Work, life-purpose, Life cannot be sold, because its worth is infinite. At bottom it must be given away. Earthly happiness, money and the means to it, are incommensurate with what is divine.

That all valuable knowledge is practical, that we should work hard without complaining, should create order out of disorder, respect industry and industrialists, insist only on a subsistence rate of payment — all these propositions may be true or false. For the moment what matters is how Carlyle leads his readers to accept them through claiming to elaborate in full the *accepted* meaning of a single crucial term. This device is essential to how he expresses the 'life-philosophy'.

Carlyle's discussion of the *Divine Comedy* of Dante [1] affords an excellent illustration of how a word, to be used as Carlyle desires, must be given a special and expanded sense. This discussion may strike some modern readers as no better than an extravagant farrago of trite or senseless paradoxes; but, whatever its defects, it has an elaborate symmetry, and a closely woven rhetorical structure. Carlyle has previously been speaking of the 'Hero' as a Divinity or a Prophet; here his intention is to exalt the poet's office until we think of poets and prophets as equals, and then to show that among poets, Dante is pre-eminent. The task is essentially, therefore, one of praising. The method is to say first that poetry in general, then that Dante's poem itself, is 'Song'. 'Song' is the key-word throughout. This being so, a special sense is elaborated for it; and as usual, the word is actually put to use in the passages that develop its sense. It occurs in stating and then in supporting three paradoxes: first poetry itself is called song; then this is

[1] HH. 66-70, 75-6.

rendered more plausible by saying that all speech is song; then, when the special senses of the words appear to be confirmed, the thesis is applied to the *Divine Comedy*. Carlyle begins with the characteristic appeals to meditate upon the full meaning of the crucial term, and then, in each of the three sequences, follows a single pattern of argument with quite remarkable fidelity. Each time he moves in the same way from literal senses to metaphorical. The metaphorical senses — not original, but among the traditional commonplaces of speculation — combine to suggest that true poetry is something grand and splendid because it gives us a deep and penetrating insight into the universe. The Table printed on pages 48–9 makes these movements plain, though to some extent it abridges them. It contains, besides the introductory remarks, three extracts from Carlyle's discussion; these run consecutively across the table, and there is no omission between the columns unless one is indicated by the sign '. . .'. Many of Carlyle's favourite metaphors have an obvious importance, and so have expressions like 'namely', 'what one calls', 'in all senses', which reveal the author's control over the senses of his words. The really important point appears in the last two columns: as expansion of the sense reaches completion, the rhetorical purpose for which it was expanded proves to have been achieved; when we fully understand what, according to Carlyle, we committed ourselves to in agreeing that poetry was 'song', we find ourselves with an exalted and reverential notion of poetry in general and Dante's poem in particular:

[TABLE

Purpose:

To disprove the assertion that the Poet must 'hold a poor rank among us, in comparison with the . . . Prophet'; to show that one is as much a 'Vates' as the other; and thus to exalt Dante.

1. *Introductory Remarks:*

'The Poet has an infinitude in him . . . this . . . if well meditated some meaning will gradually be found in it. . . . I find considerable meaning in . . . Poetry being . . . how much lies in that !'

---

2. THESIS: *All poetry is essentially 'song', . . . and this is something exalted.*

A. States the thesis.	B. Mentions *literal* senses.	C. Adds the sense of '*essence*'.
'Poetry . . . metrical, having music in it, being a song . . . *if pressed to give a definition, one might say this as soon as anything* . . .'	. . . 'not in *word* only . . .' (*i.e.* it is song even simply in word, though also in other senses too)	'. . . a musical thought is one . . . has penetrated into the *inmost heart* of the thing . . . inmost mystery . . . namely'

3. *This argument is then generalized* as 'all inmost things are melodious . . . the meaning of Song goes deep' and this introduces the idea of speech by saying 'music . . . a kind of inarticulate unfathomable speech'. What was done for poetry is now done for speech, and 'song' exalted in just the same pattern as before :

| 'All speech, even the commonest . . . has something of song in it :' | 'not a parish . . . but has its *parish-accent* ; — the rhythm or *tune* to which the people there sing . . .' | 'observe too how all *passionate language* . . . musical . . . a Song. All *deep* things are Song . . . *central essence* of us . . . of all things.' |

4. *The same pattern recurs*, this time specifically to exalt the Divine Comedy :

| 'I give Dante my highest praise . . . his Divine Comedy . . . is, in all senses, genuinely a Song.' | 'In the *very sound* of it . . . a *canto fermo* . . . the language, his *simple* terza rima doubtless helped . . . *a sort of lilt*. . . .' | '. . . but . . . *essence* . . . rhythmic . . . *depth, rapt passion* . . .' |

Note.—My italics throughout, though often also Carlyle's.

D. Adds that of 'pattern' (this may be literal, at least in part).	E. Claims that the crucial point is thus reached.	F. Asserts the value.
'the *melody* that lies hidden in it; the *inward harmony of coherence*'	'which is its *soul*'	'whereby . . . it has a *right* to be . . . in this world.'
'The Greeks fabled of *Sphere - Harmonies*; it was the feeling they had of the *inner structure* of Nature;'	'that the *Soul* of all her voices and utterances'	'was *perfect* music.'
'. . . a true inward symmetry, *what one calls an architectural harmony* . . . which also partakes of the character of *music* . . .'	'. . . Dante's World of *Souls!* . . . deep out of the author's *heart of hearts*'	'and it goes deep, and through long generations, into ours.'

(vii) *Paradox and Truism*

Paradoxes in Carlyle are too frequent to need full illustration; but what might be called the positive paradoxes must be distinguished from the negative, because their functions are quite different. 'Nature is *preter*natural' [1] is an example of the first, while that the Poem written only for success has 'not yet become a Thing' [2] or that 'We have sumptuous garnitures for our Life, but have forgotten how to *live*' [3] is of the second. Of these two kinds of paradox, the first exalts our notion of the subject by employing a word that would normally be used only of something superior to it, the second belittles the subject by withholding a word that would normally be employed of it; and in both, the word in question serves as a term of praise. Sometimes one can find Carlyle writing two contrasting assertions, where the term of praise used in one is withheld in the other. Thus by contrast with the bad poem which is not yet a Thing, 'all real " Art " is definable as Fact'.[4]

The paradox that the commercial poem is not yet a 'Thing' has a special interest; it suggests the general value of such writing. Carlyle is at pains to make his statement acceptable to the reader and he begins by speaking only of a Poem which is being planned. 'Thy No-Thing of an Intended Poem, O Poet who hast looked only to reviewers . . . behold it has not yet become a Thing.' Since this poem is still only 'intended', the statement is true literally. But it is soon transformed into paradox, for Carlyle goes on: '. . . The Truth is not in it!'; and then comes the crucial transition, and the by now familiar claim that a special sense is the only sense: 'Though printed, hotpressed . . . to the twentieth edition: what is all that? The Thing, *in philosophical uncommercial language*, is still a No-Thing.' [5] 'Still' hides the shift from one sense of 'thing' used in an unequivocal and clearly true statement, to another sense, used of something not intended but by

---

[1] HH. 165.   [2] PP. 173.   [3] PP. 5.
[4] Quoted above, p. 43.   [5] PP. 173 (my italics).

now produced, in a paradox. Carlyle has prefaced his paradox by a non-paradoxical verbal equivalent; which we saw him also doing as he shifted from one sense of the word 'song' to another.

It is natural to ask whether in these passages at least, Carlyle is not a fraud; and one is tempted to say that he is. Yet this hardly follows. Certainly, these passages comprise trains of association that could induce an unreflecting reader to accept Carlyle's conclusion, and yet have no ground for it whatever; and sometimes perhaps, when the reader discovers himself fallen into this trap, he may reasonably claim to have been preceded there by the author. But this is interpretation at a fairly crude level, and assumes that if Carlyle's prose has any value at all, it has the value of a sequence of logically developing propositions whose sense is plain at once. What warrant is there for this assumption ?

But, it may be asked, what alternative is there to it ? An alternative does exist. It is that a discussion may consist of what might be called 'nodal' propositions, with a far from immediately plain sense, but introduced, familiarized, made easier for the reader to grasp, by a variety of techniques that would indeed be sophistical, if their interpretation could be nothing but logical; but not otherwise. The intervening passages do not prove the nodal propositions, but they work upon the reader, they quicken his insight until he can grasp their point directly for himself. This by itself, though, is insufficient. Of what value to him can these nodal propositions be, if they are not logically proved, but simply asserted, dogmatically though perhaps alluringly ? That they are important (as is seen whenever they are examined in Carlyle) in praising one object or disparaging another, in evoking the emotions of respect or disrespect, is not enough; for these emotions can be evoked by trickery.

But the solution lies along these lines : emotions are not always and necessarily evoked by trickery, and a criterion can be found to distinguish genuine from sophistical evocation. For though language can evoke emotions,

so can things themselves; and language, even when it fails
to state or describe, has a legitimate emotive power if it
operates not independently, in a beautiful though empty
mist, but by re-directing our attention to objects, concen-
trating it upon them, and thereby making us notice aspects
of them that previously we had overlooked. A vital distinction exists between one emotive use of words, as it is
called, and another. With the first, when we turn from the
language to the things of which it is alleged to speak,
experience cancels our incipient emotions, and prompts us
to discard a tissue of sophistical nonsense. With the second,
experience reinforces and completes what language began.
This distinction between usefully and fraudulently evoca-
tive language remains, even should we all disagree about
which attempts are of which kind; but many people are
likely to find themselves in agreement that certain attempts
are of one kind, and others of the other. As for Carlyle,
most readers would agree that some of his nodal propositions were aids to insight, and some of them emphatically
were not.

So much for the paradoxical element in Carlyle's work;
its apparent contrary is the element of truism. 'Truism'
means here a statement that is true solely from how the
words in it are defined; and seems the opposite of paradox,
because just as a paradox cannot really (we are inclined to
say in our down-to-earth moments) be true, so a truism
cannot really be false. But Carlyle controls the senses of
his words so thoroughly that the contrast is illusory. What
is a paradox at one extreme, interpreted in a perfectly
straightforward sense, is a truism at the other, when the
special sense given to some crucial word is made fully
explicit. This is often why Carlyle says that some apparent
extravagance will become obvious when meditated upon,
especially if the meditation is carried out in just the
required spirit.

With patience, every intermediate variety between
paradox and truism can be traced. 'Independence, in all
kinds, is rebellion',[1] is at one extreme; then, perhaps a

<hr />

[1] SR. 158.

shade less belligerently paradoxical, come those sentences quoted previously, where there is a hint that the meanings must be considered as well as the things themselves; then statements which hint that a word may have two quite unrelated senses, or a true sense and a false sense, like 'properly speaking, the land belongs to . . . God'.[1] There are two interesting specimens of the next position on the scale. One runs: 'were your Superiors worthy to govern, and you worthy to obey, reverence for them were even your only possible freedom';[2] and the other: 'Despotism is essential in most enterprises . . . they do not tolerate "freedom of debate" on board a Seventy-four! . . . yet observe . . . Freedom, not nomad's or ape's Freedom, but man's Freedom; this is indispensable. . . . To reconcile Despotism with Freedom . . . do you not already know the way? It is to make your Despotism *just*. Rigorous as Destiny; but just too, as Destiny and its Laws.'[3] These two passages are almost the same in meaning. Their interest is that they make paradoxical assertions only upon some condition which goes far to turn the paradox into a truism. To be sure, this condition is put indirectly, and is by no means conspicuous. But they could be para-phrased, at loss only of subtlety in presentation, as 'obedi-ence is freedom if of worthy subjects to worthy superiors', and 'despotism brings freedom, if it is just despotism'. In this form the tendency towards truism is plain, either because despotism failing to bring freedom would quite likely be regarded as *ipso facto* not 'just' despotism, or because anything that just despotism failed to bring would not be freedom 'properly speaking', or of the human and not merely nomadic or simian kind.

Assertions like this are common in Carlyle; and either by a word like 'true' or 'real' or by some device of typo-graphy, they indicate that a word used has a special sense and leave the question open whether or not this sense will

[1] PP. 148. The expression 'properly speaking' has several uses, but here it seems to mean not 'precisely speaking', so much as 'using the word in its true sense, not a sham sense'.
[2] SR. 158.   [3] PP. 237.

suffice to render the whole assertion a truism. For example,
'the grand problem yet remains . . . finding government by
your Real-Superiors'; [1] 'a revolt against *false* sovereigns
. . . the painful but indispensable first preparative for true
sovereigns'; [2] 'Europe requires a real Aristocracy, a real
Priesthood. . . . False Aristocracies are insupportable . . .
true aristocracies are . . . indispensable'; [3] 'A Time of
Miracle; as indeed all "Times" are . . . when there are
MEN alive . . .'; [4] 'the god-made king is needed'.[5]

These distinctive words like 'true' and 'real' — and
italics too — insist that the reader give to an assertion just
that sense which makes it true. But the insistence is
unnecessary if it is difficult for him to do otherwise, and
some words naturally carry the implication required by
the author. Carlyle speaks of struggling 'as for life in
reforming our foul ways . . . alleviating . . . our people;
seeking . . . that something like spiritual food be imparted
them, some real governance . . . be provided them!' [6]
Here 'governance' requires the word 'real' to give it a
sense in which it is a truism to call it desirable, but the
idiom of the language makes us take for granted that
'spiritual' food is desirable. Here Carlyle combines two
techniques: he precedes an assertion that is explicitly
qualified so as to be a truism, by an assertion that is a
truism through the most natural sense of the words it
contains.

Ungarnished truisms are common in Carlyle's work:
'Many things can be done . . . had we once got a soul': [7]
inability to do the things would show that *ipso facto* we
still lacked a soul. 'The . . . Wise will have . . . to take
command of the . . . Foolish' [8] — if ever it proved that
this relation ought not to hold, *ipso facto* either 'wise' or
'foolish' would have been misused. 'The one enemy we
have in this Universe is Stupidity' [9] — any apparently
stupid thing that proved useful is *ipso facto* not stupid
really, any inimical thing is *ipso facto* stupid at bottom, even
if not apparently. 'All the millenniums that I ever heard of

[1] PP. 185.   [2] HH. 102.   [3] PP. 203.   [4] CL. iii. 166.   [5] LDP. 28.
[6] PP. 157.   [7] PP. 155.   [8] LDP. 30.   [9] LDP. 86.

heretofore were to be preceded by a "chaining of the Devil"' [1]
— if the Devil proves not to have been chained, *ipso facto*
what has come is not a millennium.

Perhaps the reader will at this point lose patience once
for all with Carlyle and I fear with the analysis of him too.
Yet in spite of appearances these truisms are not worthless,
because they are not empty. There is an ambiguity in their
crucial terms that gives some point to them after all. When
these terms are given one interpretation, the sentences
follow by definition, and when another, they are controversial but substantial generalizations. Their air of incontro-
vertibility is a persuasive or rhetorical device, making the
controversial seem non-controversial; but, though Carlyle
may unconsciously trick the reader, it is not into nothing.
This can easily be seen.

'Abler men in Downing Street, abler men to govern
us' [2] — that these would help may be a truism, but after it
has been enunciated at the head of a paragraph, Carlyle
goes on to make it controversial: 'the Able Man . . . is
definable as the born enemy of Falsity and Anarchy, the
born soldier of Truth and Order'. [3] This is vague enough,
certainly; but it by no means follows by definition that
this ability is desirable in Downing Street or elsewhere;
and the definition is much further elaborated. Later,
Carlyle reverts to this topic. What is required is 'an
increased supply of Human Intellect to Downing Street', [4]
and Intellect is 'otherwise definable as Human Worth'. [5]
Further, it can be pursued only by 'devout prayer to
Heaven'; in this Christian context 'Worth', and 'Intellect'
too perhaps, have relatively precise meanings, and once
again we see how Carlyle is drawing upon an established
religious tradition. Compare '"Organization of Labour";
— which must be taken out of the hands of absurd windy
persons, and put into the hands of wise, laborious, modest
and valiant men'; [6] here there is an elaborate fusion of

[1] Niagara (ME. iii. 595).   [2] LDP. 93.
[3] LDP. 93.   [4] LDP. 98.
[5] LDP. 98. Cf. LDP. 30, 'Wisdom, which means also Valour and
heroic Nobleness . . . God's-message'.
[6] PP. 165.

what is controversial with what is not. 'Absurd', 'windy', and on the other hand 'wise' can scarcely be given senses that do not leave the whole assertion a truism; 'laborious', 'modest' and 'valiant' all introduce something of a more or less controversial nature, though Carlyle has so broken down the normal resistance of language that in reading the sentence one begins to feel how their meaning could be adjusted to make them apt by definition alone. A good deal later, Carlyle further elaborates his concept of a wise man: 'other men . . . a totally other sort of men, different as light is from dark, as star-fire is from street-mud'; [1] and this illustrates again how each more restricted assertion, in a work of this kind, tends to rely upon the whole cumulative strength of the 'Life-Philosophy', and how our understanding of the life-philosophy cannot be put into any formula or rubric, but is a sense of something, an understanding built up in us gradually by all the techniques which this chapter has been examining, and, strangely enough, revived in our minds even by what seems to draw on it.

Carlyle's truisms then, are not simply empty, just as his paradoxes are not simply false. Rather, we discover two different methods of making controversial statements leave their impress on the reader: paradox is impressive and memorable because surprising and striking, truism because incontrovertible. These assertions derive their persuasive and rhetorical power from their form. But they make a contribution of substance too, because the senses of words are manipulated until the paradox is no longer paradoxical, the truism no longer trite. The paradox is mollified, as it were, until it just relapses into a proper sense, and the truism is progressively charged with meaning until it just manages to acquire one. In both cases, the ultimate result is not very different. Once the reader is alive to this kind of ambiguity, he can see Carlyle combining and alternating between these methods with presumably unconscious skill traceable on every page.

Early in this chapter four principles were advanced as

[1] PP. 215.

a summary of Carlyle's philosophy. It is now possible to see more clearly how the whole texture and detail of his work is what really interprets them. A sense of the life and energy that pervades the world is amassed gradually for his reader by the febrile style, by the constant dramatization of apparently abstract argument, by a wide variety of metaphors, and sometimes by the bewilderingly erratic sequence of ideas and images. The integration of the universe, as Carlyle sees it, and its permeation by this cosmic life, is suggested by innumerable passing deviations from small things to great. What is almost a new linguistic continent of distinctive or even esoteric metaphor makes Carlyle's sense of a cosmic fissure between good and bad, real and sham, enter every fragment of what he wrote; and it is the living quality of the cosmos, and this great split through it, which generate Carlyle's sense of the course of history. These devices would give a vivid sense of his world view, even if he never generalized at all. But his broader assertions draw upon a remoulding of the senses of words so extensive and elaborate that it might almost be called a new linguistic continent too. As a result, the more discursive parts of his work must be seen not as logical argument, but as sequences of verbal marches and countermarches — as formulae which prepare the reader's mind for, and converge upon, some nodal or crucial assertion. And this nodal assertion will prove acceptable (if at all) not on logical grounds, but because, prepared and sensitized as he is, the reader may glimpse how, in a strained and cryptic way, it is a revelation of some important and elusive truth, an assertion which, if it is put to the test, illuminates the whole bias of experience. Finally, by the frequent use of Biblical diction, Carlyle attaches his whole exposition to a philosophy or world view which is deeply familiar and widely sympathetic. No part of Carlyle's prose seems quite unrelated to his overriding purpose.

CHAPTER III

CARLYLE AS PROPHET-HISTORIAN

(i) *Didactic History*

OBLIVION seems largely to have engulfed Carlyle's historical works, but it is because their author had one standard, and modern historians judge them by another. At first glance, the books themselves mislead in this respect. Constant demands for accuracy, impartiality, intelligible presentation, proper handling of documents, prompt the reader to suppose that Carlyle's aim was scientific historiography in the narrow sense. Yet this was exactly what he wished to avoid; exactly what was incarnated in that mythical 'Dryasdust', his constant butt. History, he insists, is the working of didactic Destiny; 'didactic . . . to this generation' [1] because it is a 'poor hag-ridden and wig-ridden generation'.[2] Properly told, it teaches men their own true nature and how they should live, it reveals to them how the world they live in is organized.

The French Revolution, in Carlyle's view, is a great object-lesson teaching us that certain conditions cannot but lead to anarchy, and that anarchy cannot but destroy itself. A great moral lesson is to be learnt from it, and Carlyle says plainly what it is : 'Wherefor let all men know what of depth and of height is still revealed in men; and with fear and wonder, with just sympathy and just antipathy . . . contemplate it and appropriate it; and draw innumerable inferences from it'.[3] The Revolution even reveals the ways of God to man; enigmatically perhaps, but clear as day when explained. 'In the whirlwind also He speaks.' [4]

[1] FG. iv. 284.   [2] FG. vi. 378.   [3] FR. 778.   [4] FR. 182.

What gives point to history is its lessons in morality and — in the widest sense — cosmology.

For Carlyle, writing this kind of history is an imaginative and creative activity that demands the powers of a poet. Prometheus attracted the gifts of Aeschylus; Frederick, 'this new Titan', was less fortunate but equally deserving,[1] and less fortunate but more deserving than Achilles and Aeneas. The task of the 'sacred Poet, or man of real Human Genius' is that of '*interpreting* Human Heroisms', and thereby drawing a true image of the hero from the 'circumambient Chaos of muddy babble, rumour and mendacity'; something of this kind Carlyle clearly sought to provide for Frederick. Nor are we left in doubt of why this is worth doing; had things gone as they should, 'I calculate, we should by this time have had a different Friedrich. . . . O Heavens, a different world of it, in so many respects!' History of the proper kind is a power for human good; as for the consequences of Dryasdust history, 'you need not go exclusively "to France" to look at them. They are too visible in the . . . sublime gilt Doggeries . . . of all modern Countries.'[2] In the deep significance of its subject-matter, and in its practical lessons, Carlyle's history is akin to his polemical writing. The dominant purpose behind each is the same. To some extent, history ties the author's hands. He selects the details which lend themselves to his historical parable, and as a rule is convinced that the rest are not genuinely important. But there is a point beyond which picking out some things and leaving out others cannot go, and occasionally the reader sees him striving to assimilate troublesome material, or suspects that the course of events might have suited his requirements better than it did. But for all this, the moralizing and prophesying form is the central and guiding strand of his work; and what does not lend itself straightforwardly to these activities is often enough made useful indirectly.

Viewed in this light, *The French Revolution* and *Frederick the Great* may seem diffuse, melodramatic, exasperating

---

[1] FG. v. 429.   [2] FG. v. 122-3.

as ever. But they reveal a quite remarkable power to organize a narrative, on a very large scale, so that it acquires a moral or philosophical significance; and they are crucially important in the present enquiry, not only because they display a variety of new methods of expressing a 'life-philosophy', but also because in a sense one has here what scientists would call a 'control'. One can watch Carlyle's view of things developing in the histories, with a knowledge, drawn already from the polemical works, of what that view will prove to be; and it is naturally easier to trace Carlyle's methods of expression, when one knows in advance what answer they are to give. Moreover, these histories seem to stand midway between the 'prophetic' essay and the novel, for here Carlyle's methods of expressing his view of things prove in many respects to be like those that novelists often use for the same purpose. The present chapter is consequently a sort of transition to those on Disraeli, George Eliot and Hardy — though this is not, by the way, to say that Carlyle's history is really fiction.

The present enquiry is restricted to *The French Revolution* and *Frederick the Great*, and will say nothing of *Cromwell's Letters and Speeches*. This is in some respects the work most satisfying to the modern historian, but Carlyle's distinctive intentions are limited in it by the duties of editorship, and as a polemical work the book does little or nothing not done more fully in the other two. These give prominence to two quite different aspects of Carlyle's world view. *The French Revolution*, in its whole design, is a grand presentation in historical form of Carlyle's convictions that the world everywhere manifests a wild and inexhaustible energy, that all change must run its appointed course, and that change is, in essence, the ousting of sham by reality. The main speculative significance is metaphysical; Carlyle's 'World-Phoenix' is the central character. These ideas inevitably find some place in *Frederick the Great*, but that book chiefly enriches Carlyle's teaching by its comprehensive picture of what is good and bad in human character or action, and for our present purpose its main significance is moral. The difference is largely dictated by the subject, but partly it occurs because Carlyle himself, in the years between 1835 and 1851, had grown less interested in such philosophical conceptions as freedom and necessity, or appearance and reality, and more interested in certain virtues of individual character.

(ii) 'The French Revolution'

Carlyle visualized the French Revolution as a single process of history, vast in scale, swift and continuous in movement, cosmic in its implications : a specimen of basic human needs bursting through a flimsy structure of social shams, driving men on irresistibly from 'phasis', as he called it, to phasis, culminating in complete anarchy which he called 'Sansculottism', and then, its impetus exhausted, relapsing into a new order. It was a memorable, minatory, monitory stage in the cosmic process that replaces the sham by the real, and a signal example of the irresistible cosmic forces and their final intolerance of half-measures. Carlyle's narrative is like a novel in its gathering speed, its climax in the so-called 'Terror' of 1793–4, and its calmer, quieter close. It is the account of a single integrated movement, of which the author's natural style here emphasizes the speed, just as in his polemical works it emphasized how the universe is alive with irresistible energy.

Quotations given in the previous chapter often showed Carlyle reminding his readers that his immediate subject had a cosmic significance : 'sooty Manchester — it too is built on the infinite Abysses'. This is precisely what he desires us to see in the Revolution; and every device is pressed into service so that we may never forget it. 'Very frightful it is when a Nation, rending asunder its Constitutions and Regulations . . . grown dead cerements for it, becomes *trans*cendental . . . it is thus that . . . we are to contemplate France . . . and all on such a scale, and under such aspect : "cloudy death-birth of a world" : . . . heaven on one side . . . on the other . . . hell-fire' ; [1] and there are, moreover, chapters of more or less philosophical digression

[1] FR. 514.

when the assertion is generalized. But overt statement like this is inconspicuous in the total deployment of resources; hints and echoes and reminders keep the principle in the reader's mind constantly. Of the first assembly of the States General, for example, he writes 'so many serried rows sit perched there; like winged creatures, alighted out of Heaven'.[1] It is a curious image, but its work is not done until it brings to mind, besides Heaven, the council of the Fallen Angels in Pandemonium. There is the same indirect significance in his ironical account of the 'Gospel according to Jean-Jacques': 'man is properly an Accident under the sky . . . without Heaven above him, or Hell beneath'; [2] in an idea of Marat's 'rooting itself in Tartarus, branching towards Heaven'; [3] or in such a remark as 'subterranean Paris, — for we stand over quarries and catacombs, dangerously, as it were midway between Heaven and the Abyss, and are hollow underground, — was charged with gunpowder'.[4]

Sometimes the net is thrown less widely, but the effect is similar. The account of celebrations in the Champ-de-Mars, July 1790, begins 'that circle of bright-dyed Life, spread up there, on its thirty-seated Slope; leaning, one would say, on the thick umbrage of those Avenue-Trees . . . and all beyond it mere greenness of Summer Earth . . . over all the circling heights that embosom Paris, it is as one more or less peopled Amphitheatre; which the eye grows dim with measuring . . . and all France properly is but one Amphitheatre'.[5] A little further on we are reminded that the 'deep azure Heavens' and 'green all-nursing Earth' with its streams and forests, is a mystic garment and dwelling-place of God. These are conspicuous but isolated specimens of a technique that in some form appears on almost every page. The Revolution exemplifies the universe. If we are allowed to forget this, we forget the main reason for writing of it.

The first feature of the Revolution, then, which Carlyle wishes to keep constantly before the reader, is that it is typical; the second, which follows from the first, is that

[1] FR. 114.   [2] FR. 127.   [3] FR. 261.   · [4] FR. 295.   [5] FR. 301.

it is inevitable. In every detail it is a determined, a necessary process. There are many direct assertions of this necessity, either general or more limited;[1] but various devices of exposition convert the bare dogma into an impression pervading the whole chronicle of events. One of these is the use of suggestive metaphor. Carlyle likens the historical process to a plant blossoming and wilting; to a gathering storm; to a self-consuming firework; to a sun or star burning out its natural course; to the natural sequence of the seasons; to a steady process of fermentation; and to the birth of 'progeny' naturally resembling their parents.[2] Some of these reveal clearly how a metaphor can adjust our historical perspective, and what importance the author attaches to that adjustment. 'Is it not a plain truth of sense . . . that human things wholly are in continual movement . . . by unalterable laws, towards prescribed issues ? How often must we say, and yet not rightly lay to heart: The seed that is sown, it will spring ! Given the summer's blossoming, then there is also given the autumnal withering: so is it ordered not with seed-fields only, but with transactions, arrangements. . . . French Revolutions. . . . The Beginning holds in it the End . . . as the acorn does the oak. . . . Solemn enough, did we think of it . . . all grows, and seeks and endures its destinies : consider likewise how much grows, as the trees do, whether *we* think of it or not.'[3] Here the oscillation between figurative and plain language is complex and striking; its effect cannot be missed; Carlyle does all he can to guard against our missing it by constantly emphasizing that it is food for thought.

More important still in vivifying this dogma is Carlyle's use of a form of dramatic irony: when King Louis is brought in procession from Versailles to Paris (6th October 1789) he writes, 'Poor Louis has Two other Paris Processions to make: one ludicrous-ignominious like this; the other not ludicrous nor ignominious, but . . . sublime'.[4]

---

[1] *E.g.* FR. 617: 'endless Necessity environing Freewill !'
[2] FR. 11, 51, 213, 274, 335, 337, 776.
[3] FR. 335.   [4] FR. 246.

Mentioning Minister Brienne's residence in 1788, he tells the reader how 'a dusky-complexioned taciturn Boy' called Bonaparte sat studying mathematics in the near-by military school.[1]   In his account of the States-General assembling, he calls on the reader to observe with 'prophetic' eyes, points him out Marat, Danton, Desmoulins and the rest, assures him in advance that Mirabeau will be the greatest of them all, Robespierre the meanest.[2]   Earlier, he has introduced the Breton Club as 'first germ of — the *Jacobin's Society*'.[3]   Describing the citizens preparing the Champ-de-Mars for the Festival of 1790, he singles out the father of Joséphine Beauharnais 'who shall get Kings though he be none'.[4]   He mentions the doorkeepers at the Jacobin Society on a particular night, because one of them later became King Louis-Phillipe.   He writes of the Legislative Assembly of 1791 as he did of the States-General: picks upon those to be important in the future, hints their coming careers in deterministic language — 'Valazé doomed to a sad end . . . Couthon, little dreaming *what* he is' and at the close gives this determinism clear expression; 'Parties *will* unfold themselves . . . forces work within these men and without . . . these . . . and all men, must work what is appointed them'.[5]   But we do not come unprepared upon this assertion; all the facts of the new Assembly have been so presented to us that it seems merely to summarize their tendency.   Dryasdust historians occasionally make such observations in passing, but for Carlyle they are quite different — they hint at the abiding realities of the world.

The last three paragraphs have done no more than give a few samples of Carlyle's exposition; but innumerable turns of phrase lend a distinctive colour to the narrative throughout.   The third general feature which Carlyle sees in the Revolution is a wild, violent, febrile irrepressible energy; and this is suffused through the whole texture of his argument more inextricably still.   This view of history simply follows from Carlyle's widest speculative conceptions, according to which there was an uninterrupted war

[1] FR. 92.   [2] FR. 115-21.   [3] FR. 90.   [4] FR. 297.   [5] FR. 422-4.

streamers, jacks, every rag of tricolor that will yet run on
rope, fly rustling aloft : the whole crew crowds to the
upper deck . . . with universal soul-maddening yell . . .
she staggers, she lurches, her last drunk whirl ; Ocean
yawns abysmal ; down rushes the *Vengeur* . . . into
Eternity.' [1] This did not occur. Carlyle knows it. He
goes straight on to reject the account as a legend, as an
inspiring piece of *blague*. Why then repeat it in detail ?
Not merely through garrulity, but because even as *blague*
it is inspiring in the way that he requires. Its riotous
wildness and confusion, the whole exciting human turmoil,
are too good for him to omit. Carlyle may have been
biased, yet at bottom he was honest to the facts as he knew
them, and this story is something that ultimately he must
discard. But Carlyle the historian-prophet uses it first.

In other words, incident can contribute as well as
metaphor to the pervasive effect. This is an important
point, and in due course will prove valid of other authors
too ; Carlyle's narrative illustrates it in both selection and
treatment. But he does not stress incidents depicting the
Revolution as merely — to use his own word — vertigin-
ous. We are not concerned with any trick of treatment
that is crude and undifferentiated, but with a complex and
comprehensive handling of material : every kind of detail
contributes something to the impression of febrile energy,
each kind makes the contribution that it can make most
effectively, each helps to complete what is ultimately a
picture of every conceivable variety of movement and
vitality. Incidents and situations are described so that they
seem facetious or degrading or impressive, pastoral or
frenzied or epic. It is as if Carlyle were passing to and fro
throughout a whole spectrum ; the examples which follow
will give some idea of its range.

At the facetious extreme there is an account of how
secret visitors to the King in the Tuileries were pitched one
after another downstairs and kicked along by the sentries,
until they landed at the bottom and were chased off home
by the mob ; [2] or of the Hotel Castries being sacked :

---

[1] FR. 718.   [2] FR. 360.

'gone distracted, devil-ridden, belching from every window, "beds with clothes and curtains", plate of silver and gold with filigree, mirrors, pictures, images, commodes, chiffoniers, and endless crockery and jingle: amid steady popular cheers, absolutely without theft'.[1] Not much different are the revelries in Paris after the Terror: women parading the streets in Greek costume, and 'little feet naked, as in Antique Statues, with mere sandals, and winding-strings of riband', and gold rings on their toes, or dancing in 'flesh-coloured drawers' with gold circlets, or using pillows and stuffing to conform to the fashion for pregnancy;[2] though this, ludicrous enough, is made to seem also a little shameful. When he writes of the crisis of 1792, he touches, amid all the excitements of war, on the 'frilled promenaders' sauntering under the trees, the girls in white muslin with their green parasols, the scampering dogs and busy shoeblacks — 'so much goes its course; and yet the course of all things is nigh altering and ending'.[3] He singles out, too, incidents of wild, riotous saturnalia: for example, a procession in 1793 of those bringing spoil from the churches to the Convention, as they ride drunkenly along, straddling asses draped in the church vestments, swilling brandy from the church chalices, eating mackerel off the sacramental plate; Deputies leaving their seats to join in and dance the *Carmagnole* with girls in the priestly robes;[4] or again, a 'Feast of Reason' in Notre Dame — 'wind-music, red nightcaps, and the madness of the world', and in other churches, tables piled high with sausages and pork puddings, and crowds of men, women and children eating or drinking everywhere, 'mad multitudes . . . whirling and spinning' as they dance half-naked in the streets or indulge in 'other mysteries, seemingly of a Cabiric or even Paphian character', along the aisles.[5]

These are Carlyle's lighter moments. While still contributing to the impression of multifariousness, he can adopt a sharper tone of satire and suggest, as in his account

[1] FR. 347.   [2] FR. 759-62.   [3] FR. 486.
[4] FR. 705.   [5] FR. 706-7.

of the *emigrés* at Coblentz, that the riot is a sham through
and through :

> Emigration, flowing over the Frontiers . . . in various
> humours of fear, of petulance, rage and hope . . . Coblentz
> is become a small extra-national Versailles ; a Versailles *in
> partibus* : briguing, intriguing, favouritism, strumpetocracy
> itself . . . all the old activities, on a small scale, quickened by
> hungry Revenge. Enthusiasm, of loyalty, of hatred and
> hope, has risen to a high pitch ; as, in any Coblentz tavern
> you may hear . . . arms are a-hammering at Liége ; 'three
> thousand horses' ambling hitherward from the Fairs of
> Germany . . . Their route of march, towards France and
> the Division of the Spoil, is marked out, were the Kaiser
> once ready.[1]

Every sentence in this passage is almost imperceptibly
adjusted to induce the attitude Carlyle seeks ; 'humours',
strumpets, taverns, fairs, abject dependence on the despised
foreigner — all these are so woven into the passage that
they determine its nature almost through concealing their
own. In contrast, this, heightened by the imperative
mood, is Carlyle's picture of the rearming Republic :

> Meanwhile, the faster, O ye black-aproned Smiths. . . .
> This man and that, all stroke from head to heel, shall thunder
> alternating, and ply the great forge-hammer, till stithy reel
> and ring again . . . pikes . . . fifty thousand of them, in six-
> and-thirty hours . . . Dig trenches, unpave the streets, ye
> others . . . cram the earth in barrel-barricades . . . Have
> scalding pitch, at least boiling water ready . . . ! Patrols of
> the newborn National Guard, bearing torches, scour the
> streets, all that night ; which otherwise are vacant, yet
> illuminated in every window by order.[2]

The contrast between the two is nearly complete. The
main impression in each is energy ; in one it is misplaced
and pitiful, in the other terrible and splendid.

To reinforce this general impression Carlyle picks on
relatively trivial details and gives them a quite special
prominence. His account of a powder-magazine exploding

[1] FR. 443-4.   [2] FR. 156.

at Lyons (August 1793) is elaborated for just this purpose:
'In the Autumn night . . . what sudden red sunblaze is
that . . .? It is the Powder-tower . . . nay the Arsenal
with four Powder-towers, which has caught fire in the
Bombardment; and sprung into the air, carrying "a
hundred and seventeen houses" after it. With a light, one
fancies, as of the noon sun . . . what a sight was that, which
the eye of History saw, in the sudden nocturnal sunblaze!
The roofs of hapless Lyons, and all its domes and steeples
made momentarily clear; Rhone and Saone streams flash-
ing suddenly visible; and height and hollow, hamlet and
smooth stubble field, and all the region round; — heights,
alas, all scarped and counter-scarped . . . blue Artillerymen,
little Powder-devilkins, plying their hell-trade there.' [1]
Sometimes he creates this same impression by quite re-
calcitrant details. This is how the French produce arms:
'The wheels of Langres scream, amid their sputtering fire-
halo . . . the stithies of Charleville ring with gun-making';
forges are everywhere in the open spaces of Paris, great
press-drills mounted in barges on the Seine; carpenters,
clock-makers, chemists, cobblers, needle-women, all are
hard at work. But the climax is that the citizens of Paris
collect saltpetre from the old plaster of their walls and by
digging in the earth of their cellars: 'Swiftly, see! The
Citoyens, with up-shoved *bonnet rouge*, or with doffed
bonnet, and hair toil-wetted; digging fiercely, each in his
own cellar, for saltpetre.' [2]

It is such passages that give *The French Revolution* its
character and make it a comprehensive statement of
Carlyle's philosophy of the historical process. But the
three characteristics distinguished so far — grand scale,
necessity, violent energy — are not always suggested in
isolation. So far we have examined passages where one
feature was very prominent and others hardly present;
but many integrate two or all three, and suggest that they
are essentially interdependent. The description quoted
above of the exploding magazine conveys not only the
violence of the event, but also how it was framed in the

[1] FR. 673.   [2] FR. 713-14.

whole landscape of France: how this is significant must by now be familiar. There is the same transition in a passage like, 'Busy is the French world! In those great days, what poorest speculative craftsman but will leave his workshop; if not to vote, yet to assist. . . . On all highways is a rustling and bustling. Over the wide surface of France . . . as the Sower casts his corn abroad upon the furrows, sounds of congregating and dispersing; of crowds in deliberation . . . rise discrepant towards the ear of Heaven.'[1] In the following account of the States-General assembling (4th May 1789) Carlyle weaves all three trends together. We are made to see the significance of the event as spreading over France and Europe, back into remote history, up to Heaven and even down into Hell; its inevitability is expressed in plain terms, and conveyed by metaphors of gestation, and of marching soldiers; of the wild violence of the scene there is no need to say anything.

Yes, Friends, ye may sit and look . . . all France, and all Europe, may sit and look. . . . Oh, one might weep like Xerxes:— So many serried rows sit perched there; like winged creatures, alighted out of Heaven:[2] all these, and so many more that follow them, shall have wholly fled aloft again . . . and the memory of this day still be fresh. It is the baptism-day of Democracy; sick Time has given it birth, the numbered months being run. . . . Behold, however! The doors of St. Louis church flung wide; and the Procession of Processions advancing . . . shouts rend the air; one shout, at which Grecian birds might drop dead. . . . Some Fourteen Hundred Men blown together from all winds, on the deepest errand . . . in that silent marching mass there lies Futurity enough. No symbolic Ark, like the old Hebrews, do these men bear: yet with them too is a Covenant. . . . The whole Future is there, and Destiny dim-brooding over it . . . it lies illegible, inevitable . . . as it shall unfold itself, in fire and thunder, of siege, and field-artillery; in the rustling of battle-banners, the tramp of hosts, in the glow of burning cities . . . ![3]

[1] FR. 105.   [2] Already discussed, p. 62 above.   [3] FR. 114-15.

It is interesting to see how a passage of Carlyle's wildest rhetoric makes a contribution at every turn to his central purpose.

Such are Carlyle's principal means of showing the historical process as vast, inevitable and violent. But, though these terms describe the character of the process, they do not determine its outcome; and the exact nature of that outcome is important, because Carlyle believes that history ultimately produces what is good. Seen at full length, the facts of history are also the lessons of morality. Here, though, Carlyle need not be particularly explicit; his chief concern is simply to make his readers heed exhortations familiar to them already. On this point his historical works, like his polemical, say little more than that history is a movement from sham to reality: prior to 1789, 'France was long a "Despotism tempered by Epigrams"'; [1] the aim of the Revolution, and whatever changes it effected permanently, comprised 'that Man and his Life rest no more on hollowness and a Lie, but on solidity and some kind of Truth'.[2] This is perfectly familiar.

But Carlyle exploits his historical material to amplify and enrich these notions. He selects and elaborates incidents which forcibly convey what is 'true' in conduct, or what sham. Of the first kind, there are not many. One instance is his account of General Bouillé quelling a riot among his troops, who were storming into their Colonel's quarters to rifle the regimental pay chest; the General, blocking their way on the stairs, motionless, hours on end, with drawn sword, 'in grim calmness . . . as a bronze General would',[3] until help arrives. Grim calmness is exactly to Carlyle's taste; here at least, he hints, is a true man. Examples of the sham are more frequent. There are the busy preparations (4th February 1790) for the King's visit to the States-General — the velvet cover, violet 'sprigged' with gold fleur-de-lis, to be 'slipped' over his chair, the 'fraction' of carpet to be spread in front.[4] There are the Champ-de-Mars celebrations, with their

[1] FR. 36.   [2] FR. 182.   [3] FR. 316-17.   [4] FR. 278.

'twelve hundred wind-musicians'. 'By what', he asks, '. . . shall miraculous fire be drawn out of Heaven; and descend gently, life-giving, with health to the souls of men? Alas, by the simplest: by Two Hundred shaven-crowned Individuals "in snow-white albs, with tricolor girdles" arranged on the steps of Fatherland's Altar.'[1] This, clearly, is History with a moral; and Carlyle's glee is unmistakable when, 'while Episcopus Talleyrand, long-stoled, with mitre and tricolor belt, was yet but hitching up the Altar steps to do his miracle, the material Heaven grew black . . . there descended a very deluge of rain. Sad to see! The thirty-staired Seats, all round our Amphi-theatre, get instantaneously slated with mere umbrellas, fallacious when so thick set: our antique *Cassolettes* become water-pots; their incense-smoke gone hissing, in a whiff of muddy vapour . . . the General's sash runs water', and the women worse off and looking sillier still: 'their snowy muslins all splashed and draggled; the ostrich feather shrunk shamefully to the backbone of a feather; all caps are ruined; innermost pasteboard molten into its original pap: Beauty no longer swims decorated in her garniture . . . but struggles in disastrous imprison-ment in it, for "the shape was noticeable"; and now only sympathetic interjections, titterings, teeheeings, and resolute good-humour will avail.'[2] To Carlyle this is a significant part of his narrative, not a digression from history to the novel; it shows up a sham for a sham.

Many other such examples occur. But for all that, the emphasis of the book is chiefly upon historical change as typical of the cosmic pattern. It is this which gives the impression of grand scale, integration and speed; moreover it seems to govern, and therefore be reinforced by, Carlyle's presentation of character. There are exceptions, but in general the men and women of the Revolution do not live through Carlyle's pages in full and lively detail; they are not clear individuals so much as adumbrations that exem-plify the general forces of history. Their individuality is volatilized and disintegrated by the abstractions of which

[1] FR. 303.   [2] FR. 303-4.

they are the vehicles. Or, to use Carlyle's own word,
most of them are to some degree *somnambulent*. Indeed,
he insists on this: 'a man, once committed headlong to
republican or any other Transcendentalism . . . becomes
as it were enveloped in an ambient atmosphere of Transcendentalism . . . his individual self is lost . . . the man's
cloak still seems to hold the same man: and yet the man
is not there, his volition is not there . . . instead . . . there is
a piece of Fanaticism and Fatalism incarnated in the
shape of him'.[1]

Thus Madame Roland's appearance is, briefly enough,
that of a 'queen-like burgher-woman'.[2] To this, as the
book progresses, is added merely that she had soft, proud,
big dark eyes and long black hair; at one time cooked her
own supper; and was brave, though with an effort, at her
trial. So far our knowledge of her is meagre enough. But
she is made to contribute amply to the pervasive effects:
she is 'unconscious of her worth (as all worth is) . . .
genuine, the creature of Sincerity and Nature, in an age of
. . . Cant'.[3] To be so is to be a moral emblem. 'Like a
white Grecian Statue . . . she too was a Daughter of the
Infinite.' [4] To be this, is to recall the scale of the historical
process. Marat's most salient feature is his 'contempt for
fine outsides', and his explosive laughter at the gentilities
and superfine airs and pedantries of the Girondins.[5]
Danton is 'no hollow Formalist . . . but a very Man . . .
fiery-real, from the great fire-bosom of Nature . . . he
walked straight his own wild road, whither it led him'.[6]
This tells us little distinctive of Danton, but it makes him
a specimen of all the three fundamental characters seen by
Carlyle in the world, and of the final reality to which it
moves through history. Drouet, in the Royal flight to
Varennes, has no distinct character but what adds one
touch more to the disorder and violence of the scene:
'an acrid choleric man . . . kept fretting (all day) . . . steps
out and steps in . . . prying into several things'.[7] The best
example is Mirabeau, by far the most completely portrayed

---

[1] FR. 616.   [2] FR. 287.   [3] FR. 287.   [4] FR. 692.
[5] FR. 621.   [6] FR. 733.   [7] FR. 394-5.

figure in the book. Carlyle mentions his black hair and shaggy brows and rough complexion, but turns almost at once to what they mean : they reveal the 'burning fire of genius ; like comet-fire glaring fuliginous'.[1] He is the 'roughest lion's whelp ever littered of that rough breed'.[2] His literary works are 'bitumenous'. His achievement is that 'like a burning mountain he blazes heaven-high ; and, for twenty-three resplendent months, pours out, in flame and molten fire-torrents, all that is in him'. He is one who has 'made away with . . . all *Formulas* . . . a Reality, not an artificiality, not a Sham'.[3]

(iii) *'Frederick the Great'*

The characters of *The French Revolution* then, are no more than schematically described ; the main emphasis is on their significance. Even their moral significance is little stressed, only to the point of showing once again how the 'sham' is bad. Unquestionably, their principal contribution is to Carlyle's picture of the historical process.

Frederick the Great is quite different. This book covers a period ten times as long as that of the Revolution, its events could not possibly form a swift-moving sequence culminating in a violent climax, and it could not possibly be made to portray history as in the clutch of irresistible necessity. There are references, of course, to the 'inexorable Fates', and to the Rhadamanthine Laws of Nature ; but they are not really part of the texture of the work. Indeed, Carlyle shows the resourceful and tenacious Frederick achieving the impossible rather than the inevitable. Eighteenth-century history is not at all the fiery operation of law. Success comes from patient watchfulness. If it comes also from rapidity of action, that is in some restricted enterprise, when a rare opportunity offers. The whole period, as Carlyle saw it, was hostile to the more spectacular or portentous manifestations of the cosmic principle. Nor, in spite of his occasional references to what is significant for 'World-History' and what is not, is he at

[1] FR. 118.   [2] FR. 118.   [3] FR. 120.

all unwilling to devote space to events or persons whom he
even emphasizes are unknown or uninfluential.   More
often than not his characters, in no way coloured with all
the iridescences of the Cosmos, are obscure, or work in
silence and isolation.   The subject seemed worth writing
about, because Carlyle saw Frederick and his associates as
outstanding if imperfect types of human virtue and
integrity.   Frederick was one who, like other heroes,
performed his 'twelve Hercules-labours'.   He was a
specimen of humanity ready-made for the moralist who
wanted to teach, on a grand scale, by the method of
example.   Throughout, this personal interest dominates
the book, and controls and subordinates every other aspect ;
though just how far it is extended and elaborated remains
to be seen.

The contrast between the methods of these two books
is clear if we compare a rather similar incident in each :
the death of Frederick himself, and the death of Mirabeau.
Carlyle's chapter on Mirabeau [1] epitomizes everything that
has been said so far about his methods and approach.   In
the first few lines he reminds his readers that men's years
are numbered ; that even those most influential in World-
History are called from '*the press of ruddy busy Life*'.   At
once, we hear the three notes of his common chord.   We
are told of how Mirabeau, in his last illness, lay 'dying as
by slow fire' ;   how the people crowded and pressed to
enquire after him ;   how before he died his mind 'lit up,
for the last time . . . his speech is wild and wondrous' ;
ultimately his death comes as the sun rises, his last effort a
'passionate demand' for opium.   But then without a pause
Carlyle reverts to the waiting multitude, to the days of
mourning throughout the city (though the detail Carlyle
selects is that the too-hurrying coachman may be set upon
by the crowd), to the funeral orations everywhere in
the streets, the ballad-singers hawking their laments, the
'immeasurable crop, thick as the leaves of Spring' of
portraits, engraved or painted or whatever else ; and next,
in elaborate detail, the vast procession of the funeral, and

[1] FR. Book III, chapter 7.

the great multitude thronging the roofs, the windows, even the lamp-irons or tree-tops; and the drums, the trombones, the gunfire. The last move is to replace narrative by meditation. Mirabeau's life 'blazes out, far-seen . . . in this World-Pyre', he lived and died 'Titanically', was 'a Reality and no Simulacrum', and was, for all his faults, if not a truly epic at least a truly tragic figure, 'if not great . . . large; large in his qualities, world-large in his destinies'. We have everything, except the Mirabeau who might have been obscure.

The account of King Frederick's death [1] is a complete contrast. First come anecdotes of what occurred at the King's last public appearances. He gets wet through, riding all day in the rain at a military review, and when his boots were taken off at evening the water 'came pouring from them like a pair of pails'. Every step in his last gradual decline is recorded. He still goes riding — ever shorter distances — and sees his friends and carries out the day's routine, beginning indeed earlier than ever, at four in the morning. His last letters, his last attentions to others, his resolve at the very end to work as usual next day, his last utterances and actions, are all given in detail. Their meaning lies in the 'grand simplicity of stoicism in him'.[2] His death was 'stern and lonely'; his body was prepared for burial by military doctors, taken by military escort through the silent crowds to the royal vault at Potsdam. Quiet and brief, the closing words of the account, and of the whole book itself, turn the reader's attention not to the World-Phoenix, but to the individual Frederick. If in nothing else, Carlyle's attempted epic runs true to type in its calm and gentle close.

The number of characters in *Frederick the Great* depicted with sharp and vivid detail is very large; and their portraits are all touched with the moral intentions behind the historical narrative. But the sweep and complexity and integration of the work from this point of view

[1] FG. Book XXI, chapter 9.
[2] FG. vi. 439. All subsequent references in this chapter are to the six volumes of *Frederick the Great*.

are quite missed, if we suppose that the author merely presents his readers with specimens of good character, or even with specimens of character both good and bad. The book contains something much more ambitious than this: it gradually amasses a multitude of individuals who collectively, in the end, give an exhaustive picture of what the human virtues are, and how in particular human beings they are sometimes unalloyed and outstanding, sometimes present only in low degree or an uncongenial environment, sometimes struggling against other forces of personality in various ways hostile to them. This is also true of the vices of mankind. What the reader sees, as the work unfolds, is a comprehensive panorama of the human virtues and the human failings, incarnated incompletely or distortedly in men and women taken one by one. This is not to say that the characters are abstractions. They are not. They have usually a simple but most vivid individuality. It is to say that in the mass these individuals display the system of the abstractions of moral virtue and vice as they appear to Carlyle in human character; and they achieve this by being so numerous, so varied, in many cases so incompletely either good or bad, and at the same time complementary to each other.

The character of Frederick himself is an example. As is well known, Carlyle portrays him sympathetically — had the book not been kinder to Frederick than he seems to have deserved it would have been belied by its focal point. But all the same he is clearly a mixture of good and bad: he chose friends unhappily, because he was too fond of *esprit* and not deeply, reverentially fond enough of wisdom; [1] of his poetry, 'nobody can wish details in this Department',[2] though when he writes verses at a time of grave crisis it at least shows that he is not 'brooding'; [3] he spends, perhaps, too much time on plans for his Opera House — but it is better to be devoted to anything rather than nothing, and it is an unusually practical opera-house, with good acous-

---

[1] iv. 310.   [2] iv. 223.

[3] v. 65. Significantly, Carlyle says here that if we avoid taking the *shell* of the fact here, and ignoring the *essence*, it throws a great light on Frederick.

tics, ventilation, and precautions against fire; [1] he makes
up fanciful names for his friends, and indulges in other
such 'cloud-work' and 'airy symbolism' — but this is
excusable in a young man, and indeed may have a 'spice
of reality', because at the same time he selected his companions rigorously on their superior merit and behaviour. [2]
This technique is remarkable. It is a method not simply
of whitewashing Frederick's character, but also of showing
how even foibles reveal sterling qualities struggling through
an imperfectly sympathetic material, and of showing in one
way more, therefore, what the sterling qualities—in Carlyle's
view — really are. For the real and important parts of
Frederick's nature are his power of practical judgement,
his steady swiftness, capacity to hold his peace and respect
'rough wisdom' in others, 'inexpugnability', indifference
to 'scenic matters', and insight into realities. [3] These
particular qualities are mentioned in describing how he
ultimately submitted to his father, how he refused to attend
the ceremonies of vowing homage to him unless at the same
time he could attend military reviews, and how in 1742 he
got what he wanted from the Pope. But the important
thing is that they are illustrated, and given point, by almost
every detail of the narrative; this is largely what made its
author think it worth reciting.

Frederick then is by no means a figure of perfection;
he is simply a remarkable specimen of how outstanding
qualities may be fused with diverting foibles. He takes
his place in what is not a simple scale of virtue but a complex order of individuals. 'Inexpugnability' can take a
multitude of forms. The elder Prince of Anhalt-Dessau
is a man of 'vast dumb faculty', of 'dreadful impetuosity';
he insists on marrying an apothecary's daughter, he murders a medical student who was his rival, he nearly murders
his tutor while on the grand tour; implacably self-pos-
sessed, tenacious, impetuous in battle, devoted to warfare,
incessantly drilling his troops, 'brooding' over military
inventions. His character shows in his look as in his deeds:
'a tall strong-boned man; with cloudy brows, vigilant

[1] iii. 413-14.   [2] ii. 403.   [3] E.g. ii. 356; ii. 507; iv. 49.

swift eyes'; his skin is a bluish tint as if from gunpowder; 'he wears long moustaches; triangular hat, plume . . . are of thrifty practical size. Can be polite enough . . . but hides much of his meaning . . . inarticulate . . . plays rough pranks . . . has a big horse-laugh.'[1] Among the other varieties are Frederick's father with his tempestuous rages, carpentry, and passion for simple cleanliness, 'an unwedge-able and gnarled big block of manhood and simplicity and sincerity';[2] General Ziethen 'big-headed, thick-lipped, decidedly ugly', a 'rugged simple son of the moorlands' — nourished, it appears, on fire, iron and oatmeal;[3] Zisca (introduced in a complete digression), with his iron battle-club, a 'great behemoth of a war-captain; one of the fiercest, inflexiblest, ruggedest creatures ever made in the form of man';[4] Walpole, more pedestrian, 'sturdy, deep-bellied, long-headed, John-Bull fashion';[5] Pitt, 'serious always' but also 'full of airy flashings, twinkles, and corus-cations';[6] the Maréchal Belleisle at the siege of Prague (1742), brisk but laconic, 'is prepared to dare all things . . . contrives, arranges', lays in immense supplies of biscuit, 'gathers himself into iron stoicism';[7] and the Emperor Charles VI, nearly devoid of outstanding ability, yet proud, patient, brave in illness, 'intensely serious; a handsome man, stoically grave . . . honestly doing his very best with his poor Kaisership, and dying of chagrin by it'.[8] These pictures of virtue in different though related forms have a cumulative significance for the reader.

The characters of whom Carlyle more or less dis-approves are varied and variegated too; as a result, they too make up a comprehensive picture — this time of the degrading or ridiculous in human nature. Few of them are bad without qualification; indeed, there is a perfectly con-tinuous transition to them, from those characters whom the author admires.

Perhaps the fullest and most closely packed portrait of one with qualities both good and bad is that of the Maréchal de Saxe. The description of him is given below:

[1] i. 290.   [2] ii. 462.   [3] iii. 260.   [4] iii. 397.
[5] iii. 242.   [6] iv. 522.   [7] iii. 433.   [8] iii. 65.

it reads consecutively line by line, with omissions only where they are indicated ; the most favourable comments are put to the left of the page, and the less and less favourable ones put further and further to the right :

   Much   wild
natural ingenuity in him ; cunning rapid   whirls
          of contrivance ; and gained Three Battles
and very many sieges   amid the loudest clapping
                    of hands that could well be . . .
perfect intrepidity . . .
             Nobody needed to
be braver . . .
   great good-nature too,
      though of hot temper   and so full
                    of multifarious
                    voracities ; . . .
inarticulate good sense withal,
      and much magnanimity   run wild, or run to seed.
      A big-limbed,   swashing,
              perpendicular
              kind of fellow :
                  haughty of face,
     but jolly too ;
   with a big,   not ugly   strut ; — captivating to the
                    French nation,
     and fit God of War . . .   for that
                  susceptible People.
     Understood their Army also . . .
           and how, by   theatricals
   and otherwise,
          to get . . .
  fire out of it . . .   whether . . . on the road to ruin
              or not . . . he did not care.[1]

In this remarkable passage Carlyle's technique and interest is clear. We are being informed of a chequered personality, in a manner that indicates at every turn just what nuance of qualified approval or disapproval we are to accord to every trait. Indeed, so conspicuous is the element of evaluation that only the word 'big-limbed' is relatively independent of it. For the present discussion

[1] iv. 217.

the crucial point is that this brings us not merely to assess the qualities of the Maréchal de Saxe, but to conceive a certain fairly specific personality, and then judge it not by our pre-existing standards, *but by the author's*.

The plainly descriptive element is often more prominent in these portraits, because Carlyle, to achieve his purpose as a moralist, must cause his reader not merely to think that this or that character is good or bad or something of both. He must make the reader adopt this attitude of a more or less specific figure, someone of whom we do something significant in adopting just this attitude, because we could possibly and consistently have had another, or even none at all. Thus portraiture and evaluation must be performed jointly; and each must lead to a result that is definite and specific and that matches the other. If these two processes are not, in every case, fully separable one from the other, it is because many expressions in our language cannot but contribute to both at once, and many more may be caused to do so by their use and context.

Some further examples will illustrate how Carlyle makes a bid to equip us with a comprehensive diagram of human nature, and at the same time to suggest definitely and convincingly how we should assess its varieties. There is, for example, the infant Frederick's governess, Mme de Roucoulles : 'respectable', 'did her function very honestly, there is no doubt' — it is not easy to say whether this is praise or the reverse; in old age given to tattle, 'the dreadfullest bore', and even at her zenith (if one may so call it), 'a clear, correct, but somewhat barren and meagre species, tight-laced and high-frizzled in body and soul . . . not very much of silent piety . . . perhaps of vocal piety more than enough'. But for all this, at least inculcating in the young Frederick 'various thin good things'.[1] In Voltaire also there seems more to regret than to praise; he is 'the brightest young fellow in the world', 'disposed to make himself generally agreeable' — chiefly by the method of 'electric coruscations' and attentions to actresses. It is not a type Carlyle readily admires; yet

[1] i. 281-2.

he also notices, with approval, Voltaire's interest in the
legendary Englishman, 'rugged, surly . . . taciturn', and
mentions that besides Voltaire's life of gaiety there was
'always some current of graver enterprise . . . going on
beneath'.[1] Elsewhere the amalgam of good and bad in
Voltaire is made explicit: 'one fancies in him a mixed
set of emotions, direct and reflex'.[2] Maupertuis is another,
further along the scale. He is pompous, self-opiniated,
pig-headed, ridiculous — the 'Perpetual President', with
his sublime solutions to metaphysical conundrums,[3] and
'flattish red countenance and impregnable stony eyes',[4]
'the red-wigged Bashaw, Flattener of the Earth', the 'big
glaring geometrical bully'; [5] yet at the same time he is
'a man of rugged stalwart type . . . of an ardour, an intelligence not to be forgotten . . . of good and even of high
talent; unlucky in mistaking it for the highest'.[6] Further
still from grace is Kaunitz, the Austrian Chancellor: '"The
greatest of Diplomatists", they all say; — and surely it is
reckoned something to become the greatest in your line
. . . the Supreme Jove, we perceive, in that extinct Olympus
. . . sparing of words, sparing even of looks . . . King of the
Vanished Shadows. A determined hater of Fresh Air;
rode under glass cover, on the finest day . . . fed, cautiously
daring, on boiled capons'; [7] or of him again 'traits there
are of human cunning, shrewdness of eye; — of the loftiest
silent human pride, stoicism, perseverance . . . but not, to
my remembrance, of any conspicuous human wisdom . . .
a man to give one thoughts'.[8]

Relatively few of Carlyle's characters seem to have
enjoyed his unmitigated disfavour. They are vain, hypo-
critical, pedantic, self-important, or preoccupied with
trivialities; but here again, there is no fixed pattern, even
here where a fixed pattern might most be expected. Their
significance lies largely in this variety. Even the worst of
them add to the panoramic effect. There is Stanislaus
Poniatowski 'airy sentimental coxcomb, rather of dissolute
habits, handsomest and windiest of young Polacks',[9] the

---

[1] ii. 386-92.   [2] iv. 252.   [3] iv. 253.   [4] iii. 21.   [5] iii. 22, 23.
[6] v. 390; cf. iii. 21.   [7] iv. 215.   [8] iv. 355.   [9] iv. 395.

Empress Catherine's *Emeritus* lover, anointed King of
Poland on a false pasteboard scalp fitted over his head, so
that he need not shave his 'ambrosial locks'; [1] 'Excellency
Montijos', Spanish delegate to the Imperial Election (1741)
'a brown little man', with a half-page of titles, and portable
tapestries and gold plate in his field-baggage — the 'bottle
holder' and 'peacock-tail' to the French Maréchal Belleisle; [2] the fastidious General Brühl, with one suit for every
day of the year, and twelve tailors permanently engaged to
care for them — Brühl the 'vainest of human clothes-
horses'; [3] Schlubhut, 'high-mannered at the wrong time',
telling King Friedrich Wilhelm that it is 'not the done
thing' to hang a nobleman, even one who has robbed the
Treasury; [4] and last, the unscholarly, vulgar, ugly, gross,
'swag-bellied' Professor La Croze.[5]

Thus, all in all, there is a continuous gradation, of a
complex rather than simple kind, through the whole range
of these characters, from the most admirable to the least.
There is no question of moral advocacy simply by showing
specimens of the good man, or condemnation by specimens
of the bad. Carlyle's method is more elaborate and comprehensive. He introduces a vast number of individuals;
he so describes them that their look, their habits, their
propensities are revealed in sharp and vivid detail; and
in the course of so doing, he in every case controls and
forms the exact attitude of favour or disfavour, qualified
or unqualified, that the reader is to take up to each. The
result determines our moral attitudes to a range of character so wide that it comprises a very large proportion of the
combinations occurring in life itself. In other words,
Frederick the Great makes an implicit bid to provide a
comprehensive moral estimate of our experience. As far
as the individuals in the book seem to incarnate, in various
configurations, abstract virtues and vices, this moral outlook
can be expressed as definite moral principles, as general-
ities about stoicism, inexpugnability, powers of decision,
energy, taciturnity, earnest endeavour, humility — or, on
the other hand, shallowness, conceit, sloth, self-importance,

[1] vi. 237.   [2] iii. 272-3.   [3] iv. 71.   [4] ii. 183-4.   [5] ii. 379.

hypocrisy, spiritual myopia, dissolute habits and the rest. The panorama of individuals, developed and detailed as it is, explains the very meaning of these words by providing a variety of instances of their use. In Carlyle's other writings the real import of the key moral terms can be no more than hinted at by some single vivid detail or suggestive example. In *Frederick the Great* they are gradually, comprehensively, exhaustively explained by what is really a grandiose process of definition by examples. This, of course, is only one-half of the story; as they are progressively defined they are progressively used in controlling the reader's attitudes. But here more than elsewhere in his work we really see exactly what Carlyle's favourite moral terms are used to indicate. It is impossible not to conclude that, despite its fearsome dimensions, frequent wearisomeness, and sometimes even ridiculous history, *Frederick the Great* provides the richest and most detailed indications of Carlyle's outlook, if not as historian, or philosopher, at least as moral sage.

CHAPTER IV

DISRAELI

(i) *Is Disraeli a Sage at all?*

EXOTIC fantasies like *The Rise of Iskander* or *Alroy*, the fantastic 'Wanderjahr' politics and adventures of *Vivian Grey* or *Contarini Fleming*, the dandiacal politics of *The Young Duke*, high-life romances like *Henrietta Temple* or *Venetia*, politics and society in *Coningsby* or *Sybil*, religion, travel and speculation in *Tancred* or *Lothair*, and the objective and subtly felt panorama of *Endymion* — all these together make Disraeli one of the liveliest and most versatile novelists of his period. He could scarcely seem more different from Carlyle. Indeed, it is not at first clear that Disraeli wrote much, or indeed anything, which gives expression to a point of view not merely political, but genuinely speculative or philosophical. And just as Carlyle would not have concerned this enquiry had he been merely an opponent of Free Trade and Parliamentary elections, so Disraeli would not, had he been merely a romancer or merely a protagonist of the Tory party.

But there is usually more to his work than this; as there must be, perhaps, in any serious political writer and as indeed there was in the novelists of the 'dandy' and the 'silver-fork' schools even before Disraeli, exploiting their materials, did a good deal to deepen their impact. An outlook that is more than political, and is proved to be more than political because it finds as natural an expression in the German forests, on the Italian sea-shore, or among the Arabs or Syrians, as it does at home in England, runs through all his work — except, strangely enough, the quite untendentious *Endymion*. It is not, to be sure, there alone;

Disraeli lacks the insistence of Carlyle. He has not Carlyle's singleness and earnestness of purpose. The line of
his polemical interest runs waveringly athwart his work,
and often it is hidden by Disraeli the romancer or Disraeli
the more narrow politician. But for all that it is there :
and although it must be disentangled from other elements
and then seen in the context of them, its intermittent
nature results in a colourful, irresponsible brilliance that
is not without its relevance, as we shall see.

Disraeli's novels, one after another (though some much
more clearly than others), contain a pattern of enquiry
typical of the moralist or seer raising 'ultimate' questions ;
and one must see how it is to these ultimate questions that
his novels suggest an answer, not only to more circum-
scribed political issues. The elements of the pattern are
those traced already in Carlyle : Disraeli creates the same
sense of perplexity, the same unsureness about fundamentals, and the same dissatisfaction with conventional answers
on the ground that they are shallow. Sooner or later his
heroes tend to find themselves confronted with questions
about ultimates. Tancred says : 'It is time to . . . renovate
our communications with the Most High . . . I . . . would
lift up my voice to heaven, and ask, what is DUTY, and
what is FAITH ? What ought I to DO, and what ought
I to BELIEVE ?' [1] Charles Egremont, disappointed in love,
begins to detect his illusions, to stop and think, 'to observe,
to enquire, and to reflect . . . he discovered that, when he
imagined his education was completed, it had in fact not
commenced'.[2] For the young Coningsby, 'What were his
powers ? What should be his aim ? were often . . . questions infinitely perplexing . . .'; he 'loved to pursue every
question to the centre'; [3] he had 'a mind predisposed to
enquiry and prone to meditation'.[4]

Through his characters, Disraeli not only suggests
these problems, but also indicates what frame of mind can
hope to solve them. His view here is, once again, typical
of the 'prophet'. Coningsby, 'sustained by a profound,
however vague, conviction, that there are still great truths,

[1] T. 55.   [2] S. 40.   [3] C. 123.   [4] C. 151.

if we could but work them out',[1] pursues his questions to
the centre 'not in a spirit of scepticism . . . on the contrary,
it was the spirit of faith'. He 'found that he was born in
an age of infidelity in all things . . . he needed that deep
and enduring conviction that the heart and the intellect,
feeling and reason united, can alone supply'.[2] Tancred
also unites these qualities; and 'life is stranger than I
deemed' [3] is the epitome of what is essentially his religious
education. Lothair, though intellectually complacent at
first, is really 'of a nature profound and inquisitive, though
with a great fund of reverence'; [4] he says (with an air of
distress) 'We live in dark times'; [5] and the novel of which
he is hero portrays a quest for something that will remove
his perplexity. What he seeks is a religion, a 'Life-
Philosophy' — this is still true, even though he chiefly
makes his enquiries among the women he falls in love with.

There is thus no doubt that at least these four novels
present the prophet's familiar, basic problem, although
they do so in novel form, and of course do much else too.
The doctrine advanced by Disraeli in answer to this problem is revealing. It illuminates with particular vividness
the contrast between abstractly stating a view of life, and
something which will really evoke it in the reader's imagination. For, put in its baldest terms, Disraeli's central pre-
miss about the human situation is only that human society
as a whole is like a live thing. Its essential qualities are
continuity and *vitality*. From this all the rest would follow
logically, if logic were relevant. Disraeli makes this point
explicitly in the *Vindication of the English Constitution*.
The individual's character, he says, produces a salutary
consistency of conduct without 'that organized philosophy
which we style *system* . . . the blended influences of nature
and fortune form his character; 'tis the same with nations'.
Wise nations from time to time reflect on the sources of
institutions that flourish in them, and 'in this great national
review, duly and wisely separating the essential character
of their history from that which is purely adventitious, they
discover certain principles of ancestral conduct . . . and

[1] C. 147.   [2] C. 123.   [3] T. 424.   [4] L. 376.   [5] L. 62.

. . . resolve that these principles shall be their guides and
their instructors . . .'.[1]   But the nearest that he ever gets to
this in his novels is, once only, to draw for an explanation
on a more limited and only half-explicit version of the
principle.   In a speculative discussion between the two
philosopher-poets of *Venetia*, Cadurcis and Herbert, he
makes the latter say : 'All the inventive arts maintain a
sympathetic connection between each other, for, after all,
they are only various expressions of one internal power,
modified by different circumstances either of the individual
or of society'.[2]   Here, for once, the key principle shows
itself in the relatively plain form beyond which such
cryptic generalizations can never go.   What makes this the
key principle, however, is not that it is proved or reiterated,
but that the whole quality and texture of Disraeli's work
mediates it to the reader.

Like Carlyle, and like Newman or George Eliot too,
though more expressly than any of them, Disraeli insists
upon the barrenness of abstractions, and the rich wisdom
inherent in practice.   'Eschew abstractions'[3] he argues
in the *Vindication* : 'remember instead how entirely the
result of a principle depends upon its method of application'.[4]   Characters, in the novels, serve as mouthpieces for
the same opinions.   Vivian Grey belittles 'the progress of
liberal principles . . . your philosophy, your philanthropy,
and your competition',[5] by arguing that a simple fall in
stocks can sweep them all away.   Contarini Fleming, at
the very beginning of his life-history, writes, 'when I turn
over the pages of the metaphysician, I perceive a science
that deals in words instead of facts . . . imaginary principles
establish systems that contradict the common sense of
mankind'.[6]   Incidents bring this to life : in *Vivian Grey*
idealist metaphysicians fall victim to a crafty and satirical
Nature which makes them desert their principles and admit
materiality by eating 'kalte schale'.[7]   The false outlook can
be dramatized as easily as the true : in *The Young Duke*,
the odious Mr. Duncan Macmorrah, stupid, aggressive,

[1] WW. 120.   [2] V. 436.   [3] WW. 147.
[4] WW. 139.   [5] VG. 140.   [6] CF. 3.   [7] VG. 398.

self-opinionated, and after all sychophantic — 'an acute utilitarian', in short — orates in praise of first principles [1] in the not altogether appropriate environment of an early morning coach to London. We are shown Disraeli's hero, the Duke himself, winning the argument merely by calm replies and well-bred smiles. In *Sybil* Stephen Morley, champion of Moral Force and the principle of association, is a consistently ineffective figure until he abandons his theories, and Sybil herself who also theorizes and idealizes in the beginning, has after a time 'seen enough to suspect that the world was a more complicated system than she had preconceived . . . found to her surprise that great thoughts have very little to do with the business of the world'.[2]

Tancred, on the other hand, is significantly less intellectualist than Sybil. Though he is insistent for truth, he is accommodating about abstractions :

> 'You are going into first principles,' said the Duke, much surprised.
> 'Give me then second principles,' replied his son ; 'give me any.' [3]

This distaste for dogmatic generalizations shows itself sometimes even unexpectedly. *Lothair* is the story of a youth for whom at first 'one conclusion . . . was indubitable : life must be religion' — 'life should be entirely religious'.[4] But after some experience he 'now felt that he had started in life with an extravagant appreciation of the influence of the religious principle on the conduct of human affairs'.[5] Coningsby, we are left to hope, will at the end of all his experiences 'denounce to a perplexed and disheartened world the frigid theories of a generalizing age that have destroyed the individuality of man'.[6] The characters, the incidents, the author's explanations display everywhere that excogitated rationalisms are artificial, naïve, crude, something that experience and maturity necessarily correct.

---

[1] YD. 292-3.   [2] S. 335.   [3] T. 49.
[4] L. 73, 91.   [5] L. 376.   [6] C. 477.

(ii) *Tradition and Change*

On the other hand, traditional continuity as a guide in
life is exalted throughout Disraeli's work both directly and
indirectly. 'It is useless to argue the question abstractedly.
The phrase "the people" is sheer nonsense. It is not a
political term. It is a phrase of natural history. A people
is a species ; a civilized community is a nation. Now, a
nation is a work of art and a work of time. A nation is
gradually created by a variety of influences. . . .'[1] Many
scenes and incidents in the novels bring this creed to life.
Tancred's vision in the desert (nothing less, I fear, than
a gigantic angel slowly waving a palm-tree sceptre) utters
the same message : 'the eternal principle that controlled
barbarian vigour can alone cope with morbid civilization'.[2]
Tradition accounts also for all that is best in Tancred's
own ancestral town of Montacute, set in a fertile clearing
in its age-old north-country forest, a neat, stone-built
town with an ancient church, a modern one in the best
traditional style (modern readers may be sceptical of this),
a bridge provided by a munificent ancestor of the present
Duke, a charter, with 'under the old system' a representative stake in Parliament, and the towers of the ducal castle
rising high over the whole scene before the forest begins
again.[3] Westminster Abbey has similar associations ; its
instructiveness, indeed, is made explicit.[4] Pen Bronnock,
the Duke of St. James's great isolated country residence,
standing in its antiquated park by the sea, once the scene
of a Royal Council, exerts the same influence :[5] 'am I not
standing here among my hereditary rocks', its owner
meditates, 'and sighing . . . to be virtuous !'[6] Chateau
Desir[7] with its prominent muniment room, family arms in
the gateway spandrils, mixture of Gothic and Italianate
architecture (traditional and exotic), and setting of ancient
forest trees, is the scene of Vivian Grey's early political
manœuvres. Coningsby's house Hellingsley is 'one of
those true old English Halls . . . during many generations

[1] WW. 343.   [2] T. 291.   [3] T. 22-3.
[4] S. 266.   [5] YD. 220-21.   [6] YD. 228.   [7] VG. 36-8.

vigilantly and tastefully preserved by its proprietors'. No scene could recall 'happier images of English nature, and better recollections of English manners'.[1] Sometimes the significance of these scenes is given point (rather stiltedly) in conversation :

> 'There are few things more pleasing to me than an ancient place,' said Mr. Temple.
> 'Doubly pleasing when in the possession of an ancient family,' added his daughter.[2]

Sometimes, as in the Duke of Bellamont's henchman Colonel Bruce, who has all the functions and understanding of a great landowner's assistant, and thinks the Duke and Duchess the best people in the world, Disraeli portrays a character who both incarnates and sets a true value on these various traditional activities and virtues.

But the traditional position of the great landed noble is not admired as merely picturesque or conventionally proper. It has more significant qualities : it is, or at least can be, grand and patriarchal. These qualities may appear also in other settings, but for Disraeli, wherever they appear, they are always praiseworthy. That these are the real grounds of his admiration will become plainer from seeing how Disraeli shapes the movement of entire novels, one after another.[3] But also he emphasizes it by details. The great landowner is a great public servant. Tancred 'long pondered' his 'duties as a great proprietor of the soil' ;[4] with regard to 'a great estate, no doubt it brings great cares' ;[5] among Mr. Dacre's distresses on account of his entailed property was the thought of the numerous tenantry 'who looked up to' him 'with the confiding eye that the most liberal parvenu cannot attract'.[6] There is also a good deal of cottage visiting in the novels. The Duke of St. James goes with May Dacre when she visits her cottagers as Lady Bountiful, Ferdinand accompanies Henrietta Temple on the same errand, Vivian Grey relieves the cottager's distresses single-handed, Egremont

[1]. C. 360.   [2] HT. 87.   [3] See below, Section iv.
[4] T. 14.   [5] YD. 229.   [6] YD. 60.

visits the cottage children with Sybil, 'their queen'.[1]
When Tancred comes of age there is a great festival, the
country people foregather from miles around, pavilions are
erected in the ducal gardens for their dinner, each parish
by itself, with its flag and band — 'an immense but well-
ordered fair' — there are village sports and games, cricket
matches, morris dancing, and a complimentary visit by the
mayor and councillors of Montacute.[2] Other examples
must be reserved for later on. All in all, the great house
and its occupants are the focus of a vigorous patriarchal
society.

If there is any doubt that the aristocratic society of the
great estate was for Disraeli typical of society at its best,
it is dispelled by an explicit comparison that he draws in
the *Vindication*: the great statesmen of English history,
he says here,[3] 'looked upon the nation as a family, and upon
the country as a landed inheritance. Generation after
generation were to succeed to it, with all its convenient
buildings and all its choice cultivation, its parks and
gardens, as well as its fields and meads, its libraries and its
collections of art, all its wealth, but all its encumbrances.'
The significant metaphor of the treatise simply becomes a
significant example in the novels; seeing its point is for
Disraeli the basis of rightly ordering human society.
To complete the parallel with this analogy between good
society and family, Disraeli has in *Tancred* a portrait, full
of interest, of the Baroni family of musicians and per-
formers. They live a humble nomadic life in a caravan,
but when the great merchant and financier Sidonia visits
them, father Baroni says, 'I rule and regulate my house like
a ship'; the children honour their parents, the family
lives by an ordered system of invariable rules, and all
pursue those arts which are their traditional mode of
livelihood.[4]

In this visit to humble compatriots (for the acrobat and
the financier are both Jews) Sidonia too is a patriarch:
and it is he also who encourages Tancred to visit Palestine

---

[1] YD. 269; HT. 115-16; VG. 54-6; S. 211.　　[2] T. 26-39.
[3] WW. 124.　　　　　[4] T. 327-8.

and the Levant as the traditional land of wisdom. Moreover, he represents another tradition, that of the great
London merchants, an aristocracy of its own, builders of
mansions, Disraeli says, even more than the landowners;
and Sidonia's own noble house, though indeed 'agitated
with the most urgent interests of the current hour', has
an elegance, dignity and peace that give it 'something of
the classic repose of a college'.[1] After he arrived in the
East, Tancred finds that tradition and the patriarch can
take still other forms. He visits the 'superb Saracenic
castle' of Fakredeen, Emir of Canobia ('This is the first
gentleman's seat I have seen since I left England' his
man-servant significantly observes).[2] The young Emir,
elsewhere quite puerile and unreliable, here lives up to his
great position : he is 'brilliant, sumptuous, and hospitable,
always doing something kind . . .'[3] and all the Emirs and
Sheikhs ride in to pay him their respects. There is a great
hunting party, conducted with elaborate and hieratic
orderliness, and afterwards a grand banquet. Preparations
for this illustrate both the decorum and the kindly con-
descension of a patriarchal society. Disraeli's account is
too colourful, too characteristic, and too pointed, not to
quote in full : 'the huntsmen were the cooks, but the
greatest order was preserved ; and though the Emirs and
the great Sheikhs, heads of houses, retiring again to their
divans, occupied themselves with their nargillies, many
a mookatadgi mixed with the servants and the slaves, and
delighted in preparing this patriarchal banquet, which
indeed befitted a castle and a forest'.[4]

But the tradition to which Disraeli finds himself
attracted is not one of unvarying institutions, or a rigid
and immutable class hierarchy. It is a tradition of energy,
insight and adaptability, and its aristocratic or patriarchal
virtues could find expression in new forms and institutions
as easily as in old. It is so far from being hostile to popular
movements, that it is exactly what they make essential.
In the eighteenth century, when the common people could
be safely ignored (so the argument runs), an oligarchy

without either talent or ideals might survive. 'But we live in a different age: there are popular sympathies, however imperfect, to appeal to; we must recur to the high primeval practice, and address nations now as the heroes, and prophets, and legislators of antiquity.'[1] A popular and democratic age must find its own aristocrats.

Of these, Millbank in *Coningsby* is an example.[2] His seat, of residence as of operations, lies in a parkland in Lancashire where 'a clear and powerful stream flows through a broad meadow land'. Here, among the traditional setting of ancient elms, rises 'a vast deep red brick pile . . . not without a certain beauty of proportion and an artist-like finish'. But over the 'principal entrance' — 'a lofty portal of bold and beautiful design' — stands a statue of Commerce: for this is not Mr. Millbank's ancestral home, but his principal factory. Disraeli, portraying his ideal for the new industrialized world, still adopts the patriarchal pattern of society, though he modifies its form. Salubriously away from the factories (there were three in all) stands the new village, its architecture neat and 'even picturesque', with gay gardens everywhere, a 'sunny knoll', a church, rectory and school 'in the best style of Christian architecture' and — the new and old again organically fused — what would now be called a community centre. 'The mansion of the millowner' completes the plan; and this, with its situation 'on an agreeable and well-wooded elevation', its beautiful meadows, its variety of gardens and conservatories, is — though 'in the villa style' — the typical home of an improving landlord.

Disraeli emphasizes this aspect of the millowner: Coningsby is taken round the factory by a Mr. Benson, whose conversation is chiefly of how its owner builds churches, schools and houses ('on a new system of ventilation') for his work-people; and the factory itself is not simply a means of making money, but an emblem of the new industrial aristocracy. 'The building had been fitted up by a capitalist as anxious to raise a monument of the skill and power of his order, as to obtain a return for the great investment.' And over a glass of claret, after a dinner 'perfect of its kind', Millbank explains to Coningsby the theory that lies behind this picture: he asserts that the country requires not a nominal aristocracy of meaningless titles, nor an 'artificial equality', but a genuine aristocracy of virtue, ability and power — of this, Millbank himself [1] in his whole setting is an example, and his sincere and powerful personality lends support to the special sense of 'aristocracy' which the discussion puts forward.

That the aristocracy which Disraeli admires is one of quality, not lineage, is clear also in *Sybil*. Here the present landed aristocracy is portrayed in one of its failures. Lord Marney is a harsh and inconsiderate landowner, the town of Marney (so different from Montacute) is neglected, squalid and abjectly poor, the agricultural labourers are sullen and burn the ricks. His brother and a stranger, among the ruins of Marney Abbey, recall how the monks of an earlier time, before their expropriation, were kindly, altruistic, improving landlords, and in addition were patrons of the arts and great architects. They formed a genuine aristocracy; and that most of the mitred abbots were 'sons of the people' seems even an advantage, for it contributed something to 'the principle of the society'. At length this conversation advances the words 'association' and 'gregariousness' as names for the good and the bad patterns of society; and it is clear that for Disraeli an aristocracy is something of value not for snobbery, but for its patriarchal and integrating functions.

In *Henrietta Temple*, Disraeli (it is one of his lighter moments) can even trace the aristocratic virtues in a

[1] Disraeli has something similar (not identical) in mind when in *The Spirit of Whiggism* he argues that no wise industrialist will interfere with the social pyramid within which he may himself contribute to a new aristocracy, and writes sympathetically of manufacturers who try to become landed gentry: 'when passions have a little subsided, the industrious tenpounder, who has struggled into the privileged order of the Commons, proud of having obtained the first step of aristocracy, will be the last man to assist in destroying the other gradations of the scale which he or his posterity may yet ascend; the new member of a manufacturing district has his eye already upon a neighbouring park, avails himself of his political position to become a county magistrate, meditates upon a baronetcy, and dreams of a coroneted descendant' (WW. 349).

moneylender. Mr. Levison is one of the rich boors of his
profession. He neglects his fine old city house,[1] 'in that
gloomy quarter called Golden Square . . . a noble yet now
dingy mansion' — jumbles his portraits and *genre* paintings,
crowds his rooms with ugly furniture and his furniture with
ponderous ornaments, juxtaposes a faded Turkey carpet
and a handscreen with a view of Margate. In person he
is the same — a little stout, a little bald, garish clothes, too
many rings, too big a gold chain, too keen an interest in
selling coal. Mr. Bond Sharpe,[2] with his meticulously
cared-for residence in Cleveland Row, pursues the same
profession in the other and proper style. His footman is
impeccable, his exquisite dinners (the knives and forks
have Dresden china handles!) are famous, his gold plate,
though rarely on display, is elegant and superb — furniture, flowers, gardens, everything is the perfection of
refined opulence, and so is Mr. Bond Sharpe. 'His figure
was slight but compact. His dress plain, but a model in
its fashion. He was habited entirely in black, and his only
ornaments were his studs. . . .' He lends the hard-pressed
Ferdinand fifteen hundred pounds in the coolest possible
manner, and invites him to dinner into the bargain.
Although Bond Sharpe is making his fortune, started life
as a prize-fighter, and lends money generously so as to
get into good society, Disraeli portrays him in an entirely
amiable light. He is good because he knows how to live
and act in the grand manner: he has taste, respects good
society, seeks the public responsibilities of wealth (he will
be in the next Parliament), and for Disraeli is an admirable
example of how a new but genuine aristocracy can be
conceived and born from nothing.

(iii) '*A motley sparkling Multitude*'

But one element in the portrait of Mr. Bond Sharpe
has so far been ignored; and although less tangible than
the others, it is of crucial importance, for it takes us beyond
an external survey of the forms and institutions which

[1] HT. 350-51.   [2] HT. 357-63.

Disraeli admired, to their inner and essential quality. We advance from the mechanisms to the 'feel' of things. This new element is the freshness, the brilliance, the life and colour and movement that Disraeli lends his whole portrait. The cabriolet that brings Ferdinand to Bond Sharpe's house goes dashing and twisting and whirling through the streets; it draws up with beautiful ease before the door; the staircase is perfumed with flowers, the gold plate glitters with gems; in one room they are busy preparing for dinner, in another the table is covered with papers. This quality of animation is sustained by Disraeli's choice of words in the most trivial places: 'The chairs had been *rifled* from a Venetian palace; the couches were part of the *spoils* of the French revolution'.[1] Even more important for Disraeli's view of things than the formal outlines, is this vivid animation filling them through and through.

That Disraeli sees this life and energy not opposed to long-rooted tradition, but an essential aspect of it, is something quite distinctive in his outlook. It is unmistakable in his account in *Coningsby* of the great house of Lord Monmouth.[2] This the reader sees first with 'the beautiful light of summer' shining over it . . . 'there was not a point which was not as fresh as if it had been renovated but yesterday'. It was a Tudor house, a medley of architecture 'with a wild dash of the fantastic in addition'. The surrounding countryside is 'sparkling with cultivation'. Coningsby himself wanders out into the gardens in a beautiful, calm evening, but 'the mitigating hour that softens the heart made his spirit brave'. When the moon rises, it is 'a pale and then gleaming tint . . . and soon a glittering light flooded the lawns and glades'. The chapter ends as Coningsby reaches 'a rushing river, foaming in the moonlight, and wafting on its blue breast the shadow of a thousand stars'. There are no ancestral slumbers here.

Lothair's visit to his country seat, Muriel Towers, has the same brilliant colour and animation. 'Muriel Towers', the chapter begins,[3] 'crowned a wooded steep, part of a wild and winding and sylvan valley at the bottom of which

[1] HT. 359 (my italics).   [2] C. 360-63.   [3] L. 189-204.

rushed a foaming stream' and 'the park, too, was full of life', with deer and fierce white cattle roaming among the glens and dells and savage woods, or by the glittering lake. Lothair arrives in his barouche: the postilions dash through the park, the startled deer scud away across the grass. There is a 'sinuous' lake with green islands and golden gondolas, the principal gateway was once 'the boast of a celebrated convent on the Danube'. Later that day, as he wanders over the castle, 'What charmed Lothair most . . . were the number of courts and quadrangles . . . all of bright and fantastic architecture, and each of which was a garden, glowing with brilliant colours, and gay with the voice of fountains or the forms of gorgeous birds'. On another day, he and his friends explore the place together. They go everywhere in the interior, but all is so novel and beautiful that no one is tired; and no one, he repeats, is tired that afternoon, when they drive for hours in the park. The gardens 'had been formed in a sylvan valley enclosed with gilded gates . . . the contrast between the parterres blazing with colour and the sylvan background, the undulating paths over romantic heights, the fanes and the fountains, the glittering statues, and the Babylonian terraces, formed a whole much of which was beautiful, and all of which was striking and singular'. Some of this, of course, is nonsense, but Disraeli's nonsense, as we shall see, has a certain method in it.

This love of what is brilliant and colourful does not find expression only in the scenes of aristocratic traditionalism. It pervades the novels, is perhaps their most striking quality, and produces innumerable descriptions, incidents and conversations, all with this distinctive bias. It is supported by Disraeli's swift, vigorous, staccato style. It lies behind the extraordinarily large number of fine mornings in these books — it is a fine morning when Ferdinand Armine surveys his ancestral park after coming home at last ('the tall trees rising and flinging their taller shadows over the bright and dewy turf'),[1] when the Duke of St. James sets off to give his maiden speech in the House of

[1] HT. 71.

Lords,[1] when Tancred leaves Jerusalem,[2] when Lothair
first sees it,[3] and each time it is the glitter and gusto and
life of the morning that Disraeli wants to secure.   He
pursues these same qualities in describing, for example, the
rivers of Damascus :

> They gleam amid their groves of fruit, wind through their
> vivid meads, sparkle among perpetual flowers, gush from the
> walls, bubble in the courtyards, dance and carol in the
> streets :   everywhere their joyous voices, everywhere their
> glancing forms, filling the whole world around with freshness,
> and brilliancy, and fragrance, and life.

— and, as so often, he goes straight on to indicate how this
scene provokes meditation and gives it a certain bias :

> One might fancy, as we track them in their dazzling
> course, or suddenly making their appearance in every spot
> and in every scene, that they were the guardian spirits of
> the city.[4]

Because of the contrast it offers with other novelists,
Disraeli's description of an early morning coach ride [5] is
illuminating :

> Away whirled the dashing Dart over the rich plains of our
> merry midland ;   a quick and dazzling vision of golden corn-
> fields and lawny pasture land ;   farmhouses embowered in
> orchards and hamlets shaded by the straggling members of
> some vast and ancient forest.   Then rose in the distance the
> dim blue towers, or the graceful spire, of some old cathedral,
> and soon the spreading causeways announce their approach
> to some provincial capital.   The coachman flanks his leaders,
> who break into a gallop ;   the guard sounds his triumphant
> bugle ;   the coach bounds over the noble bridge that spans a
> stream covered with craft ;   public buildings, guildhalls, and
> county gaols rise on each side.   Rattling through many an
> inferior way they at length emerged into the High Street,
> the observed of all observers, and mine host of the Red Lion,
> or the White Hart, followed by all his waiters, advances from
> his portal with a smile to receive the 'gentlemen passengers'.

---

[1] YD. 289.   [2] T. 222.   [3] L. 407.   [4] T. 379.   [5] HT. 33-4.

'The coach stops here half an hour, gentlemen : dinner is quite ready !'

'Tis a delightful sound. And what a dinner ! What a profusion of substantial delicacies ! What mighty and iris-tinted rounds of beef ! What vast and marble-veined ribs ! What gelatinous veal pies ! What colossal hams ! Those are evidently prize cheeses ! And how invigorating is the perfume of those various and variegated pickles ! Then the bustle emulating the plenty ; the ringing of bells, the clash of thoroughfare, the summoning of ubiquitous waiters, and the all-pervading feeling of omnipotence, from the guests, who order what they please, to the landlord, who can produce and execute everything they can desire. 'Tis a wondrous sight.

George Eliot used coaches to introduce quite a different picture of life, as we shall see ; and so did Dickens, for he catches the same richness and plenitude as Disraeli, but adds to it the humane and whimsical geniality of a mood that is quite different.[1]

Another way of seeing how carefully selective Disraeli's situations are usually, is to examine chapter 66 of *Lothair* ; for here, in a grand Catholic procession and service at Rome, he has exactly the sort of opportunity he seizes so often with gusto, but it so happens that this time he wishes to present the scene unsympathetically. Despite all the lavish colour and excited movement, the touches that secure this effect are easily seen. The cardinal's coaches were 'brilliant equipages', but this time it was because they had had to be recently replaced, Garibaldi having burnt the traditional ones ; a phrase here and there — 'monsignori and prelates without end' — suggests that the procession is grandiose rather than grand ; the congregation in church flutter their fans, eat sugar plums, take snuff ; Lothair's escort is clearly a schemer ; the marshals are 'experienced' and business-like ; the cardinals' train-bearers are 'exhibiting with the skill of artists the splendour of their violet robes'. All that seems achieved by the brilliant ceremony is that this long service 'could not be

---

[1] Cf. *Felix Holt*, the Introduction (discussed below, p. 117), and *Pickwick Papers*, chap. 28.

said to be wearisome'. The whole incident is important because here Disraeli refuses to find the qualities of life that he finds so often, and this exceptional case throws the usual case into sharp relief.

Sometimes Disraeli, or one of his characters, expresses this view of things explicitly. 'Life is adventurous. Events are perpetually occurring, even in the calmness of domestic existence, which change in an instant the whole train and tenor of our thoughts and feelings',[1] he writes; or 'how full of adventure is life! It is monotonous only to the monotonous.'[2] 'The sense of existence' alone is the charm of life to Sidonia.[3] Lord Monmouth finds the world 'a masquerade; a motley sparkling multitude, in which you may mark all forms and colours, and listen to all sentiments and opinions';[4] for him, the driving force behind this is only a desire for plunder, but in adding this he ceases to speak for the author. Perhaps the clearest passage of this kind is in *Venetia*, when the two poets indulge in philosophical remarks as — one early morning — they sit together on the Italian coast and look out over the sea:

'. . . The great secret, we cannot penetrate that with all our philosophy, my dear Herbert. . . . And yet what a grand world it is! Look at this bay, these blue waters, the mountains, and these chestnuts, devilish fine! The fact is, truth is veiled, but like the Shekinah over the tabernacle, the veil is of dazzling light.'

'Life is the great wonder,' said Herbert, 'into which all that is strange and startling resolves itself. The mist of familiarity obscures from us the miracle of our being. Mankind are constantly starting at the events which they consider extraordinary. But a philosopher acknowledges only one miracle, and that is life . . .'[5]

Herbert (he is in part a portrait of Shelley) then leads the conversation on further, to life in the biologist's sense; but it is clear that for a moment the two men's conversation has been moulded so as to express the author's own view; and the word 'miracle', applied to life as a whole, shows

[1] HT. 19.   [2] T. 459.   [3] C. 248.   [4] C. 201.   [5] V. 415-16.

by itself how much, at this point, Disraeli has in common
with Carlyle — and with Newman.

It is on this exuberance, this almost boisterous zest for
life, that one must rely in order to meet an obvious criticism
of Disraeli as a novelist with any considered view of the
world; for in many of his books there are remarks or
incidents that seem thoroughly melodramatic and irresponsible — seem nonsense, in fact, like the fanes and glittering statues and Babylonian terraces of Muriel Towers.
Coningsby first met Sidonia, for example, after a tramp
in the forest that was interrupted by a thunderstorm:
the wild-fowl and deer were in panic, the forest trees
roared and shrieked, 'the passion of the ash was heard in
moans of thrilling anguish'. Coningsby, under a sky
black as ebony, took refuge in a forest farmhouse. There,
as he stood at the window, 'a flash of lightning illumined
the whole country, and a horseman at full speed, followed
by his groom, galloped up to the door' [1] — Sidonia has
arrived. Sybil, sitting on a bench in St. James's Park (it
was a beautiful summer morning, with shining clouds,
glittering waters, and prismatic wild-fowl), reads Egremont's moving speech in the House of Lords. There
were tears in her eyes; she looked up 'as it were for relief',
and 'before her stood the orator himself'.[2] Earlier in the
same novel Egremont, Morley and Gerard converse among
the ruins of Marney Abbey.[3] One of them enunciates
the doctrine of The Two Nations. A sudden flush of rosy
light suffuses the grey ruins, the twilight star glitters
through a vacant arch, a lovely voice is heard singing the
evening hymn to the Virgin. It proves to be Gerard's
daughter; no one can take all this very seriously.

One is tempted by their humour, presumably half-
conscious, to quote other instances. Tancred and Fakredeen go to visit the Queen of the Ansarey: both dress in
their best, one is a blaze of shawls and jewelled arms, and
Tancred 'retained on this, as he had done on every other
occasion, the European dress, though in the present
instance it assumed a somewhat more brilliant shape than

[1] C. 114.   [2] S. 337.   [3] S. 67.

ordinary, in the dark green regimentals, the rich embroidery, and the flowing plume of the Bellamont yeomanry cavalry'.[1] Vivian Grey, at seventeen, 'a young and tender plant in a moral hothouse . . . paced his chamber in an agitated spirit, and panted for the senate'.[2] Glastonbury, in *Henrietta Temple*, wanders on foot as a young man through Switzerland and Italy; we are told that he is probably driven by an unconscious desire to discover the ideal: what he brings back, after three years, is several thousand sketches, and a complete Alpine Hortus Siccus.[3] When Ferdinand is under arrest for three thousand pounds, he is offered the money by the girl he thinks has abandoned him for another man, is sent it by the girl whom he has abandoned himself, and receives the following note from the elegant and imperturbable Count Mirabel, who went gambling the previous evening in an effort to win something to lend him:

> Berkeley Square, half-past 7, morning
>
> Mon ami. Best joke in the world! I broke Crocky's bank three times. Of course; I told you so. I win 15,000 l. Directly I am awake I will send you the three thousand, and I will lend you the rest until your marriage. . . .[4]

— the marriage is to the richest heiress in England.[5] These are a few examples of a quality that really runs through the novels; many passages quoted earlier in other contexts resemble them; and many readers are likely to feel that

[1] T. 418. There is no doubt that Disraeli saw the fun of this. Compare the intentionally comic Sir Vavasour Firebrace's glowing description of the glories of a resuscitated 'equestrian order': '"Picture us for a moment, to yourself, going down in procession to Westminster, for example, to hold a chapter. Five or six hundred baronets in dark green costume, — the appropriate dress of *equites aurati*; each not only with his badge, but with his collar of SS; belted and scarfed; his scarf glittering; his pennon flying; his hat white, with a plume of white feathers; of course the sword and the gilt spurs. In one hand, the thumb-ring and signet not forgotten, we hold our coronet of two balls!"

'Egremont stared with irrepressible astonishment at the excited being. . . .' (S. 58-9). Here Disraeli is enjoying the fun of an idea about which, in the *Vindication of the English Constitution* (WW. 151-61), he writes with full seriousness.

[2] VG. 17. [3] HT. 15. [4] HT. 444.
[5] See HT. 81, 'Language cannot describe the startling symmetry of her superb figure'.

as a result, Disraeli's novels are to some degree in the realm of farce or fantasy. If this is where they belong, they can hardly also mediate a serious view of the world — or at the very least, these rollicking irresponsibilities must surely detract from their power to do so.

But on reflection, the problem seems more complex : for while it is clear that these incidents cannot be taken seriously *in isolation*, as specimens of what life is like, it is less clear that, in an unexpected and indirect way, they do not encourage the reader to accept the whole tenor of the novels in which they occur. This may appear paradoxical ; but less so, if we bear in mind the rather distinctive view of things to which Disraeli wanted to give expression. He was an optimist about both the quality of life, and its ultimate results : he saw the world as an exciting, exhilarating place, and a place that characteristically supplied happy endings. A twofold cheerfulness of this kind, however, is extremely likely to put readers out of sympathy : they can too readily call exceptions to mind, or they are too familiar with people who advance these controversial opinions with a complacent pomposity that is revolting. Disraeli's farcical and fantastic touches are a kind of safety-valve ; they provide for scepticism because they do not have to be taken in full seriousness ; they invite us to suspend disbelief for the sake of fairy-story pleasures, and so they provide for a margin of disagreement within the frame of a general agreement. And they also modify the reader's impression, not of the world, but of the author : it is so obvious in these passages that Disraeli is enjoying himself, and his attitude to the world is infectious through a direct contact with his sanguine personality. In other words, these intrinsically flippant touches in the novels help to control Disraeli's tone : and thereby they adjust both the general character of his work, and our sense of himself.

(iv) *Ideals and Realities*

What this general character is, however, has still not quite been identified, for Disraeli's thoroughgoing optimism has another significant result. It means that he need not make depicting the world as it is, and suggesting to his readers how they ought to behave in it, two distinct tasks. Probably he had a less detailed interest in the moral implications of his view of things; but for an optimist the 'painful right' of George Eliot does not exist; there is no inescapable contrast between what is and what should be, and in depicting the former an optimistic author tends to depict the latter. The two coalesce. Coningsby is sometimes an example of this process: meditating on the spectacle of King's Chapel, Cambridge, by moonlight, he says: 'Where is the spirit that raised these walls? . . . Is it indeed extinct? . . . But I cannot believe it. Man that is made in the image of the Creator, is made for God-like deeds. Come what may, I will cling to the heroic principle. It can alone satisfy my soul.'[1] But only a few pages before this, we read that Coningsby had 'the heroic feeling', 'born in the heart'.[2] In a sense, then, he already is the noble figure that he strives to become. This ambivalency between the normative and the descriptive runs through the novels, and qualifies Disraeli's extravaganzas in another way: when his work cannot be accepted as describing the world as it is, one accepts it as having shifted for a moment to describing the world as it should be. Like any optimist, Disraeli often finds the transition from one to the other imperceptible; and very often his work carries conviction because we are brought to see it as somehow a portrait of what is, and of what should be, all in one.

This is reinforced by the general pattern of the novels (for in this respect they have a remarkable — indeed a revealing — sameness), and in their basic selection of material. Every one of Disraeli's novels is centred upon a young man's growing to maturity, forming his views on the world, and finding his right place in it (*Sybil* is different only in that this happens to both the hero and the heroine). As, each time, this takes place, Disraeli's sense of the brilliance and variety and colour of the world finds expression not only in the details of incidents, but also in their

[1] C. 266.   [2] C. 259.

juxtaposition.[1] All the novels involve a considerable
variety of scene — a sharp contrast to the rigidly circum-
scribed locale of the typical George Eliot novel. The large
majority of them are novels of travel; and (except for
Vivian Grey, set in England and Germany) it is travel
always in the same direction, to Paris, Rome, Greece and
the Levant. But their variety comes from changes in mode
of life, as well as in scene: the great country house, the
London season, high life in Paris, aristocratic business
and industrial society, cottage scenes, industrial slums
as in *Sybil*, the world of servants (*Tancred* opens with a
delightful scene from the private life of Leander, the
celebrated cook), inns and coaching scenes (*The Young
Duke*), a Dickensian spunging-house (*Henrietta Temple*),
a drunken carouse among German barons (*Vivian Grey*),
fishermen, artists, an Italian patriot army (*Lothair*) — in
every novel, Disraeli exploits the varieties of place and
class to make his panorama as changeful and colourful as
he can.

But it is not a systematic changefulness: Disraeli does
not explore how the elements of society are interrelated.
Even *Sybil* has a good deal of the picaresque in its form.
The novels rarely develop through any internal logic:
they turn on casual events, on delightful, exhilarating
operations of chance. The Duke of St. James is rescued,
at the nadir of his fortunes, by lucky financial accidents,
the unexpected ability to make a brilliant speech on
Catholic Emancipation, and a rise in the price of coal;
the deadlock in *Venetia* evanesces because Lord Herbert
is reconciled to his wife though everything has made this
seem impossible; Coningsby's problems are solved by the
opportune death of his grandfather, and his quite unexpected ability to become a future Lord Chancellor, apparently at no trouble to himself; Ferdinand, in *Henrietta
Temple*, escapes ruin through a chance introduction to his
munificent moneylender, and then another to the wonderful
Count Mirabel; *Lothair* turns upon a moonlight vision in

[1] Compare how Carlyle secures an effect through telling juxtaposition,
discussed above, p. 30.

the Coliseum at Rome, *Endymion* on an opportune loan
of twenty thousand pounds; Egremont's life is transformed
by a chance meeting in the ruined abbey; *Vivian Grey*,
Contarini Fleming and — very differently — *Tancred*, are
picaresque fantasies from beginning to end. But although
Disraeli's situations do not develop through any inner
necessity, they mediate a definite view of things nevertheless. The world may be largely one of chance, but it is
one of chance that is exhilarating, colourful and benign —
of Chance fit for heroes to live on.

Disraeli's view of the world is conveyed through what
he omits as well as what he presents. In some of the novels,
one finds the seclusion, rich with tradition, of the remote
country house; but there is never any drabness — even
in *Sybil* the working-classes are fierce and colourful. And
there is really no badness either. Mrs. Felix Lorraine in
Vivian Grey, Sir Lucius Grafton in *The Young Duke*,
Joseph Diggs in *Sybil*, are all quite secondary and not
perhaps wholly serious figures; and they all come to bad
ends in just the same casual, chance way that the good
characters come to good ends. The Young Duke's gambling bout, Ferdinand's disappointments in love, even the
angry scenes in *Sybil*, are incidentals that are cancelled
out by the whole trend of the novels in which they appear.
Disraeli does not explore that part of human experience
which comprises sin, guilt, depravity or misfortune; they
are not primary data in the view of life which his work
conveys.

Disraeli's polemical interest is often somewhat fitful;
his high spirits and optimism and brilliance often serve the
needs only of a happy romantic *Wanderjahr* or love-story.
But nearly all his novels sooner or later concentrate on that
self-renewing traditionalism that he regarded as key to the
good life. That this is true, in various ways, of the *Young
England* trilogy needs no proof; [1] but the other novels are

---

[1] Though the well-known last sentence of *Tancred* ('The Duke and
Duchess of Bellamont had arrived in Jerusalem') has perhaps been misunderstood in part: it is surely not just a rhetorical flourish, but indicates,
besides this, that Tancred's parents have at last felt the power of those
traditional influences that meant so much to their son.

polemical in this respect also. The essential line of their plots recommends their author's scheme of values. The Young Duke abandons his thoughtless extravagance for an interest in politics and the life of a territorial magnate. Cadurcis and Venetia settle down as country nobility and repair their ancestral home. Ferdinand Armine becomes an improving landlord, and his successes in public affairs seem likely to revive the family barony. Lothair finds a solution to his perplexities in the duties of a great land-owner, and the traditional anglicanism that goes with them. *Vivian Grey* is no exception : the upshot of all Vivian's German experiences is that whatever was good in the traditionalism of the petty princes can be transferred without loss to the greater princes. Even *Endymion* has some-thing of it, for the hero, rising from poverty to become Prime Minister, is only restoring the tradition of his father ; while the great industrialist, Job Thornbury, becomes a landed patriarch and is jokingly called 'Squire' by his sons. One novel after another bears witness, in its whole contour, to the view that life is colourful and kindly, and that the right ordering of it lies in an active and adaptable traditionalism.

But this is to say that Disraeli's fiction has a much more genuine integration than is sometimes allowed. It does not break into two unrelated halves, empty political general-ities on the one hand, and irresponsible though picturesque frivolities on the other. Disraeli's respect for tradition is inseparable from his zest for what is colourful and lively, because it is the latter which interprets the former. For him, this light-hearted brilliance is the world's enduring and traditional quality. The serious and the rollicking parts of his work unite ; and this fact enables one to see two things, first that a more or less serious expression of his outlook is diffused quite widely through the novels, and second that Disraeli's qualities as a light entertainer, so far from destroying the more overtly serious and con-sidered of his works, do something to clarify, and even I think to deepen their meaning. Moreover, they do this not merely in a quite abstract way. It is these qualities which largely control the tone in which Disraeli expresses his message, and the frame of mind of the reader approaching that message. The lighter side of Disraeli's work both interprets, and makes more sympathetic, the side which is more in earnest.

CHAPTER V

GEORGE ELIOT

(1) *Preliminary: 'Silas Marner'*

GEORGE ELIOT is quite plainly a novelist who is also a sage. She speaks in her letters of 'The high responsibilities of literature that undertakes to represent life'; [1] she writes 'it is my way . . . to urge the human sanctities . . . through pity and terror, as well as admiration and delight',[2] or 'My books have for their main bearing a conclusion . . . without which I could not have dared to write any representation of human life — namely, that . . . fellowship between man and man . . . is not dependent on conceptions of what is not man: and that the idea of God, so far as it has been a high spiritual influence, is the ideal of a goodness entirely human'.[3] But there is really no need to turn to the letters. The didactic intention is perfectly clear from the novels alone.

In *Adam Bede*, for example — and it is George Eliot's first full-length work — she says that so far from inventing ideal characters, her 'strongest effort is . . . to give a faithful account of men and things as they have mirrored themselves in my mind'.[4] Realistic pictures of obscure mediocrity serve a didactic purpose: 'these fellow-mortals, every one, must be accepted as they are . . . these people . . . it is needful you should tolerate, pity and love: it is these more or less ugly, stupid, inconsistent people whose movements of goodness you should be able to admire'.[5] Finally, she gives the lesson an autobiographical import: 'The way

[1] To John Blackwood, 30th March 1861 (quoted in J. W. Cross, *George Eliot's Life*, vol. ii, p. 293).

[2] To Frederic Harrison, 15th August 1866 (*ibid.* vol. ii, p. 442).

[3] To the Hon. Mrs. Ponsonby, 10th December 1874 (*ibid.* vol. iii, p. 245).   [4] AB. 177.   [5] AB. 178.

in which I have come to the conclusion that human nature
is lovable — . . . its deep pathos, its sublime mysteries —
has been by living a great deal among people more or less
commonplace and vulgar'.[1]

But George Eliot is not interested only in people and
in their good and bad qualities; she wishes, beyond this,
to impart a vision of the world that reveals its whole design
and value. Her teaching may be partly ethical, but it is
ethics presented as a system and grounded on a wider
metaphysical doctrine. Her early novels emphasize how
an integrated scheme of values is a help to man — 'No
man can begin to mould himself on a faith or an idea
without rising to a higher order of experience' [2] — and she
vividly indicates the forces in her own time that impelled
men to seek such a scheme. For one class to be cultured
and sophisticated another must be 'in unfragrant deafening
factories, cramping itself in mines, sweating at furnaces
. . . or else, spread over sheepwalks, and scattered in lonely
houses and huts . . . where the rainy days look dreary.
This wide national life is based entirely on . . . the emphasis
of want. . . . Under such circumstances there are many . . .
who have absolutely needed an emphatic belief: life in this
unpleasurable shape demanding some *solution* even to
unspeculative minds . . . something that good society calls
"enthusiasm", something that will present motives in an
entire absence of high prizes . . . that includes resignation
for ourselves and active love for what is not ourselves.' [3]
This is an interesting passage for the social historian,
and for the critic of nineteenth-century capitalism too;
but its present importance lies in showing what was of
concern to George Eliot as she wrote, and how we are
justified in searching her novels for philosophy as well as
ethics.

Moreover, she clearly saw that these principles did not
lend themselves to abstract presentation; to be convincing
they needed the methods of the imaginative writer. A
striking passage in *Janet's Repentance* asserts that the
influence which really promotes us to a higher order of

[1] AB. 186.   [2] SCL. 339-40.   [3] MF. 314 (my italics).

experience is 'not calculable by algebra, not deducible by logic, but mysterious . . . ideas are often poor ghosts . . . they pass athwart us in thin vapour, and cannot make themselves felt. But sometimes they are made flesh; they . . . speak to us in appealing tones; they are *clothed in a living human soul, with all its conflicts, its faith.* . . . Then their presence is a power . . . and we are drawn after them with gentle compulsion.' [1] We cannot but recognize, even in passing, how Dinah Morris, Maggie, Dorothea and others of George Eliot's characters are just such incarnations. And when, in *The Mill on The Floss*, she writes of the influence of Thomas à Kempis, this appeal of a non-logical kind is related directly to how books are written. The *Imitation* still 'works miracles' because 'written down by a hand that waited for the heart's prompting'; [2] expensive sermons and treatises that lack this essential carry no 'message', no 'key' to 'happiness' in the form of a key to understanding; their abstractions consequently cannot persuade.

Thus it is clear that George Eliot wished to convey the kind of message, and knew that she must use the distinctive methods, with which this enquiry is concerned. But in examining how her novels are moulded to conform to these requirements, there is something which is here of first importance as it was not with Disraeli. For George Eliot was a profoundly, perhaps excessively serious writer, and her novels are coloured through and through by her view of the world, and devoted in their whole dimensions to giving it a sustained expression, whereas most of Disraeli's novels are of lighter weight, and give expression to his more serious views more or less fitfully. It would, with George Eliot, be therefore a mistake to begin by noticing incidents, metaphors, snatches of conversation, or similar details. What must be given primary stress is the broad outline, the whole movement of her novels as examples of life that claim to be typical. 'How unspeakably superior', wrote Matthew Arnold, 'is the effect of the one moral impression left by a great action treated as a

<hr />

[1] SCL. 393-4 (my italics).   [2] MF. 313.

whole, to the effect produced by the most striking single thought or by the happiest image.' [1] This is as true of the work of the sage-novelist as it is of classical drama or the epic poem. To ignore it is to miss the wood for the trees.

Silas Marner, perhaps because it is simple and short, shows this most plainly. It is worth examining in some detail. Silas the weaver, expelled from his little nonconformist community through a trick of blind chance, settles as a lonely bachelor in the obscure Midland village of Raveloe; one son of the local landlord steals his savings but is unsuspected, and Eppie, the daughter of another by a secret marriage, appears as a foundling at his cottage and he adopts her. Many years after, when she is a young woman about to marry, and her father Godfrey is middle-aged and has married again, the truth about her birth and about the robbery comes at last to light. Various things lend the tale its distinctive quality. First, the characters and their doings seem to belong to the same order of things as the non-human world that surrounds them. The little village, off the beaten track in its wooded hollow, is half submerged in the world of nature. The villagers are 'pressed close by primitive wants'.[2] The passage of time and the rotation of the seasons affect humans and animals and plants all alike. Individuals are dominated by their environment. 'Marner's face and figure shrank and bent themselves into a constant mechanical relation to the objects of his life, so that he produced the same sort of impression as a handle or a crooked tube, which has no meaning standing apart.' [3] It follows from this that all the people in the book are humble and obscure; they may be attractive or virtuous, but they are all nobodies. Silas is a poor weaver who finds hard words in the prayer-book, Godfrey Cass is a squireen's son and a barmaid's husband, Eppie marries a gardener — even Nancy Lammeter, Godfrey's second wife, is only a trim farmer's

---

[1] Preface tc the 1853 Edition of the poems (reprinted in *Irish Essays*, etc., *Works*, vol. xi. pp. 288-9).
[2] SM. 6.   [3] SM. 25.

daughter who does the baking and says "'oss". Such, the tale implies, is the staple of men and women.

The pattern of events in which these people are involved is one of 'poetic justice': vice suffers, virtue is rewarded. Silas, though unfortunate at first, is a good man, and at last is made happy. Godfrey Cass, who refused to acknowledge his daughter, has no children by his second marriage. Dunstan Cass the rake, stealing Silas's money at night, falls into the pond and is drowned. But this justice is rough and partial. It is not vindictively stern, so much as impersonal and aloof and half-known; it takes a slow chance course, and meets human imperfections not with definite vengeance but with a drab pervasive sense of partial failure or limited success. For the peasantry of such places as Raveloe 'pain and mishap present a far wider range of possibilities than gladness and enjoyment'. For Silas in his time of misfortune the world is a strange and hopeless riddle. His money is taken, Eppie arrives, through the operation of forces that he venerates without comprehending. Done injustice by a sudden twist of fate, he comes to trust in the world again over a long period of years, as the imperceptible influence of Eppie gradually revives long-dead memories and emotions; over the same period his estrangement from the other villagers is slowly replaced by intimacy. His life is governed by habit, and so is theirs. We never learn whether his innocence ever became clear to the congregation that expelled him as a thief.

Though the book is so short, its unit of measurement is the generation: Silas young and old, Eppie the child and the bride, Godfrey the gay youth and the saddened, childless husband. The affairs of one generation are not finally settled except in the next, when Silas's happiness is completed by Eppie's marriage, and Godfrey's early transgressions punished by her refusal to become Miss Cass. Dunstan Cass's misdeeds are not even discovered until, twenty years after the robbery, his skeleton is found clutching the money-bags when the pond is drained; and this is brought to light through, of all things, Godfrey's activities as a virtuous, improving landlord. Well may the parish-clerk say 'there's windings i' things as they may carry you to the fur end o' the prayer-book afore you get back to 'em'. All in all, the world of the novel is one which, in its author's own words, 'never *can* be thoroughly joyous'. The unhappiness in it comes when natural generous feelings are atrophied by selfishness: Dunstan steals, Godfrey denies his daughter. And the consequences of sin are never quite obliterated; Godfrey must resign himself to childlessness, though resignation is itself a kind of content. Real happiness comes when numb unfeeling hardness, the state of mind for example of the grief-stricken and disillusioned Silas, slowly thaws to warmer emotions of kindliness and love.

This novel contains, therefore, though in little, a comprehensive vision of human life and the human situation. It does so through its deep and sustained sense of the influence of environment and of continuity between man and the rest of nature, through its selection as characters of ordinary people living drab and unremarkable lives, and through the whole course of its action, working out by imperceptible shifts or unpredictable swings of chance to a solution where virtue is tardily and modestly rewarded, and vice obscurely punished by some dull privation. The details of George Eliot's treatment operate within this broader framework.

(ii) *General Features of the Novels*

Most of George Eliot's other books express the same vision of life, some of them amplifying it through their greater length or complexity. All except *Romola* and *Daniel Deronda* are set in the same historical period — that of the immediate past. This choice is significant. It is a time sufficiently near the present for manners to be familiar, dull and unremarkable, and for nothing to have the excitement or glamour of the remoter past; and yet sufficiently remote for the rhythm of life to be slower, and for man to be more fully subservient to nature. *Felix Holt* (1866) has the 1830s for its period. 'The glory had not yet departed from the old coach-roads.' [1] But besides their glories, the coaches evoke other memories; they take us back to the shepherd 'with a slow and slouching walk, timed by the walk of grazing beasts . . . his glance accustomed to rest on things very near the earth . . . his solar system . . . the parish',[2] back to the great straggling hedgerows that hid the cottages, to the hamlet that 'turned its back on the road, and seemed to lie away from everything but its own patch of earth and sky',[3] and the villagers, free alike from popish superstition, and from 'handlooms and mines to be the pioneers of Dissent'. The third chapter of this book is devoted entirely to a survey of historical trends at the time of the story, with the comment, 'These social changes in Treby parish are comparatively public matters . . . but there is no private life which has not been determined by a wider public life . . . that mutual influence of dissimilar destinies which we shall see gradually unfolding itself'.[4] *Adam Bede* (1859) opens in the year 1799, when the village carpenter sings hymns as he works in his shop, and travellers go a-horseback, and 'there was yet a lingering after-glow' from the time of Wesley. The actions of *Middlemarch* (1871–2) and *The Mill on the Floss* (1860) seem also to be set in the 1830s; while *Silas Marner* (1861) is a story of the early nineteenth century 'when the spinning wheels hummed busily in the farmhouses' and pallid weavers, 'like the remnants of a disinherited race', were to be seen 'far away among the lanes, or deep in the bosom of the hills' and 'to the peasants of old times, the world outside their own direct experience was a region of vagueness and mystery'.[5]

The total impact of the novels also owes much to the sense they create of historical change; and of how, slowly, indirectly, in unexpected ways, it touches the lives of the characters. Inconspicuous as it is, this does much to suggest an integrated social continuity, of which personal relations between characters are only one part. *Janet's Repentance* portrays the gradual permeation of rural life

[1] FH. 1.   [2] FH. 2.   [3] FH. 3.   [4] FH. 51.   [5] SM. 3-4.

by Evangelicalism; it records one instance of a general social change. The background of *The Mill on the Floss* is the expanding prosperity and material progress of the whole nation; and when the fortunes of the Tulliver family are at their lowest, Tom is carried up again by the rising prosperity of the firm he works for, with its many interrelated and developing commercial activities. At one point the story hangs upon whether or not to install steam plant in the Tulliver's old watermill. When Silas Marner goes back at last to the chapel in Lantern Yard where he worshipped as a young man, he finds everything swept away to make room for a modern factory with its crowds of workpeople. In *Felix Holt*, personal experience is determined by the Reform Bill's gradually taking effect, and still more by the slow shift of population from agriculture to industry.

But in this respect there is a more massive contribution. Real historical change is quite important in these novels, but it is less important than the complex interaction of town and countryside, of the pleasures or amusements of life with its work and business, of the various classes of society, and of social institutions like the church, the village inn, the bank, the chapel, the manor, the school and the workshop. It is an interesting contrast with Dickens. Varied though his social panorama may be, he is really interested in the occupations of only one social class — his business men are rarely seen in their offices, and if they are, it is usually not to work — and an occupation interests him not for its distinctive niche in the scheme of things, but for what it has of odd or picturesque or *macabre*. His characters sell curiosities or optical instruments or skeletons; they drive coaches or keep inns; they are ham actors, dancing-masters, fishermen; or if simply clerks or schoolmasters, they tend to be oddities or rogues in themselves. But for George Eliot every character has his distinctive occupational niche, and it is this which determines his nature and gives him what leverage he has upon the course of the action. Lawyer Dempster in *Janet's Repentance*, Mr. Tulliver in *The Mill on the Floss*, Lawyer Jermyn in

Felix Holt, Bulstrode and Mr. Vincy and Caleb Garth and Lydgate in *Middlemarch*, Tito in *Romola* even — all of them have their livelihoods to earn, and their actions are largely governed by the need to do so in a world that is complex and slow to change.

Often these complexities are not treated fully in the novel, but they lend it a depth and variety of social colour. Adam Bede's getting a wife and following a career are not two processes, but one; and as the story proceeds, the relation between him and Arthur Donnithorne is a product of how they stand as rival lovers, and how they stand as landlord and bailiff. In *Middlemarch*, the love-affair of Lydgate and Rosamond is largely a projection of their social and economic standing. Similarly in a minor work like *Brother Jacob*: the story centres upon how a new shopping habit gradually spreads through a country town. 'In short,' writes George Eliot, 'the business of manufacturing the more fanciful viands was fast passing out of the hands of maids and matrons in private families, and was becoming the work of a special commercial organ.'[1] Mr. Freely, who is responsible for this 'corruption of Grimworth manners',[2] 'made his way gradually into Grimworth homes, as his commodities did'.[3] His engagement to a prosperous farmer's pretty daughter is an aspect of economic success.

Seeing the characters thus enmeshed in a wider context develops in George Eliot's readers the sense of a tortuous, half-unpredictable, slowly changing world of a thousand humdrum matters. 'Anyone watching keenly the stealthy convergence of human lots, sees a slow preparation of effects from one life on another . . . old provincial society had its share of this subtle movement; had not only its striking downfalls . . . but also those less marked vicissitudes which are constantly shifting the boundaries of social intercourse, and begetting new consciousness of interdependence . . . municipal town and rural parish gradually made fresh threads of connection — gradually, as the old stocking gave way to the savings-bank, and the worship

[1] *Op. cit.* (printed in SM, p. 332).   [2] *Ibid.* 329.   [3] *Ibid.* 333.

of the solar guinea became extinct . . . settlers, too, came from distant counties, some with an alarming novelty of skill, others with an offensive advantage in cunning.' [1] Lydgate exemplifies the first of these types, Bulstrode the second. The author, illustrating the general order of life by particular cases, is at pains to ensure that we see the wider drift.

George Eliot also uses the temporal scale of her novels for didactic ends. The slow movement of the natural world is stressed by the great span of time with which every novel deals — a span not packed with events in their variety, but necessary if we are to watch the full working out of even one event. *Silas Marner*, *The Mill on the Floss* and *Amos Barton* (if we take count of its epilogue) actually narrate events over a full generation. All of the other novels or *Scenes*, except *Adam Bede*, plunge back a full generation to depict the circumstances that originally created the situation of the novel. In *Felix Holt*, for example, the fortunes of all the chief characters except Felix are settled by the liaison, thirty-five years ago, between the local landowner's wife and her lawyer, and by the elderly minister's marriage as a young man to a Frenchwoman whose infant daughter is now a grown woman. *Daniel Deronda* tells how Daniel recovered the Judaic heritage of which he was deprived at birth. It is the same with the others.

The sense of a deterministic world where everything happens of necessity is increased in these novels by their stress on kinship. George Eliot is never tired of emphasizing how the nature of the parents fixes that of their children. *Felix Holt* depends for its climax on a visible resemblance between father and son. The earlier pages of *The Mill on the Floss* are full of the power of family tradition, the manner in which children reproduce and yet modify their parents' characters, and above all, the sense that kinship by blood is the basis of just such a slowly operating, half-inarticulate interdependence between things as George Eliot desires us to recognize everywhere. The reader who

[1] Mid. 68.

responds to this will see an added point when Maggie
rescues Tom from the flood. The details of the narrative
may leave much to be desired. But Maggie's action shows
how a deep sentiment of kinship may overcome years of
hostility ; and in essence, it is apt in the same way as Aunt
Glegg's sudden change to helpfulness when her niece is
in trouble. It is not pure melodrama or pure sentimentalism
at all. Again, in *Adam Bede*, the author is careful to bring
out the partial resemblance and partial contrast between
Adam and his mother, or Mr. Irwine and old Mrs. Irwine,
or Mrs. Poyser and her niece Dinah the Puritan. There is
a sustained sense of continuity by blood decisive in its
influence but almost too obscure and subtle for observation.
If there were any doubt that this contributes to a general
impression of nature, the point is made explicitly in
Daniel Deronda. When Daniel tells Mordecai, his Jewish
future brother-in-law, that he too is a Jew, Mordecai's
first words indicate how this kinship adumbrates a wider
system : 'we know not all the pathways . . . all things are
bound together in that Omnipresence which is the plan
and habitation of the world, and events are as a glass
where-through our eyes see some of the pathways'.[1]
Kinship is an aspect of the system of Nature.

(iii) *The Basic Selection*

The chief general feature which gives expression to George
Eliot's view of things has yet to be mentioned. It is the
very strict selection she makes of what characters or events
she is prepared to tell of at all.[2] This preliminary selection,
necessarily made by almost any artist, is easily overlooked ;
but of crucial importance. We may perhaps allow the
amplitude and solidity of George Eliot's best work to
blind us to all that is rigidly excluded from it ; yet a large
part of human nature she never touches. In all her work,
no one is coolly, calmly, deliberately selfish, like Becky

[1] DD. 543.
[2] *The Lifted Veil*, in many respects quite exceptional, is not taken into
account here.

Sharp;[1] the least lovable characters are merely half-aware
of the pain they cause others. No one except Mr. Tulliver
and Baldassare are even alleged to know real hatred, and
their feelings are constantly thwarted and attenuated by
the course of events. Apart from them, no one feels the
sudden, violent passions of anger, or jealousy, or revenge,
or spitefulness, or infatuation. (Stephen Guest perhaps
feels this for Maggie at one instant, when he kisses her arm,
but in the main the situation between them is different.)
No one consciously finds pleasure in doing wrong, or in
inflicting pain on themselves or others. No one is savage,
no one is depraved. The world of serious characters
divides into the good and the weak; being weak is essentially being stupid, being blinded to all the consequences.

Necessarily, the incidents are as distinctive as the
characters. There are no adventures, almost no scenes of
violence, no picaresque episodes or isolated romances.
The staple of the books lies in slowly ripening, intermittent,
half-unconscious things like disillusion, the quest for
insight, growing affection, reformation, or, above all,
temptation. Dorothea slowly learns that Casaubon is a
false god; Maggie, and Gwendolen Harleth in *Daniel
Deronda*, learn that happiness lies in renunciation; Silas's
starved affections unfold again in the presence of Eppie;
Fred Vincy reforms. To the slow mounting of temptation
George Eliot returns again and again. It is a temptation
like this which makes Arthur Donnithorne seduce Hetty
and Hetty abandon her child; Maggie and Stephen Guest
yield to a similar erosive process; so too with Bulstrode,
at both the beginning of his life when he makes his fortune
at the expense of others, and later when he occasions the
death of his former confederate. It is through this kind of
slow weakening, even, that Gwendolen Harleth fails to

---

[1] 'Rosamond . . . think no unfair evil of her, pray: she had no wicked
plots, nothing sordid or mercenary . . . she never thought of money except
as something necessary which other people would always provide' (Mid.
194-5); 'there may be coarse hypocrites, who consciously affect beliefs and
emotions for the sake of gulling the world, but Bulstrode was not one of
them. He was simply a man whose desires had been stronger than his
theoretic beliefs' (Mid. 448). (Compare the account of real heroes in
Janet's Repentance; SCL. 341.)

throw the rope to her drowning husband. So it is with Dunstan Cass stealing Silas's money. *Romola*, of course, is more than anything else an account of how Tito sins more and more deeply without ever really intending evil at all. No one, in the moment of yielding, fully sees the significance of his act; insight is dulled by the pressure of circumstance.

When George Eliot is thinking of how her characters relate to each other, though, two processes interest her chiefly, and they are of this same gradual and half-unseen kind. They are, estrangement, and — in its widest sense — endearment. *The Mill on the Floss* depicts the growth of affection between Maggie and Phillip Wakem, and then Maggie and Stephen Guest; and the waning of affection, except at the end, between Maggie and her brother. *Romola* records how Tito's position is slowly consolidated in his marriage with Romola, and then how she gradually becomes estranged from him. The relations between Adam and Dinah, or Arthur and Hetty in *Adam Bede*, between Felix Holt and Esther, between Gwendolen Harleth and her husband in *Daniel Deronda*, or between Dorothea and Casaubon and Ladislaw and Rosamond and Lydgate in *Middlemarch*, are of a similar kind. They are not phases or episodes, their resolution makes the substance of these novels from beginning to end. George Eliot cares for those aspects of human nature which come nearest to the *geological*. Such relationships may be crucial, but they are certainly distinctive. That by virtually confining herself to them she suggests that they are typical, is what contributes so much to her view of the human situation.

To sum up, then, George Eliot gives expression to her 'philosophy of life' by such broad and general features of her work as its characteristic setting in the recent past; its habit of linking a particular story to known historical conditions; its meticulous charting of social and economic patterns; its interest in slow changes and events that have remote consequences; its pervasive sense of the tie of kinship; and its being rigorously confined to characters and happenings of a quite distinctive kind. If we now turn

from these features to the details of presentation, we find
that they too play an important part; but as might be
expected, they indoctrinate us less with the speculative
than with the moral aspect of the author's teaching. In
doing so they reveal that, as is natural but important, this
moral teaching is at all points a consequence and inference
from her metaphysics.

The general reason why this is so could not be clearer.
For George Eliot, Man is a part of Nature, and Nature is a
vast and complex system of which the parts are subordinate
to impersonal forces governing the whole. The individuals
that belong to such a system cannot be heroes; they have
to be obscure and petty, and their characters cannot but
mingle good and bad. George Eliot never tires of saying
so. In *Mr. Gilfil's Love-Story*, describing Tina at the
height of her grief, she interrupts the story with 'Nature
was holding on her calm inexorable way'; and in this
'mighty torrent' Tina is no more important than an
amoeba or a sparrow.[1] And in *The Mill on the Floss* she
writes, 'It is a sordid life . . . this of the Tullivers and
Dodsons — irradiated by no sublime principles, no romantic visions . . . emmet-like . . . oppressive narrowness'.[2]
But if we have a full understanding, we see fine human
qualities, though they are inevitably moulded and adjusted
by the system. 'In natural science . . . there is nothing
petty to the mind that has a large vision of relations, and to
which every single object suggests a vast sum of conditions.
It is surely the same with the observation of human life.'[3]
In *Middlemarch* ordinariness actually creates the remarkable: 'That element of tragedy which lies in the very fact
of frequency, has not yet wrought itself into the coarse
emotion of mankind'.[4] But in *Amos Barton* another point
is made: people of this 'insignificant stamp', even so
'bear a conscience, and have felt the sublime prompting
to do the painful right'.[5] What is crucial is that George
Eliot's preoccupation with those whose life is obscure or
frustrated determines her portrait of human duty.

[1] SCL. 167-8.   [2] MF. 292-3.   [3] MF. 293.
[4] Mid. 141.   [5] SCL. 51.

(iv) *The Ethics*

First of all, in this complex world, duty is not always easy to recognize.[1] We might expect not. But sometimes it *is* easy. As Mrs. Farebrother is made to say, 'Keep hold of a few plain truths, and make everything square with them. When I was young, Mr. Lydgate, there never was any question about right and wrong.'[2] This proud, kindly, distinguished old lady is a reliable authority. George Eliot is fairly clear about what leads in moral questions to definite answers. Objectively, duty is settled by fixed and unalterable circumstances — by the constants in the system of Nature. We require 'that knowledge of the irreversible laws within and without . . . which, governing the habits, becomes morality'.[3] Sometimes the relevant circumstance is an established human tie or bond. 'She had rent the ties that had given meaning to duty';[4] 'It was as if he had found an added soul in finding his ancestry'.[5] But duty is determined, in the sense of *recognized*, less by ingenuity or logical acumen than by deep true feeling. 'That signifies nothing — what other men would think,' says honest Caleb Garth in *Middlemarch*, 'I've got a clear feeling inside me, and that I shall follow.'[6] In *Theophrastus Such* comes the formal — and as it is called, 'persuasive' — definition: '*Let our habitual talk give morals their full meaning* as that conduct which . . . would follow from the fullest knowledge and the fullest sympathy'.[7] Knowledge itself, if we may judge from an observation in *Middlemarch*, is in these matters a kind of feeling; and the passage quoted from *Theophrastus Such* goes on immediately to relate duty to the natural system, for it says

[1] 'A thick mist seemed to have fallen where Mr. Lyon was looking for the track of duty.' FH. 170.

[2] Mid. 123.   [3] MF. 310.   [4] MF. 512.

[5] DD. 540; see George Eliot's 'Notes' to *The Spanish Gypsy*: 'Meanwhile the subject had become more and more pregnant to me. I saw *it might be taken as a symbol* of the part which is played in the general human lot by hereditary conditions in the largest sense, and of the fact that what we call duty is entirely made up of such conditions.' (Cross, *op. cit.* vol. iii, p. 43; my italics.)

[6] Mid. 408.   [7] TS. 158 (my italics).

that this 'meaning' is 'perpetually corrected and enriched by a more thorough appreciation of dependence in things, and a finer sensibility to both physical and spiritual fact'. The word 'sensibility' is significant. According to George Eliot, we cannot fully unravel the system of 'dependence'; we must know it by the partly non-logical comprehension appropriate to it.

So much for what factors determine duty and what processes of thought discover it. In both, George Eliot's view follows from her whole metaphysics. This is true also of what she says about the behaviour that constitutes duty. To her, dutiful behaviour is renouncing pleasures in excess of our obscurity and unimportance, and resigning ourselves to the privations of a system of nature where personal happiness is subordinate and accidental. Resignation is a duty because Nature is as it is. 'Our life is determined for us,' says Maggie, 'and it makes the mind very free when we give up wishing and only think of bearing what is laid upon us'; [1] 'She was experiencing some of that peaceful melancholy which comes from the renunciation of demands for self, and from taking the ordinary good of existence . . . as a gift above expectation'. [2] Renunciation, for George Eliot, is the essential part of virtue; and it is the chief moral reality implied by her whole outlook.

Vice and virtue contrast with each other point by point. Wrong actions, like right ones, are determined by all the slow complexity of events: this determines them, however, not in the sense of making them wrong, but in the plainer sense of bringing them about. Lydgate sees himself 'sliding into that pleasureless yielding to the small solicitations of circumstance, which is a commoner history of perdition than any single momentous bargain'. [3] This too is how the thought of a sinful course of action grows in the mind. There is no need to reflect; sin proffers itself freely as what is most attractive. But according to George Eliot, what makes it possible for the sinful thought to dawn and to influence is the converse of what enables us

[1] MF. 327.   [2] DD. 577.   [3] Mid. 567.

to see the path of righteousness. It is not deep feeling but a lack of feeling, it is an insensibility blinding us to feelings and sufferings in others, and causing us to face life with excessive demands. 'He was . . . back in those distant years when he and another . . . had seen no reason why they should not indulge their passion and their vanity, and determine for themselves how their life should be made delightful in spite of unalterable external conditions.'[1] Bulstrode, in *Middlemarch*, could combine wrong-doing with evangelicalism because 'he had argued himself into not feeling it incompatible . . . the years had been perpetually spinning . . . intricate thickness, like masses of spider's web, padding the moral sensibility'. And it is emphasized that his aptitude for wrong followed from a combination of excessive demand and defective emotion: '. . . age made egoism more eager but less enjoying'.[2] Every word of that phrase directs us to something in the outlook of the author.

The consequences of virtue and of vice are the one point in George Eliot's view that remains to be stated. Here the case of vice is clearer. Righteousness may be rewarded, or may have to be its own reward,[3] but the ultimate consequences of wickedness are never in doubt. No one in George Eliot's novels ever sins and escapes; even though punishment may be long delayed and its local source quite unexpected. Tito Melema, Mrs. Transom, Bulstrode, in a sense Lydgate, Grancourt — however tardily or unpredictably, Fate ultimately chastises them all. The fate of other sinners is of course less circuitous. And clearly enough, the general action of her stories is largely modified to bring this about. At the close of *Brother Jacob* she says plainly that this is something to make a story worth telling: 'Here ends the story of Mr. David Faux . . . and we see in it, I think, an admirable instance of the unexpected forms in which the great Nemesis hides itself'.[4]

Thus George Eliot has a detailed theory of human

[1] FH. 226.   [2] Mid. 447.   [3] See R. 602-3, quoted below, p. 155.
[4] See SM. 363.

morality, and a detailed account of how it follows from
what the world is like. It may seem as though in summariz-
ing this outlook we have first surreptitiously wandered
quite away from the methods of presenting it, and then, in
the final quotation from *Brother Jacob*, wandered surreptitiously back. But a fuller survey of the confirmatory
passages quoted throughout the discussion disproves this :
for the great majority of those passages were not isolated
reflections, but embedded in the texture of the novels.
They commented upon a concrete situation, were uttered
by a distinctive character, or appeared in a fictitious
argument with a definite pattern of its own. Their significance was always controlled by methods of suggestion
that are George Eliot's because she is a novelist. We have
sampled them only in preliminary and fragmentary manner,
disregarding their context. This abstractedness must now
be remedied.

(v) *The Methods: Character*

The main kinds of literary material which George Eliot
manipulated so that it should convey her speculative or
moral outlook are five in number. They are, the characters ; the incidents ; the settings or scenes in which
incidents occur ; the situations ; and the dialogues. It is
necessary to distinguish incidents and situations because
every memorable phase of a novel is not necessarily a
striking event ; it may equally well be a deadlock where
nothing happens or can happen. This is only to say that
the course of events impresses the reader sometimes by
moving on, and sometimes by not moving on ; and an
impasse may be peculiarly important, since it may lead to
discussions between characters in which the author can
transmit her vision to the reader with the greatest im-
mediacy and power. Necessarily, these are divisions of
emphasis rather than essence, and we could take them in
any order, because any good novel is a continuous narration
and any good reader takes it as a continuous imagined
reality.

It seems convenient, though, to begin by seeing what contribution is made by the characters, as far as this can be isolated. This contribution is apparently fourfold.

First : a character may stand in a novel as a vividly striking *specimen* of how the general scheme of things proceeds. If we are unconvinced that nature is a system determined through and through by law, Arthur Donnithorne is a living witness to the fact. 'Are you inclined to ask whether this can be the same Arthur ? . . . The same, I assure you, only under different conditions. Our deeds determine us.' [1] If we are unconvinced that natural forces pursue a constant course despite superficial changes, there is Bardo de' Bardi, 'the family passions lived on in him under altered conditions',[2] pride and self-assertion show in the scholar as in the warrior. The infant Eppie evokes a sense of awe like 'some quiet majesty or beauty in earth and sky' ; [3] but if so, she is a specimen of how man resembles the rest of nature. Tom Tulliver and his prejudices show what must happen to those who 'can get no sustenance out of that complex, fragmentary, doubt-provoking knowledge which we call truth',[4] and we see something of the system in how he comes to terms with the truth about it. If a vivid particular case will persuade us that Nemesis is a reality, there is Nicholas Raffles, Nemesis incarnate to Bulstrode : 'Now, as if by some hideous magic, this loud red figure had risen before him in unmanageable solidity — an incorporate past which had not entered into his imagination of chastisements'.[5] Adam Bede looks like this to Arthur. 'Adam . . . stood like an immovable obstacle against which no pressure could avail ; an embodiment of what Arthur most shrank from believing in — the irrevocableness of his own wrong-doing.' [6] 'Incorporate' and 'embodiment' — in each case there is a word to emphasize the exact point.

Second (really something akin to Carlyle's 'calls to meditation' or Disraeli's young men) : many of George Eliot's novels are actually written round a character who

AB. 319.   [2] R. 48.   [3] SM. 158.
MF. 496.   [5] Mid. 380.   [6] AB. 317.

comes to an understanding of things. Our sense of the
value of this wisdom is quickened by being shown men
or women earnestly seeking it out. Maggie 'wanted some
explanation of this hard, real life . . . some key that would
enable her to understand' [1] and success lay in 'making
out a faith for herself'.[2] Romola has 'a sort of bitter
desire to know that there was some sufficient reason why
. . . the world was barren for her'.[3] Dorothea 'yearned
. . . after some lofty conception of the world which might
frankly include the parish of Tipton and her own rule of
conduct there'.[4] Interestingly enough, Lydgate's medical
researches are for a similar end: not any specialized
question of science, but to discover something general or
fundamental and significant for philosophy: 'what was
the primitive tissue' — the answer would be something
'showing the very grain of things'.[5] This is not a need
confined to the literate or sophisticated. Dolly Winthrop
the simple countrywoman has it too; 'If there's any light
to be got . . . we've need of it i' this world, and I'd be glad
on it myself, if you could bring it back'.[6] And these
characters, seeking their scheme of things, also remind us
occasionally of Carlyle's assertion that profound notions
require meditation: even if only in Dinah Morris's ineffable 'thoughts are so great — aren't they sir? They seem
to lie on us like a deep flood.' [7] In short, we are constantly
shown examples of the kind of person and the mode of
thought for which George Eliot as a speculative moralist
is actually writing.

Third: as the stories proceed it becomes clear that
many of the characters in them, like Carlyle's in *Frederick
the Great*, are *exemplars* of the good or bad. Adam Bede
is 'a stout-limbed clever carpenter with a large fund of
reverence'; [8] Caleb Garth's 'virtual divinities were good
practical schemes, accurate work, and the faithful completion of undertakings . . . he had a reverential soul with
a strong practical intelligence'.[9] Dorothea Brooke, from
her appearance in the first paragraph of *Middlemarch*, is

---

[1] MF. 308.   [2] MF. 314.   [3] R. 329.   [4] Mid. 4.   [5] Mid. 108.
[6] SM. 235.   [7] AB. 89.   [8] AB. 165.   [9] Mid. 182.

also an instructive figure. Her moral tone is conveyed by
a device we found in Carlyle:

> Miss Brooke had that kind of beauty which seems to be
> thrown into relief by poor dress. Her hand and wrist were
> so finely formed that she could wear sleeves not less bare of
> style than those in which the Blessed Virgin appeared to
> Italian painters; and her profile as well as her stature and
> bearing seemed to gain the more dignity from her plain
> garments, which by the side of provincial fashion gave her
> *the impressiveness of a fine quotation from the Bible* . . . in a
> paragraph of to-day's newspaper.[1]

George Eliot finds it unnecessary to say which quotation:
a general reminder of the Bible is enough to fix our attitude.
The earlier part of this extract also shows especially well
how an author can use the appearance of a character to
evoke in the reader a response proper really only for moral
qualities. This is like Carlyle's account of the Maréchal
de Saxe.[2] In a simple way, Adam's stout limbs are the
same.

None of these characters is ideal — especially not
Dorothea, who for all her fineness labours under foolish
and disastrous delusions. As once again in Carlyle, instruction by exemplar proceeds not through portraits of perfection, but through a complex system of characters good
within their limits or in some significant respect. The
method thus acquires vastly more adaptability, conviction
and power. Figures with very mixed qualities can instruct
— even the Dodsons, even Mrs. Glegg, even Aunt Pullett.
'The Dodsons were a very proud race, and their pride
lay in the utter frustration of all desire to tax them with a
breach of traditional duty or propriety. A wholesome
pride in many respects, since it identified honour with
perfect integrity, thoroughness of work, and faithfulness
to admitted rules.'[3] Their creed is incomplete and crude,
but it has its merits. 'Mirah's religion was of one fibre
with her affections, and had never presented itself to her

---

[1] Mid. 3 (my italics).   [2] See above, p. 81.
[3] MF. 294.

as a set of propositions' [1] — limited, but basically right. Within one continuous system of character, therefore, we can be shown bad in the good and good in the bad, and progressively instructed in what to follow or avoid, until even the villain of the piece can display something of each. Tito 'made almost everyone fond of him, for he was young, and clever and beautiful, and his manners to all were gentle and kind. I believe, when I first knew him, he never thought of anything cruel or base. But because he tried to slip away from everything that was unpleasant . . . he came at last to commit some of the basest deeds.' [2] His good qualities were no sham, no mere cloak for bad, but integral to his nature. Indeed, we should expect George Eliot to give most attention to mixed characters, mixed because of how they conform to the environment that controls them.

Fourth, and last of the contributions made by characters to the persuasive technique: once the general outline of their personality is clear to the reader, they are used as *authorities* for the views their creator wishes to defend. Any novelist, by creating the illusion of reality, can thus introduce as many reliable witnesses as he wants. But just as a succession of perfect exemplars would pall on the reader and arouse his suspicions, so a succession of unimpeachable authorities would too. We therefore find systematic variety. At one end of the scale perhaps is Savonarola: 'Romola was so deeply moved by the grand energies of Savonarola's nature, that she found herself listening patiently to all dogmas and prophecies, when they came in the vehicle of his ardent faith and believing utterance'.[3] This shows, perhaps, what George Eliot must have relied on some of her characters to do for us. Adam Bede is perhaps her most deliberately created authority. She even introduces him in total abstraction from the story to argue with his own creator about her characters and the problems they raise. 'Religion's something else beside notions. It isn't notions sets people doing the right thing — it's feelings,' [4] he says (thereby asserting in

[1] DD. 260.   [2] R. 603.   [3] R. 404.   [4] AB. 182.

words what we saw Mirah asserting in her substance).
He does this, 'broadening his chest and throwing himself
back in his chair',[1] just as, while Caleb Garth speaks of
'the soul of man', he uses a 'deep tone and a grave shake of
the head'[2] or is 'looking on the floor and moving his feet
uneasily with a sense that words were scantier than
thoughts' as he becomes our authority for the doubtless
deep, though I fear also bald, thought, 'things hang together'.[3] But after all, this is a plain man's version of a
momentous faith; and George Eliot's viewpoint becomes
far more massive and comprehensive and catholic because
we see it expressed by a great variety of characters, in a
simple or a more sophisticated form, depending on their
abilities. 'Things out o' natur niver thrive', says simple
Luke, the head miller in *The Mill on the Floss* — 'a tall
broadshouldered man of forty, black-eyed and black-
haired, subdued by a general mealiness'.[4] 'Life isn't cast
in a mould — not cut out by rule and line, and that sort
of thing',[5] or 'there's something singular in things: they
come round, you know',[6] says Dorothea's guardian, the
lovable, egregious Mr. Brooke. Among the most elaborate
of all these speculative pronouncements is one by the
humble cottager Dolly Winthrop, telling Silas Marner how
'it come to me all clear like, that night when I was sitting
up wi' poor Betsy Fawkes, as is dead and left her children
behind, God help 'em'.[7] Here, mixed up with gossip and
digression and ignorance and reiteration, we have in all
essentials a version of the author's own world view. And
this complex use of characters as authorities has a special
aptness. To be expressible in a simple or a subtle form,

---

[1] AB. 183.

[2] George Eliot's comment on this is interesting, and throws further
light on some of Carlyle's methods (see p. 24), and on her account of
Dorothea's plain garments (see the passage quoted on p. 131): 'It was one
of Caleb's quaintnesses, that in his difficulty of finding speech for his
thought, he caught, as it were, snatches of diction which he associated with
points of view or states of mind; and whenever he had a feeling of awe, he
was haunted by a sense of Biblical phraseology, though he could hardly
have given a strict quotation' (Mid. 298).

[3] Mid. 294.   [4] MF. 30, 27.   [5] Mid. 28.
[6] Mid. 590.   [7] SM. 191.

so as to suit the needs and capacities of the most sophisticated people and the least, is perhaps essential to any
significant view of life.

(vi) *Incident and Scene*

But characters usually deliver themselves of these aphorisms
in a particular situation which makes them apt. Adam is
almost alone as a mouthpiece *in vacuo*. What the characters contribute is thus intimately linked with what the
incidents of the story contribute. To begin with, incidents
(just like characters) are striking specimens of the scheme
of nature. That the individual is set in a wider context is
demonstrated when Deronda's new interests as a Jew
take him from Gwendolen on a visit to remote places. It
is Gwendolen's lesson as well as ours : to her 'The world
seemed getting larger . . . and she more solitary and helpless
. . . before the bewildering vision of these wide-stretching
purposes in which she felt herself reduced to a mere
speck'.[1] We see again how things move according to a
hidden plan when Dunstan's skeleton is found with
Silas's gold in the pond (Godfrey recounts the incident
'as if he felt some deep meaning in the fact'),[2] and in
the gold's being discovered just pat for Eppie's wedding
('it's been kept — kept till it was wanted for you . . . our
life is wonderful' — this is how Silas 'improves' the
situation),[3] and in the orphan Eppie's arriving as a consola-
tion to Silas for his lost gold (this time Dolly Winthrop,
'with soothing gravity' says 'it's like the night and the
morning . . . sleeping . . . waking . . . rain . . . harvest —
one goes and the other comes, and we know nothing how
nor where').[4]

In *Felix Holt* there is a vivid and unexpected incident
showing how long-past events leave their trace still. The
elderly, doting Mr. Transome is confronted with lawyer
Jermyn, his wife's lover thirty-five years ago : 'he stood
still in the doorway, as if he did not know whether entrance

---

[1] DD. 583.   [2] SM. 215.   [3] SM. 220.   [4] SM. 163.

were permissible. The majority of his thoughts were but ravelled threads of the past . . . said, with a bewildered look . . . "Mr. Jermyn ? — why — why — where is Mrs. Transome ?"' [1] For a moment the effect is electrical; but the potential is speculative as well as dramatic. If we are not fully convinced that events move slowly and steal upon us unawares, there is Lydgate's courtship of Rosamond ('in the meanwhile the hours were each leaving their little deposit and gradually forming the final reason for inaction, namely that action was too late'), [2] or the slow accumulation of his debts, or the gradual seduction of Hetty by Arthur and Arthur by circumstance, or the slowly developing intimacy between Tito Melema and Tessa ('he had spun a web about himself and Tessa, which he felt incapable of breaking'). [3] And, as the narrative constantly stresses, the point about Hetty, about Tito's desertion of his guardian, and about Bulstrode's youthful vagaries, is that what has happened is irrevocable.

Tragic, ironical twists of Fate also play a large part in the stories. Mrs. Tulliver tries to persuade her husband to be reconciled with Mrs. Glegg, and tries to persuade Wakem not to buy up their mill. Each time she causes what she hopes to avoid. [4] Arthur Donnithorne tries to confess his philanderings to Mr. Irwine, and fails because the latter is scrupulously careful not to pry. [5] Phillip Wakem is ill, and Lucy Dean decides to go shopping, on the last morning that Maggie and Stephen have to resist their attraction for each other. [6] Finally, there are innumerable incidents that suggest a continuity between human life and the rest of nature. One example will suffice: Lydgate nearly eludes Rosamond, but a chance turn of

---

[1] FH. 411.   [2] Mid. 361.   [3] R. 312.
[4] MF. 78, 270.   [5] AB. 176.
[6] It is easy to see that this last example genuinely represents an ironic twist of Fate, and is not a mere coincidence. *Romola* is full of coincidences — chiefly chance meetings — but they are quite different. Their remarkableness is not emphasized and given a philosophical import; they merely serve the ends of plot and so far as possible they are made unobtrusive. The contrast is striking, in that this constant intrusion of the convenient though insignificant fluke is perhaps what chiefly disintegrates *Romola* as a sustained vision of life.

events caught him at the eleventh hour. The comment is 'that moment of naturalness was the crystallizing feather-touch: it shook flirtation into love'.[1] Throughout this discussion, one or two striking and unequivocal examples have been given where many could have been found.

Rather as the suggestiveness of the characters was enriched by setting them in a social and historical context, so the suggestiveness of action and incident is enriched by setting them in a carefully and evocatively described scene. In *Theophrastus Such*, conveniently enough, George Eliot actually discusses how a scene — in the sense of scenery — can stir our emotions and so have a moral significance:

> My philosophical notions, such as they are [this is a typical phrase for the kind of speculative concept we are concerned with] continually carry me back to the time when the fitful gleams of a spring day used to show me my own shadow . . . riding . . . over the breezy uplands . . . or along by-roads with broad grassy borders . . . I often smile at my consciousness that certain conservative prepossessions have mingled themselves for me with the influences of our midland scenery, from the tops of the elms down to the buttercups . . . our national life is like that scenery which I early learned to love, not subject to great convulsions, but easily showing more or less delicate (sometimes melancholy) effects from minor changes. Hence our midland plains have never lost their familiar expression and conservative spirit for me. . . . But because our land shows . . . this readiness to be changed, all signs of permanence . . . raise a tender attachment. . . . A crumbling bit of wall where the delicate ivy-leaved toadflax hangs its light branches, or a bit of grey thatch . . . is a thing to visit. And then the tiled roof of cottage and homestead . . the broadshouldered barns where the old-fashioned flail once made resonant music . . . the roofs . . . among the elms and walnut-trees . . . or below the square stone steeple, gathering their grey or ochre-tinted lichens and their olive-green mosses under all ministries.[2]

This is surely an important and revealing passage. It shows first, how George Eliot believes that in many ways scenery

[1] Mid. 219.   [2] TS. 24-30.

reveals the course of nature (as needless to say it does by any standard); second, how she regards scenery as something that readily creates the emotions and attitudes she wishes to create; and third, how she thinks these attitudes are first acquired in childhood, but since then perhaps overlaid or weakened. Nothing betrays more clearly how, and where, and why persuasive technique renders proof superfluous.

What now remains is to see the use made of scenery in the novels.

That descriptions of nature can be moving is well known. But they can be more. To the unthinking modern reader, the storm in *King Lear* simply makes Lear's madness more exciting, because storms are exciting. But it was also an implicit gloss on Lear's madness and on what had produced it. Between the madness and the storm was a real analogy, and recalling that analogy was recalling a whole view of how the world was arranged and ordered. Perhaps it is odd that devices which are praised in an Elizabethan writer as evidence of an 'integrated sensibility' should be quite so readily condemned in a Victorian as cheap. But however that may be, George Eliot certainly attempts to use the natural scene in this more significant way too. Once the analogy is made explicit: 'To a superficial glance, Milby was . . . dreary . . . a dingy town . . . flat fields, lopped elms . . . but the sweet spring came to Milby notwithstanding: the elmtops were red with buds . . . *and so it was with the human life* there, which at first seemed a dismal mixture . . . looking closer, you found some purity, gentleness, and unselfishness'.[1] And upon this principle she intertwines scene and incident to give her account richer, fuller significance. In *Janet's Repentance*, Lawyer Dempster and his mother walk in their garden. Certain factual details are important: the son's kindness is no more than momentary and out of character; yet even so it indicated 'how hard it is to kill the deepdown fibrous roots of human love and goodness'. These two facts are explicitly given as, in order, reasons why we

[1] *Janet's Repentance* (SCL. 269; my italics).

should feel two distinct emotions — should find the scene 'sad, and yet pretty'. The setting is a shady garden full of old apple-trees, and it reflects our contrasting emotions as we see the two figures 'passing out of the shadow into the sunshine, and out of the sunshine into the shadow again'.[1] Indeed, this alternation has a further meaning; the reader will easily see it himself.

Similarly, when Adam Bede and Arthur, after Hetty's downfall, chance to meet in the woods, beside the very tree where they met before,[2] it is not an idle coincidence melodramatizing the story. The tenor of their lives deprives the incident of coincidence. The tree marks the enduring sameness of the world around them, and by implication of their own lives too. The winter mist which helps Dunstan Cass to steal Silas's gold [3] may raise the reader's excitement, but it also deepens his sense of how the whole story occurs in remote obscurity, and how the apparent course of things, so far from being providential, makes the offence easiest just when it has grown most attractive.

Adam and Seth finding their father drowned in the brook is a more elaborate incident of the same kind. It is a careful fusion of peasant custom and superstition, of the country scenery and the event itself, all combined so that this shall seem both probable and significant. Adam has been working alone through the night to finish a coffin that his father had promised to have ready, but had neglected so as to go drinking. First we see him and his brother cheerfully carrying it away very early next day — red sunlight, flowery lanes and fields, singing birds, 'the fresh youth of the summer morning . . . peace and loveliness, the stalwart strength of the two brothers in their rusty working clothes, and the long coffin on their shoulders' — '*it was a strangely-mingled picture*'.[4] But Seth adjusts the image — he notices the gathering clouds, remembers the recent rain, thinks how the standing hay may be flooded,

---

[1] SCL. 314.   [2] AB. 473.   [3] SM. 47.
[4] AB. 49-50, my italics. The strangeness arises because the picture suggests a strange complex of emotions.

sees that the water in the stream is rising and will soon
make their plank across it impassable — and at that
instant they find Thias Bede's body floating in the current,
driven against a willow tree. It was 'a smart rap, as if
with a willow-wand' that Adam had fancied he heard against
the door, as he worked on into the previous night; we saw
him then, caught up in the ancient rustic superstition, and
wondering if the odd sound was really a sign of death.
The scenery is not simply to make the incident vivid, but
to reflect and elucidate its 'mingled' youth and age, gaiety
and tragedy, beauty and drabness. The total effect is a
control of the reader's experience, over a wide front, such
as transmits the writer's whole outlook on life even in this
one event.

Occasionally George Eliot achieves this through the
scene alone. 'I like to go and work by a road that'll take
me up a bit of a hill,' says Adam, 'and see the fields for
miles round me . . . or a town, or a bit of a steeple here and
there. It makes you feel the world's a big place, and there's
other men working in it . . . besides yourself.' The
Quaker Seth, agreeing, likes hills because 'it seems to me
as if that was Heaven where there's always joy and sunshine, though this life's . . . cloudy'.[1] The conversation
makes the technique explicit, and reveals particularly that
scenes evoke emotions not *in vacuo* but through their
factual detail. Again, the cosmic picture transpires in the
account of Fred and Rosamond riding to Stone Court:
'. . . through a pretty bit of midland landscape . . . meadows
and pastures. . . . Little details gave each field a particular
physiognomy, dear to the eyes that have looked on them
from childhood: the pool . . . the great oak . . . the huddled
roofs and fences of the homestead without a traceable way
of approach; the grey gate and fences against the depth
of the bordering wood; and the stray hovel, its old old
thatch full of mossy hills and valleys . . . these are the
things that make the gamut of joy in landscape to midland-
bred souls'.[2] By now the ride itself is incidental: the
description has central importance and its aim is to make

us understand the system of nature, and therefore love it better. The clearest transition from facts to emotions, and perhaps one of the most charming, is the description of the Rectory in *Felix Holt*: 'a fine old brick-and-stone house, with a great bow-window opening from the library on to the deep-turfed lawn, one fat dog sleeping on the door stone, . . . the autumn leaves duly swept away, the lingering chrysanthemums cherished . . . a Virginian creeper turning a little rustic hut into a scarlet pavilion. It was one of those rectories which are among the bulwarks of our venerable institutions — which arrest disintegrating doubt . . . and rally feminine instinct and affection to reinforce masculine thought.' [1]   To this no comment need add point.

But while the scenic background can do much to enrich our understandings or modify our feelings about the order of the world, it is much less important in incidents or situations whose main point is simply moral; and it is time to turn to these. To use incident as simply an example of what constitutes good or bad conduct is so well-known a device that little need be said of it. There is an explicit reference in *Daniel Deronda*, where Daniel tells Gwendolen that she has seen, in her recent sad experiences, specimens of the kind of conduct she must avoid — seen them as if shown her for her instruction by an angel.[2]   It is a significant and largely overlooked criticism of this novel that it does so little to create a genuine vision of an order of nature bringing a moral order as its corollary, and is yet so full of haphazardly introduced models for the details of conduct. Klesmer the tame musician, for example, has agreed to consider Mirah's singing abilities, if she will agree to sing for him. Then: '"I shall be very grateful," said Mirah, calmly, "He wants to hear me sing, before he can judge whether I ought to be helped." Deronda was struck with her plain sense in these matters of practical concern' [3] — and, clearly enough, the reader is meant to be struck as well. Deronda himself has all the tedium of a paragon:

[1] FH. 236-7.   [2] DD. 558.   [3] DD. 338.

Deronda was mute : to question her seemed an unwarrant-
able freedom ; he shrank from appearing to claim the authority of a benefactor, or to treat her with the less reverence
because she was in distress.[1]

' I want to know nothing except what you like to tell me,'
he said.[2]

Few men were able to keep themselves clearer of vices
than he ; yet he hated vices mildly.[3]

And Gwendolen is sometimes almost as dull — which is
remarkable, since her conduct at least has the supposed
relish of wrong-doing :

'Pray go to church, mamma. . . . I prefer seeing Herr
Klesmer alone. . . .'
'That is hardly correct, I think,' said Mrs. Davilow,
anxiously.
'Our affairs are too serious for us to think of such non-
sensical rules,' said Gwendolen, contemptuously. '. . . trust
my judgement, mamma.'
Gwendolen had her way, of course. . . .[4]

The *minutiae* of mid-Victorian propriety were hardly
such as to encourage too detailed an examination of the
copy-books for it.

But sometimes George Eliot gives the events she
narrates a more interesting and deeper moral significance.
When this is so, what happens is not a model for us to ape
or steer clear of : but an event in a situation, or a situation
in itself — an *impasse*, say — that lays bare the issues
fundamental in all conduct of any significance, and casts a
flood of light upon those essential and invariable factors
present in all moral choice.

(vii) *Situation and Dialogue*

When Romola, horrified at Tito's faithlessness to the
memory of her father, leaves him and slips out of the city,

[1] DD. 138-9.   [2] DD. 139.
[3] DD. 261.   Deronda's virtuous aphorisms are exasperatingly numerous.
[4] DD. 180.

she is accosted on the hillside by Savonarola.[1] What he
says to her clarifies the moral realities of what she has done.
She claims as her justification that Tito has broken his
pledge to her father. But she is ignoring her own duties to
him and to Florence too ; her renunciation of pleasure is
skin-deep. In running away, she is seeking her own will.
Her plea that to stay was psychologically impossible is a
delusion ; the very difficulty of this course is what will
make it easy, if she once really sees the light. The implications of what Romola has done extend to the whole of the
moral life. But as the circumstances of her own lot change,
they throw other general issues into relief — and so do the
circumstances of Savonarola himself. 'It flashed upon her
mind that the problem before her was essentially the same
as that which had lain before Savonarola — the problem
where the sacredness of obedience ended, and where the
sacredness of rebellion began.'[2] Two further examples
will suffice. Esther Lyon, rightful heir to the Transome
estates, debates whether to accept Harold Transome's
advances. Her situation is too complex for her to distinguish duty merely by abstract thought, and she is obliged
to judge by feeling : but then, of the two possible courses
of action, she slowly realizes that one has only a skin-deep
illusory appeal, and the other is chosen for her by the sure
and irresistible promptings of all that is most enduring in
her nature.[3] The other example affords insight into the
consequences of misjudging or ignoring the moral situation.
Because Harold's election agent arranged free beer for his
supporters, the high-minded Felix, through a long and
indirect chain of events, has to go to prison. Mr. Lyon
points the moral : 'I pray you mark', he says, 'the poison-
ous confusion of good and evil which is the wide-spreading
effect of vicious practices'.[4]

From the nature of her world, George Eliot's characters
are naturally most fully themselves in what they say, and
what they argue. In several novels the climax to a whole
character's development is a confession, a confidence, a
proposal that can only come because deep and natural

[1] R. 370 ff.   [2] R. 487.   [3] FH. 413.   [4] FH. 375.

feeling has at last conquered egotistic reserve or desiccating
conventionality.   This is how, after all her obduracy,
Hetty in prison tells Dinah Morris how she abandoned
her child.[1] 'Melt the hard heart ; unseal the closed lips',
Dinah prays ; Hetty's confession answers both prayers at
once.   Gwendolen Harleth's confession [2] has a similar
significance in itself, though it also tells us what to think of
other acts.   In a sense the climax of *Middlemarch* comes
when Rosamond reveals to Dorothea that Ladislaw was
not making love to her, but telling her that his affections
were set once for all elsewhere,[3] and she makes this revelation because Dorothea's own 'self-forgetful ardour', disintegrates her normal selfish hardness.   'Pride was broken
down between these two.'   Rosamond was 'taken hold of
by an emotion stronger than her own . . . urged by a
mysterious necessity to free herself from something that
oppressed her as if it were blood-guiltiness . . . delivered
her soul under impulses that were new to her'.   Like
Gwendolen when she hears that Deronda is going to the
East, she spoke under 'a sense that she had been walking
in an unknown world which had just broken in upon her'.
Dorothea herself has a similar struggle.   Marrying Ladislaw would justify the notion that her former husband had
well-grounded suspicions about her fidelity, and would
shock her conventional relations.   But because her love
for him is rich and generous, she can do this at last ; and
even defy all female decorum too, by telling him outright
that she wants him.[4]

But as the issue of right and wrong becomes less plain
— and we remember that for George Eliot it need not be
plain at all — the conversations turn progressively into
debates.   The characters are protagonists whose task is to

---

[1] AB. 460.   [2] DD. 499-505.   [3] Mid. 577-9.

[4] Mid. 588. Her actual words are not happily chosen. The critical
reader may see in them an example of the financial mechanics that hamstring
so many English novels ; and the generous reader, a sign that Dorothea —
who is, after all, still no more than twenty — is only a little less immature
than at the beginning of the book. Perhaps the words, 'the flood of her
young passion bearing down all the obstructions that had kept her silent',
do something to vindicate the kindlier interpretation.

bring conflicting factors to life. It can almost be said that they dramatize moral theories. Of this kind are the tortured arguments between Maggie Tulliver and Stephen after their escapade in the boat.[1] What is to decide how Maggie shall act, now that the initial harm is done? Stephen argues that to all appearances they have eloped, and no practical good can come of returning. They cannot have a duty to thwart their mutual attraction, because they simply cannot thwart it. The emotion of love is itself a genuine claim upon duty. Formal claims not justified by living emotion are insignificant, are claims that neither of the two people they have left behind would want to enforce. These points are not meant by the author simply to confuse, like Tito's remarks to Romola; they are genuine and formidable. But Maggie answers that an emotion which ought never to have arisen cannot justify anything; that there is a whole range of emotions in her which Stephen overlooks; that it is intrinsically wrong to take happiness for oneself when one has brought sorrow to others; and finally, that in any case, her conscientious feelings prevent her marrying him, even if her arguments were false. As these characters talk, they dissect the situation before the reader. He sees the moral realities of the case through their eyes, and his vicarious insight is sharpened by a pre-existing sympathy with their personalities. Maggie's earlier conversations about her friendship with Phillip, either with Tom Tulliver or with Phillip himself, also explore the moral contours of the case in just the same way.[2] The question is, when do the demands of others become so extravagant or unreasonable as to forfeit any claim on us?[3] As the characters converse and argue together we explore the situation through them; we identify the relevant points, appreciate their strength; and see the factors that determine any moral situation reflected vividly and typically in one.

[1] MF. 514-20.   [2] MF. 326-8, 352-8, 370-77.
[3] See Letter to John Blackwood, 4th April 1861. 'The exhibition of the right on both sides [i.e. Tom's and Maggie's] being the very soul of my intention in the story.' (Cross, op. cit. vol. ii, p. 296.)

But the full range of George Eliot's treatment, the breadth of front upon which she assails the reader's outlook, is missed if we think of these discussions between characters as mere expositions in dialogue form of the abstract *pros* and *cons*. No moral consideration is ever telling, save because it impinges on the emotions; but by this dramatic presentation the effective strength of every argument is maximized, since the reader sees it used by someone to whom it is vitally important. Every *pro* and *con* is the passionately held conviction of a familiar character. And there is also another perhaps even more important point.

It is that these characters are necessarily *placed* by the author. Their limitations, their obtuseness, their weakness or selfish myopia are the things that make the problem. The considerations they urge are generated within them, and have the quality of their source. Their strength or weakness, what part of the whole situation they do justice to, is implied in our knowledge of the character. And it is probably when the author places her characters with most detachment, and lets each display his perspicuity and blindness in turn, that our sense of the situation and of its moral structure is most complete and balanced and subtle. This is what makes the conversations about their debts between Lydgate and Rosamond the most mature work that George Eliot ever produced.[1] Each of them is conscious of their own rights, of their infringement, and of the other's shortcomings. Neither sees, except by vague and intermittent glimpses, that perhaps they themselves should retrench, or be willing to lose face in the very respects that they care about most or think most intimately linked with their higher life or inalienable privileges. But this very blindness is something through which the reader powerfully learns. Elsewhere, George Eliot's favourite doctrines are usually mediated to us by one character with whom the author is in large part identified; and the others proffer objections — perhaps powerful ones — to the authentic view. Here that view is suggested by what is wanting in all the characters. From oblique remarks,

[1] Mid. 469-72, 476-8, 480-83.

from what is dismissed as irrelevant, from what is left unsaid or ignored, a sense is built up in us of the maze of claim and counter-claim, of what emotions and attitudes and actions the situation demanded, and of the wrong in what it exhibited instead. This time the reader is instructed not from the wisdom of the characters, but through their ignorance.

(viii) *Metaphor*

The remainder of this chapter examines two devices of persuasion in George Eliot that may be used by any polemical writer. These are analogy or metaphor, and changing the meaning of terms. Each is greatly modified in its effect, because it is used within the texture of a novel ; and neither is of really vital importance in George Eliot's work, though analogy is fairly important. But examining them leads to several interesting minor points, and confirms some earlier discoveries.

Obligingly enough, George Eliot provides two superficially similar examples which exactly reveal how metaphor will sometimes suggest a whole world view, and sometimes be nothing but a vivid or amusing parallel. (1) In *Amos Barton* we find :

> Mr. Pilgrim generally spoke with an intermittent kind of splutter . . . but when he came to . . . the point, he mouthed out his words with a slow emphasis ; *as a hen* . . . passes at irregular intervals from pianissimo semiquavers to fortissimo crochets.[1]

(2) In *Silas Marner* we read of Dolly Winthrop :

> viewing the stronger sex in the light of animals whom it had pleased Heaven to make naturally troublesome, *like bulls and turkey cocks.*[2]

Now it is a silly mistake to see in the first any suggestion of the continuity between man and Nature, just as it would be, to see a reflection of the complexity of Nature in the analogy of 'Probabilities are as various as the faces to be

---

[1] SCL. 13-14 (my italics).   [2] SM. 107 (my italics).

seen at will in fretwork or paper-hangings'.[1] But Dolly Winthrop's notion is different. Men, bulls and turkey-cocks, it suggests, appear similar because they really are similar : they make three varieties in the same basic type. There is an analogy of causes to create the analogy of qualities ; and of course the word 'make' clearly indicates that this cause is in the author's mind (or at least Mrs. Winthrop's), and the phrase 'it has pleased Heaven' not only indicates what it is, but puts it beyond all question that the simile mediates a world view. We shall find something of this kind fairly often in Newman.

Such comparisons are common in George Eliot, but they tend to be all of one kind. They all liken human life to those parts of nature that are gradual or complex or that take place unseen. The slowly growing tree is one of the commonest, and sometimes it is ingeniously developed : 'One of those old, old towns . . . carries the traces of its long growth and history like a millennial tree' ; [2] 'it is with men as with trees : if you lop off their finest branches . . . the wounds will be healed over with some rough boss, some odd excrescence . . . many an unlovely oddity has come of . . . sorrow' ; [3] 'we poor mortals are often little better than wood-ashes — there is small sign of the sap, and the leafy freshness . . . once there ; but whenever we see wood-ashes, we know that all that early fulness of life must have been'.[4] 'Have we not from the first touched each other with invisible fibres . . . leaves from a common stem with stirrings from a common root ?' says Mordecai.[5] 'I shall never hold up my head no more — I'm a tree as is broke,' says Mr. Tulliver.[6] Another common comparison is with the river : 'human feeling . . . like the mighty rivers that bless the earth . . . flows with resistless force and brings beauty with it' ; [7] 'two human souls approach each other gradually, like two little quivering rainstreams, before they mingle into one' ; [8] 'Maggie's destiny, then, is at present hidden, and we must wait for it to reveal itself like the course

---

[1] Mid. 220. The statement of course *states* that Nature is complex.
[2] MF. 122.   [3] SCL. 247.   [4] SCL. 108.
[5] DD. 415.   [6] MF. 286.   [7] AB. 180.   [8] AB. 502.

of an unmapped river : we only know that the river is full
and rapid, and that for all rivers there is the same final
home'.[1] These metaphors supplement the world view in
various respects. They add to our sense that human affairs
are slow-moving, or irrevocable, or frustrated, or governed
by unseen forces, or set in a wider pattern ; and they do
so not merely through being vivid illustrations of these
qualities, but through hinting that they are diffused everywhere in nature and hinting also at why.

Another interesting image confirms a point made
earlier — that the same philosophical suggestiveness may
attach to a metaphor or to an incident.[2] Esther Lyon, at
first highly scornful of Felix Holt, is subsequently attracted
enough to go walking with him along the river. 'Esther
was a little amazed . . . at what she had come to. So our
lives glide on : the river ends we don't know where, and
the sea begins, and then there is no more jumping ashore.'[3]
Here a metaphor, this is exactly what happens in fact to
Maggie and Stephen in *The Mill on the Floss*. If we are
sensitive to the wider suggestiveness of either, this parallel
should make clear that the other has it too. Another
interesting comparison occurs in the description of Joshua
Rann, shoemaker and parish clerk : 'The way he rolled
from a deep rich *forte* into a melancholy cadence . . . I
can compare to nothing for its strong calm . . . but the rush
and cadence of the wind among the autumn boughs'.
This time George Eliot does all she can to bring out how
the comparison is pregnant, and what is the source of its
fuller meaning. She continues : 'This may seem a strange
mode of speaking about the reading of a parish-clerk. . . .
But that is Nature's way.'[4]

This permanent sense of the root cause of an analogy
and of its fuller import can add an overtone even to the
purely sentimental image, and this is an important point
which will have to be made again later on. Writing in
Daniel Deronda of Mirah's charms, the author says, 'how
could the rose help it when several bees in succession took

[1] MF. 436.   [2] See above, pp. 67 and 93.
[3] FH. 264.   [4] AB. 202 (my italics).

its sweet odour as a sign of personal attachment ?' [1] Tina in *Mr. Gilfil's Love Story* is like a little fledgling bird or a 'delicate plant'; [2] but the point is that she too may fly straight into trouble through immaturity, that she too 'had been too deeply bruised, and in the struggle to put forth a blossom . . . died'. In all these, the visual likeness or the sentimental link is subordinate; the main analogy is that Mirah and the flower or the fledgling bird are differentiated products with a common origin and a comparable function in the plan of Nature.

That the colourful, 'scenic', sentimental metaphors have this philosophical import is perhaps confirmed by the number of metaphors where colour and sentiment are lacking. George Eliot, at least after her earliest novels, seems to use nature chiefly as a source of scientific processes with which the people or events of the story can be compared. 'In . . . machinery . . . there is often a small un-noticeable wheel which has a great deal to do with the motion of the large obvious ones. Possibly there was some such unrecognized agent secretly busy in Arthur's mind.' [3] 'We are poor plants buoyed up by the air-vessels of our own conceit'; [4] 'the endless minutiae by which her view of Mr. Casaubon . . . was gradually changing with the secret motion of a watch-hand'; [5] 'duty, which is to the moral life what the addition of a great central ganglion is to animal life'; [6] 'he was still in his fresh youth, with soft pulses for all charm and loveliness . . . the poison could only work by degrees'; [7] 'passion is of the nature of seed, and finds nourishment within'; [8] 'this speech . . . had taken shape in inward colloquy, and rushed out like the round grains from a fruit when sudden heat cracks it'. [9] Here metaphor again hints at the general character of things. That the obscure is often crucial; that human change is like a natural process, physical, mechanical or chemical; that moral consciousness is a product of evolution — these are the principles of which the metaphors remind us as they pass. The examples were arranged

[1] DD. 355.   [2] SCL. 236, 246.   [3] AB. 175.   [4] SCL. 16.   [5] Mid. 142.
[6] SCL. 339.   [7] R. 124.   [8] DD. 487.   [9] Mid. 147.

above so as roughly to alternate between comparisons with natural and comparisons with artificial processes. The bursting seed might be either. Nothing could show better how much George Eliot is concerned with nature in the scientist's sense, rather than the conventional painter's or poet's.

The reader is occasionally reminded of nature's complexity by the metaphor of the web. We saw earlier on how the years had been 'perpetually spinning' Bulstrode's pleas of extenuation 'into intricate thickness, like masses of spider-web'.[1] Lydgate 'was now beginning to find out what [Rosamond's] cleverness was — what was the shape into which it had run as into a close network aloof and independent'.[2]   As almost always, the metaphors are developed to show resemblance not in a superficial appearance but in a fundamental process. It is this emphasis on process that gives the analogies their point, and at least once it brings the author near to literary disaster. 'Rosamond . . . was in the water-lily's expanding wonderment at its own fuller life, and she too was spinning industriously at the mutual web.'[3]   The machine is overworked, and creaks.

This is the main function of metaphor so far as our enquiry goes. But there are two less important effects. Each is connected with what should really be called *decorum* in the choice of analogies; and each is important chiefly as a secondary technique, sustaining a sense in the reader's mind of something more general already conveyed to him. The first is the use of images chosen so as to be 'in character', important because it focuses or re-focuses our vision of the character himself, and does so specifically in respect of his trade or position in society. Therefore it sustains our sense that he is set in a wider context, and that his attitudes and opinions need to be read as those of someone 'placed' as he has been placed. 'A maggot

---

[1]   Mid. 447.   [2]   Mid. 423.
[3]   Mid. 250. Tina, in *Mr. Gilfil's Love-Story*, is also likened to a water-plant, again in respect not of appearance, but a property and a process — the property of languishing out of one's native element and flourishing when returned to it. (SCL. 242.)

must be born i' the rotten cheese to like it, I reckon', says Mrs. Poyser, famous for dairying, of her own rickety farmhouse.[1] 'You can never do what's wrong without breeding sin and trouble more than you can ever see. It's like a bit of bad workmanship — you never see th' end o' the mischief it'll do', says Adam.[2] 'Dost think thee canst go on so all thy life, as if thee wast a man cut out o' timber?'[3] says Lisbeth Bede — wife and mother of carpenters. 'God overflowing my soul — as the pebbles lie bathed in the Willow Brook' (Dinah Morris).[4] For Dolly Winthrop, girl-children can be kept out of mischief by being tied up, but boys tied up would 'make a fighting and a crying as if you was ringing the pigs'.[5] 'To the receptive soul the river of life pauseth not', says Mr. Lyon — hinting his acquaintance with scripture, not rivers.[6] Perhaps this second function of the image is made clearest by an image grossly out of character, and therefore lacking this function, but nevertheless suggestive in the general way; and by contrast one in character but lacking the general significance. The first is 'you would have hampered my life with your young growth from the old root' (given to Deronda's mother, the Princess Halm-Eberstein!);[7] and the second, Farmer Hacket's 'You're like the wood-pigeon; it says do, do, do, all day, and never sets about any work itself',[8] in which it is quite fanciful to see any wider philosophical import. Thus the former is an example of the first function without the second, and the latter of the second without the first.

Images that sustain our notion of a character also resonate more generally to the *milieu* of the book as a whole. But some metaphors do only this; which therefore constitutes a third function of imagery, and the last to concern us. An image can sharpen and enrich the whole panoramic effect of the story. Two examples from *Silas Marner* will be enough: 'Marner's thoughts . . . were baffled by a blank like that which meets a plodding ant when the earth has broken away on its homeward path';[9] and 'Nancy

[1] AB. 354.   [2] AB. 169.   [3] AB. 509.
[4] AB. 89.   [5] SM. 165.   [6] FH. 376.
[7] DD. 483.   [8] SCL. 11.   [9] SM. 101.

. . . carried these decided judgements within her . . . they rooted themselves in her mind, and grew there as quietly as grass'.[1] Both of these add another light touch to the over-all picture of the setting — the latter an echo of the quiet pastoralism, the former of the bewildering frustrations this unexpectedly contains. The point is made plainer still, perhaps, by a remark of Godfrey Cass: 'While I've been putting off and putting off, the trees have been growing — it's too late now'.[2] Is Godfrey's reference to trees literal or metaphorical? Either he is likening his personal affairs to the growth of his own trees — then the general setting is suggested narrowly, but quite indisputably; or to trees in general — then the suggestion is wider in scope but more oblique; or, by one metaphor within another, to slowly developing tree-like affairs of every kind — then the suggestiveness is at its very widest, and very faintest. The phrase is of quite remarkable interest, if we scrutinize it closely.

Middlemarch contains many images that also sustain the *milieu*: these remind us of Lydgate's seduction from the life of medical research or Casaubon's part in the tale, or both together. The novel is packed with images drawn from science, some of them very elaborate. 'The crystallizing feather-touch' was quoted earlier. But studio life in Rome is 'like a small fresh vegetation with its population of insects on huge fossils'.[3] The selfish eye sees events like scratches on a mirror when a candle is held to it: 'the scratches will seem to arrange themselves in a fine series of concentric circles round that little sun . . . these things are a parable'.[4] It is necessary, says the author, to change one's point of vantage through the novel sometimes, just as 'in watching effects, even if only of an electric battery, it is often necessary to change our place and examine a particular mixture or group at some distance'.[5] Odds and ends in everyday life may have the same sort of long-term influence as an ancient inscribed stone that at last comes 'under the eyes of a scholar'.[6] We remember Mr. Casau-

[1] SM. 207.   [2] SM. 232.   [3] Mid. 155.
[4] Mid. 191.   [5] Mid. 288.   [6] Mid. 298.

bon's story this time. Lydgate's estrangement from his wife is at first 'as if a fracture in delicate crystal had begun'.[1] By these comparisons the author reminds us in passing of the tenor of the entire novel; she reinforces and emphasizes its general quality. Again, something similar will be found in Newman.

These three modes by which imagery contributes to the whole effect of suggestion are a good deal clarified by two more examples. First, we saw that metaphors could reinforce the impression of character without contributing to the general portrait of nature;[2] that is, perform the second of the three functions, but not the first. One example, at least, performs the first and rather conspicuously omits the third. In *Silas Marner*, of which the predominant note is a certain drab pastoralism, the sentence 'human beliefs, like all other natural growths, elude the barriers of system'[3] relates human beliefs very directly to the whole system of things and has a genuine speculative import. Virtually, this comparison *states* why beliefs are as they are; and on the other hand does almost nothing to describe them. But the abstract quality of the phrase 'other natural growths' actually avoids a contribution to the pastoral note, where a comparison with lichen on a thatch, or running water (among the author's favourites, after all) would have contributed with inescapable directness. While powerfully reinforcing the tone of the narrative, though, these comparisons would have been much less clear in indicating why beliefs elude the barriers of system. Suggestiveness comes from vivid particularity, and logical power from classification and generalizing. One function of the image tends to be served only as the other is not served.

Finally, these three functions perhaps become clearer if we notice that one of George Eliot's favourite analogies performs none of them, although for purely descriptive purposes it suits her needs well. This is the analogy with chess: 'Will could not like to leave his own chessmen in

[1] Mid. 471.
[2] See above, p. 151.　　[3] SM. 209.

the heat of a game'; [1] 'there was an evident selection of statements, as if they had been so many moves at chess.' [2] These are the author's remarks, so that there is no question of their being in character; and fairly clearly, they add nothing to the novel's pervasive tone. But nor do they hint at any aspect of the system of nature. They are purely descriptive metaphors, illustrating the subject by comparing it to what we know better. They indicate its quality, but are silent about its cause, because they say nothing of its place in the scheme.

Once, George Eliot recognizes some of the effects to be obtained from analogies. 'What a different result one gets by changing the metaphor! Once call the brain an intellectual stomach, and one's ingenious conception of the classics and geometry as ploughs and harrows seems to settle nothing.' [3] In this passage, she goes on to deprecate figurative, and to praise plain language. But clearly enough, when it served her turn she could enlist the former with great ingenuity; and although the units of metaphorical language are small, and they rarely come in numbers, their total effect is very considerable.

(ix) *The Control of Meaning*

Carlyle showed the enormous importance in persuasive argument of re-defining terms. This is not unimportant in George Eliot too; but like analogical argument, it is subordinated to the overriding demands of the novel form. She herself notices its significance in *Theophrastus Such*, in an essay called *Moral Swindlers*, where she attacks those who call men virtuous for their private life only, and disregard their business life. 'The informal definitions of popular language', she writes, 'are the only medium through which theory really affects the mass of minds'; she mentions 'the influences that . . . retard . . . right . . . judgement', and allots a prominent place to 'the degradation of words which involve praise and blame'. 'Let our

[1] Mid. 361.   [2] Mid. 384; cf. DD. 329.   [3] MF. 148.

habitual talk give morals their full meaning . . .' she concludes.[1]

Insistence, sometimes on the full, sometimes on the exact meaning of moral terms weaves its way into the texture of the novels. For example, Romola's closing words :

> We can only have the highest happiness . . . by having wide thoughts, and much feeling . . . and this sort of happiness often brings so much pain with it, that we can only tell it from pain by its being what we would choose before everything else, because our souls see it is good.[2]

or this from *Middlemarch* :

> 'Few men . . . would think it a duty to add to their anxieties in that way, Caleb.'
> 'That signifies nothing — what other men would think.'[3]

Both of these show the characteristic trend of defining a moral term in a novel. In the first, it sums up the whole book — it is Romola's own *Apologia pro Vita Sua*. In the second, it is developed by the interplay of known and different personalities conversing together. There is another good example of this in *Felix Holt*; though here the personalities and their situation both contribute something :

> [Esther] 'Oh ! . . . I know you are a person of right opinions.'
> [Felix] 'But by opinions you mean men's thoughts about great subjects, and by taste you mean their thoughts about small ones : dress, behaviour, amusements, ornaments.'
> 'Well — yes — or rather, their sensibilities about those things.'
> 'It comes to the same thing ; thoughts, opinions, knowledge are only a sensibility to facts and ideas.'[4]

Here Felix re-defines two pairs of terms : he makes 'opinion' one of the words that 'involve praise' and makes 'taste' involve none ; and he then ensures that the involvements of 'thought' and 'sensibility' shall be in this respect

[1] TS. 154-8.   [2] R. 602-3.   [3] Mid. 408.   [4] FH. 126.

identical. We are not, however, wooed by Felix's arguments alone, but by constant indications on the author's part that he is a good man; while we can see Esther ill at ease, unsure of her ground, rude to him because she is thrown on the defensive, and being steadily persuaded that his point of view is truer than hers. What manipulates the terms is the whole tissue of the story.

The same is true of the quarrel between Romola and Tito about selling her father's library. Tito contrasts 'substantial good' and 'brain-wrought fantasies'. Romola re-defines his terms for him:

'You talk of substantial good, Tito! Are faithfulness, and love and sweet grateful memories no good?... Is it no good that a just life should be justly honoured? Or, is it good that we should harden our hearts against all the wants and hopes of those who have depended on us? What good can belong to men who have such souls?' [1]

But what gives Romola's sense of 'good' a tangible content and makes it readily and really significant is that the novel frames it in a developed situation. Romola relates 'good' to 'a just life', 'memories', and so forth; but her own predicament is crying out to be described in these terms, and therefore is surreptitiously explaining them all the time.

It is scarcely too much to say that re-definition can sometimes furnish the whole logic of an argument. The dispute between Tom Tulliver and Phillip Wakem [2] is thrown into the form of which of them is more truly 'befriending' Maggie. Earlier in the book, when Maggie and her father argue, she says that to curse and bear malice is wicked — he, that the prosperity of rascals is wicked.[3] But the best instance is again the frequently renewed argument between Lydgate and Rosamond. Sometimes the shift is explicit: 'I think it is enough that I say you are not to go', Lydgate says.[4] Rosamond's manipulations are implicit, and they are deadlier: 'I shall do everything it becomes me to do'; [5] 'it cannot be good to act rashly'; [6]

---

[1] R. 297. [2] MF. 375. [3] MF. 287.
[4] Mid. 422. [5] Mid. 432. [6] Mid. 478.

and even 'I think you ought to have told me before we were married that you would place me in the worst position, rather than give up your own will'.[1] These utterances do not add new facts to the discussion; their function is to introduce and interrelate, though perhaps only by suggestion, tendentious expressions. Yet this seemingly abstract linguistic operation is what provides the drama and intransigence of the battle. Each protagonist has his — or her — contrasting scheme of relevances; each embodies it in his use of terms; and about relevances and meanings neither is, on the whole, open to persuasion. If the reader is induced to adjust his own vocabulary of 'words that involve praise and blame', it is towards some independent position indicated by the defects of both of theirs. The really influential factor in fiction tends to be no recurrent device of exposition (important though this may be) but the whole developing situation and its resolution — the novel from beginning to end.

[1] Mid. 477.

CHAPTER VI

NEWMAN

(i) *The System of Reality and Knowledge*

THIS chapter is devoted, for reasons given already, solely to Newman's writings as a Catholic; and the first thing to notice is the impression one is likely to get from opening these writings at random. It is that Newman is not a sage at all. He seems always to be arguing for some detail, and seldom if ever to commit himself generally to opinions of a sage-like kind. There are obvious reasons for this. The details of his view were on points of dogma or ritual, and both Newman and many of his adversaries agreed that salvation probably depended on truth in these matters, and therefore that no detail was too small and no pains too great. Moreover, he worked against keen hostility, and could not — at least at first — be too ambitious. 'I am on the defensive, and only insist on so much as is necessary to my purpose.' [1] Finally, he had no need to argue or even explain his outlook fully; it was a great victory if he could persuade a reader or listener to make contact with the Roman Church. 'Come and see. That is my keynote from first to last.' [2] Once this was done, he could leave further explanations to others.

But this seeming preoccupation with detail is quite deceptive, and if Newman has recently been gaining more and more admiration from non-Catholics, it is because he proves to have had perhaps the most comprehensive, detailed and integrated view of things — in the sage's sense — of any English writer of his century. This integration, indeed, is so complete that the beginning and end of his outlook can in an abstract way be stated by a single

[1] PPC. 136. [2] PPC. 349.

sentence. He believed that *reality is a great ordered system with the Creator as its apex*. 'His are all beings, visible and invisible . . . the laws of the universe, the principles of truth, the relation of one thing to another, their qualities and virtues, the order and harmony of the whole, all that exists, is from Him . . . the remote sidereal firmament . . . the primary atoms of matter . . . the most insignificant or unsightly insect . . . animalculae . . . the restless ever-spreading vegetation . . . the tribes and families of birds and beasts . . . and so in the intellectual, moral, social, and political world.' [1] Because of this order, everything in the universe has its proper nature and purpose : and the natural world, the church, the state, and the human individual, are all created on similar and analogous patterns.[2] Moreover, nothing in the created universe is self-contained. Newman attacks those who see the individual character of things but 'of their connection one with another, their hidden essence and their life, and the bearing of external matters upon each and upon all . . . have no perception'.[3] Moreover, the world is infinitely complex and varied, but everything has its allotted place ; it may be bad elsewhere, but there it is good. 'Everything has its own perfection, be it higher or lower in the scale of things ; and the perfection of one is not the perfection of another' ; [4] 'every exercise of nature or of art is good in its place'.[5]

This concept of the universe — what in one place he calls 'the providential system of the world' [6] — is the core of Newman's work. It lends credence and support to many detailed points, and they in turn argue implicitly for the underlying conception. In the first place, it provides for exactly the kind of knowledge which as a sage he needs to justify, for knowledge is naturally a replica of the system of the world itself. 'It is a characteristic of our minds, that they cannot take an object in, which is submitted to them simply and integrally' ; the more we

---

[1] UE. 55-6.
[2] See *e.g.* DCD. 52, 185-6, 417-18, 442 ; UE. 158 ; DA. i. 174 ; DA. ii. 267, among many passages expressing this idea.
[3] DA. i. 102.   [4] UE. 113.   [5] GA. 285.   [6] GA. 405.

know, the more the knowledge of one object links it for us with others.[1] 'There is no enlargement [of the mind] unless there be a comparison of ideas one with another . . . and a systemizing of them . . . it is not a mere addition to our knowledge which is the illumination ; but . . . the movement onwards, of that mental centre, to which both what we know and what we are learning . . . gravitates.'[2] And what is true of every created thing, that it is proper within its place, and not proper out of it, is true of every kind of knowledge. Each has its proper sphere, and if it is ignored, some other kind will try improperly to take its place.[3] The varieties of truth must be sought appropriately, or they will not be found.[4] But if complete knowledge is a complex order which contains many kinds of knowledge, then nothing is more likely than that some knowledge will come by logical proof and some will not. The very idea of knowledge as a complex system makes it likely that its more and also its less straightforward varieties have their place. Every writer expressing a general view of man and the world needs to draw on a source of knowledge other than science, but by this line of thought Newman makes a virtue of necessity. He presents such a source as simply one further aspect of the ordered system. Mere familiarity with facts, he asserts, is insufficient ; 'all this is short of enough ; a man may have done it all, yet be lingering in the vestibule of knowledge'. What is deficient in such knowledge is that it fails to complete the system : it leaves a man with 'no power . . . of arranging things according to their real value, and, if I may use the phrase, of building up ideas'.[5]

Newman's central principle therefore equips him to argue that in some cases 'Reason . . . is subservient to faith, as handling, examining, explaining, recording, cataloguing, defending, the truths which faith, not reason, has gained for us, as providing an intellectual expression of supernatural facts, eliciting what is implicit, comparing, measuring, connecting each with each, and forming one

[1] DCD. 55.   [2] UE. 126.   [3] UE 64.
[4] See *e.g.* DCD. 110.   [5] UE. 145.

and all into a theological system'.[1]   There is a time for
abstractions, and a time when 'we must not confine ourselves to abstractions, and merely compare notion with
notion, . . . not hurry on and force a series of deductions
which, if they are to be realized, must distil like dew into
our minds'.[2]   For these distinctive deductions, these dis-
tillations, we must look to a distinctive power — that of
conscience; and this power takes us back once again to
the grand system of created Nature, for it is not a chance
faculty, but has an allotted part in that system.   It is
distinctively constituted; it is 'adapted for the use of all
classes and conditions of men . . . independently of books,
of educated reasoning, of physical knowledge, or of philosophy'.[3]   It is a special and also infallible source of
knowledge; and characteristically once again, part of
its function is to complete and correct that imperfect
'natural informant', our observation of 'the system and
the course of the world'.[4]   Without what conscience tells
us, the world would seem a formless, hopeless disorder.
Newman, that is to say, views this special source of knowledge as part of a systematic design, specially appropriate
to its function in that system, and giving us knowledge
through its ordered relation to other forms of knowing.

It is also part of this differentiated system that while
some knowledge can scarcely be missed, some presents
itself only to those fit to receive it.   'Christianity is
addressed, both as regards its evidences and its contents,
to minds which are in the normal condition of human
nature.' [5]   This natural condition, of course, has its characteristic virtue.   'Light is a quality of matter, as truth is
of Christianity; but light is not recognized by the blind,
and there are those who do not recognize truth from the
fault, not of truth, but of themselves.' [6]   To the common
notion that those who deny speculative truths are somehow
at fault, Newman gives a distinctive turn.   It is part of the
universal design that these truths should seem irresistibly
clear.   The individual who finds them otherwise is himself

---

[1] DCD. 336. [2] GA. 314. [3] GA. 390.
[4] GA. 396. [5] GA. 490. [6] GA. 410.

an interruption in the cosmic system. As in Carlyle, the injunctions of conscience become clearer to those who obey them ; [1] we reach our conclusions 'under a sense of duty to those conclusions'. Those who start from other premisses reach other conclusions ; and can no more reach these than a crooked man can be made straight. 'Whether his mind will ever grow straight . . . whether he is not responsible, responsible to his Maker, for being mentally crooked, is another matter.' [2] Everyone should remember that revelation is 'a boon' that 'cleanses the heart' ; those who do not come to it as enquirers, as 'suppliants' even, must answer for themselves.[3] In *The Development of Christian Doctrine* [4] Newman contrasts the 'principle of philosophies and heresies' with the principle of thought which leads to truth in morality and religion, and which he calls the dogmatical principle ; and according to the latter, 'religious error is in itself of an immoral nature . . . it is to be dreaded . . . truth and falsehood are set before us for the trial of our hearts . . . our choice is an awful giving forth of lots on which salvation or rejection is inscribed'.

(ii) *The Course of Things*

Newman's idea of conscience thus develops his central idea of the universe : so far as we accept it, it seems one further proof that in the great design of the world, everything has been allotted its specific purpose. And this leads to another doctrine, one which occurred also in Carlyle and Disraeli and indeed has proved attractive to sages always and everywhere. This doctrine is that truth is certain ultimately to prevail, and that error will ultimately destroy itself or be destroyed.

To some extent Newman argues for these two doctrines directly. Once individuals or institutions have abandoned the truth, he says, their end is certain : 'dissolution is that further state to which corruption tends' ; [5] a successful issue in practice 'could not have followed an accommoda-

---

[1] GA. 390.   [2] GA. 413.   [3] GA. 425-6.
[4] DCD. 357-8.   [5] DCD. 203.

dation to what was sinful'.[1] He appeals to those who incline to his views, but are still in the Anglican Church, to find for their faith some institutional form 'which may ensure its . . . continuance to generations',[2] as if no system of truth could be valid unless it could ensure its own continued reception. Of 'Mahometanism' he argues 'no one would deny that there has been a living idea somewhere in a religion, which has been so strong, so wide, so lasting a bond of union in the history of the world'.[3] Prevailing is a test of truth, ultimately prevailing an ultimate test. This both applies and confirms Newman's general conception of the world as a grand design : the design is revealed in the world's development as much as in its structure. That this should be so affords a powerful argument for Christianity in general, and Roman Catholicism in particular. In *The Development of Christian Doctrine* Newman's systematic proof actually begins by showing how Christianity triumphed over the other religions of the Roman world ; and continues by arguing that Christianity stood to rival religions in the first century exactly as the Catholic faith stood to heresies in the fourth.[4] The success of the true religion was followed by that of its authentic version. In each case the implication of success is the same.

According to Newman, the Roman Church through history 'is the one great principle of unity and concord which the world has seen' ; [5] 'she cannot help succeeding, she cannot help being strong, she cannot help being beautiful ; it is her gift'.[6] The attacks of liberal historians pass over her without effect ; afterwards she is found just where she was.[7] The Church is sure to prosper and spread : 'grow you must ; I know it ; you cannot help it, it is your destiny ; it is the necessity of the Catholic name'.[8] To this every moment bears witness, because of 'that unfailing law of Divine Providence, by which all

---

[1] DCD. 373.   [2] DA. i. 199.
[3] DCD. 187. Cf. *ibid.* 97, on the exponents of the *via media* : 'their exception will have its weight — till we reflect that the particular theology which they advocate has not the prescription of success'.
[4] DCD. Chapter vi, Sections I and II.
[5] DA. i. 266.   [6] DA. i. 209.   [7] DA. i. 137.   [8] PPC. 389.

events, prosperous or adverse, are made to tend, in one way or another, to the triumph of our Religion'.[1] Success is not merely what comes to truth in the end, but it is brought nearer by every single event that occurs, and this is so because of the very texture, through and through, of the world.

The position and prospects of those on the wrong side are different. 'Such will not last on the long run, as are not commanded and rewarded by divine authority.'[2] Reform of the Anglican Church, for example, is hopeless ;[3] it will either reject attempts out of hand,[4] or transform them to its own principles.[5] Newman brings this home by pointing to the isolation, the futility, of the reformers : 'your plans seemed prospering . . . great things were to be ; and yet, strange to say, . . . you have found yourselves steadily advanced in the direction which you feared, and never were nearer to the promised land than you are now'.[6] Then this suave and commiserating tone changes to one of warning : '. . . look well to your footing that you slip not ; be very much afraid lest the world should detain you ; dare not . . . to fall short of God's grace'. But the tone which Newman adopts is so intimately connected with what he has to say that it warrants a section to itself.

(iii) *Newman's Personality and Tone*

'Who could resist the charm of that spiritual apparition, gliding in the dim afternoon light through the aisles of St. Mary's, rising into the pulpit, and then, in the most entrancing of voices, breaking the silence with words and

---

[1] PPC, p. vi.   [2] DA. i. 197.   [3] DA. i. 59.
[4] DA. i. 141-2.   [5] DA. i. 103.
[6] The doctrine that falsehood can survive indefinitely long, however, is also to be found ; and is doubtless a direct application of Newman's religious beliefs about the power of Satan in the world, and its continuance until the last day. PPC. 230 is interesting, because here Newman admits that there may be 'impressions', that 'are false and are uncongenial to our nature', 'similar in permanence' to those that are true, and only distinguished from them by not being universal, and not coming into the mind 'no one knows how, that is, from heaven'. In DA. i. 347, Newman suggests that what is certain for the future is that nothing can prevail but *either* Catholicism or scepticism. His whole attitude on this point is like that of Carlyle.

thoughts which were a religious music — subtle, sweet, mournful? I seem to hear him still—.' This is how Matthew Arnold describes what it was like to encounter the physical presence and speaking voice of Newman, and the same 'ineffable sentiment' of Newman's presence,[1] which to Arnold made him seem irresistible, is sustained through his books by several telling things. There is the impression gained from what he says of the frame of mind in which he approached his subject, and that too of the frame of mind in which he approached his reader or audience; and these are important partly for their own sakes, and partly because they influence the frame of mind in which readers or audience approach his subject and him. The issue is complicated because these various points are to some extent the special concern of the present enquiry, and to some extent not.

Perhaps this can be put more clearly. In part, Newman creates an impression of himself or of his frame of mind, or induces a frame of mind in his reader or listener, which simply means that he is given more sympathetic attention. This is something which would gain him a better hearing whatever it was that he wanted to say. Thus, when he says that truth is his object,[2] that he speaks simply out of concern for his listeners,[3] that others are better qualified in general though he has certain special advantages,[4] that he has thought about his subject long and hard,[5] or that his argument is a difficult one,[6] he is saying what any polemical writer might say, regardless of his message. And when, claiming that Catholics are misunderstood and slandered by Protestants, he good-humouredly takes himself as an unfortunate example,[7] he wins sympathy in a manner open to anyone. But not everything connected with his tone is as unconnected as this with his doctrine and outlook; and what concerns the present enquiry is how devices of tone can elucidate this outlook, and help to bring it vividly before us.

---

[1] See Arnold's *Works*, vol. iii, p. 65 and vol. vi, p. 33.
[2] DA. i. 65.   [3] DA. i. 3.   [4] UE. 1-3.   [5] UE. 3-4.
[6] UE. 229.   [7] PPC. 118 ff.

Consider, for example, how Newman stresses the personal nature of religious conviction, and how he admits that in principle his own line of thought may be valid only for himself. 'In religious enquiry each of us can speak only for himself . . . his own experiences are enough for himself, but he cannot speak for others . . . he can only bring his own experiences to the common stock . . . if it satisfies him, it is likely to satisfy others ; if, as he believes and is sure, it is true, it will approve itself to others also . . .' ; [1] or elsewhere 'I am going into these details, not . . . as if I called on you to be convinced by what convinced me . . . (for the methods of conviction are numberless, and one man approaches the Church by this road, another by that), but merely in order to show you how it was that Antiquity, instead of leading me from the Holy See as it leads many, on the contrary drew me on to submit to its claims'.[2] In part these passages simply display a becoming and ingratiating modesty, and so make us sympathetic to the writer regardless of what he says. But both of them do more. In the first, fused with this modesty, there is a note of confidence that although a modest claim is proper in such matters, there is an objective order of things which can make it unnecessary. *Magna est veritas et praevalebit.* In the second there is a hint that although Newman's own road may not be the road for anyone else, there is an order of things whereby some road is waiting for everyone ; and perhaps even that, sooner or later, everyone will begin to move along the road that is waiting for him. The picture, that is, which Newman shows us of himself seems also to depict an example of what follows from his system.

The same is true, on a far larger scale, of the *Apologia pro Vita Sua*, and the whole autobiographical section in *The Difficulties of Anglicans*.[3] In both of these, Newman describes himself seeking patiently and earnestly, over a period of years, for the truth in religion, and makes his readers enter into his confusion, unhappiness or isolation. This is enough to win sympathy for his sincerity, humility, and persistence, but it is not all he does. In its entirety

---

[1] GA. 384-5.   [2] DA. i. 344.   [3] DA. i. 71-2, 324 ff.

the final point of the account is that someone as honest and clear-sighted and persevering as he was found himself driven, in a direction almost against his will, by arguments that were many in number and complex and subtle in their nature, but that all combined ultimately into one great system with one irresistible conclusion. The portrait of Newman's religious biography becomes a map of knowledge.

A writer need not of course resort to explicit description if he wants to create an impression of himself; he can do so by every turn of phrase, through the tone in which he seems to utter what he has to say. Newman's tone seems to have two qualities, and both of these (besides being what would increase respect for anyone, whatever opinions he might be expressing) do something to convey the frame of mind which results from believing in his first principles, and therefore do something to make these real to the reader. In the first place, there is the note of modesty, of a realization that his subject-matter is really too vast for his powers: 'This, then, is the answer which I am prepared to give . . . I am prepared to maintain . . . and, as I conceive, I have now begun proving it'; 'if I am then arguing . . .'; 'this then is how I should solve the fallacy, for so I must call it'; 'if we would investigate the reason, I suppose we must first take into account Lord Bacon's own explanation'; 'such at least is the lesson which I am taught by all the thought which I have been able to bestow on the subject'.[1]

But this modest and unassuming demeanour can modulate quietly into something rather different. One can see this, and see how closely Newman brought these two qualities together, simply by completing some of the quotations already used to illustrate his modesty. The gentle 'if I am then arguing' is modified at once by the quiet firmness of *and shall argue*'; a passage quoted earlier to the effect that religious convictions are personal but that what satisfies one man is likely to satisfy another, ends on the firmer note of *for there is but one truth*'.

[1] UE. 105, 159, 160, 216, 230.

Newman wrote of the principle that religious doctrine naturally develops as a 'grave' and 'winning' hypothesis. These qualities that so attracted him are his own. Colouring his modest and winning style everywhere is a note of grave calm, of quiet confidence, of steady and imperturbable advance. 'I shall continue my investigation, and I shall introduce what I have to say by means of an objection . . .'; 'this is what will be said; and I reply as follows :— . . .' [1] Again, examples come most readily from the *Scope and Nature of University Education*, and this is significant because it is perhaps the book which does most to convey his general as opposed to his religious outlook. 'My reason for saying so runs, *with whatever abruptness*, into the form of a syllogism :—'; 'A University, I should lay down . . . professes to teach universal knowledge'; 'I will throw my argument into another form . . . this is the thesis which I lay down, and on which I shall insist . . . I think this will be found to be no matter of words . . .'; [2] 'this then is how I should solve the fallacy, for so I must call it'. [3] Such turns of phrase are trivial in themselves, but strike us by their number and continuity. They combine with the quiet, confident, unadorned finality of 'such ideas of religion seem to me short of Monotheism'. [4] And the following passage adds the vitally important note, for it hints at the source and the ground of this confidence : 'how do I propose directly to meet the objection ? Why, gentlemen, *I have met it already*, viz., in laying down, that intellectual culture is its own end.' [5] No device of tone could remind the reader more strongly that truth is a system, and that the parts of that system interrelate and confirm each other.

(iv) *Forms of Argument*

(a) *Enlisting the Negative Evidence.*—At the end of Section (ii) Newman was quoted as asserting that resistance to Catholicism had only led his hearers towards it. He

[1] PPC. 86, 87.   [2] UE. 11-13 (my italics).   [3] UE. 160.
[4] UE. 31.   [5] UE. 155 (my italics).

says the same sort of thing elsewhere — for instance that his opponents were 'however much against their will, like Caiaphas, prophesying for us'; or, as we saw, that 'all events, prosperous *or adverse*, . . . tend . . . to the triumph of our religion'.[1] This is a further application of the principle that the world is a system, and is one of the most frequent, effective and yet unobtrusive of Newman's persuasive methods. Every polemical writer, sooner or later, finds himself obliged to account for the facts which apparently argue against him. To disregard these facts usually seems too high-handed, to admit them as plain exceptions is not high-handed enough. What Newman does, again and again, is to treat them as positive though recondite illustrations of the principles they appear to discredit. They are *enlisted*; they appear as merely some less obvious aspect of the single grand system, working out the same laws as ever, but in a slightly new way.

What this means must not be misunderstood. It is not simply that Newman can deal with apparent exceptions — this would be of no interest at all. It is, rather, that he employs this distinctive means so often that it colours his whole work; and moreover, it is apt to a peculiar degree. Every time it comes, the reader seems to find confirmation that the universe is a system. This mode of argument applies that doctrine. Nor is it unrelated to Newman's tone. When even the exceptions work in one's favour, how can one fail to write with a grave and quiet confidence? Apparent reasons for perturbation always turn out to be fresh evidence. The link between this kind of argument and Newman's tone is especially clear in a passage already quoted: Newman's grave confidence stood out most plainly when he claimed to have provided in advance for an objection.

Occasionally Newman asserts it as a general truth that exceptions or contradictions are really indirect confirmations. When they show sufficient vitality and persistence, he writes, even mistakes carry information; for 'they are cognate to the truth, and we can allow for them'.[2] Fully

---

[1] DA. i. 27; PPC, p. vi (my italics).   [2] DCD. 224.

mastering an objection means putting it to actual use :
'here was at once an answer to the objection urged by
Anglicans against the present teaching of Rome ; and not
only an answer to objections, but a positive argument in
its favour'.[1] We should think that weak evidence or none
is a handicap to proof, but sometimes, Newman suggests,
it can strengthen proof : 'It is no paradox to say that there
is a certain scantiness, nay an absence of evidence, which
may even tell in favour of statements which require to be
made good . . . it frequently happens that omissions proceed
on some law, as the varying influence of an external cause ;
and then, so far from being a perplexity, they may even
confirm such evidence as occurs, by becoming, as it were,
its correlative'.[2]

It is perhaps worth while to quote a few illustrations of
this kind of argument, because this will show how often a
point of detail can also sustain a sense of a writer's whole
outlook. This is what happens when Newman claims that
the existence of evil in the world does not weaken the
arguments for God's existence, but strengthens them by
suggesting that He is estranged from his creatures ;[3] that
it was peculiarly appropriate to Christ's nature not to fulfil
the Old Testament prophecies too slavishly ;[4] that the
inchoateness of scripture, so far from weakening the
evidence for religion, gives the strongest proof of that true
form of it which insists upon doctrinal development.[5]
These are general arguments for religion. More frequently he makes the weak points of Catholicism add to its
strength : that the Roman Church now seems superstitious
to its enemies merely confirms its continuity with the
first-century Church, so superstitious in the eyes of Tacitus,
Suetonius, Pliny and other pagans ;[6] the very hostility to
Catholicism, because hostility to it through and through,

[1] DA. i. 346.   [2] DCD. 115 and 117.   [3] GA. 397.
[4] GA. 448.   [5] DCD. 62.
[6] DCD. 208 ff. Milman, in his essay on Newman's *Development of
Christian Doctrine*, violently attacked the author at this point, on the ground
that his boasted continuity with the early church was, by his own confession,
a continuity only with its superstitious excrescences. But he missed the
comprehensive nature of Newman's discussion, which attempts to trace a
double continuity: to unsympathetic outsiders, then as now, the Roman

proves it good at least in its unity ; [1] quarrels within the
Church, because they are within it, merely confirm its
strength ; [2] the rarity of Oecumenical Councils and ex-
communications, so far from proving them (as Gladstone
had maintained) 'rusty tools', merely confirms their
supreme solemnity and importance ; [3] borrowing pre-
Christian rites merely confirms the vigour and self-confidence of the Roman Church ; [4] pictures of saints being
forbidden in church 'lest what is worshipped . . . be painted
on the walls', so far from proving that saints were not to
be worshipped, merely confirms that they should be ; [5]
Anglo-Catholics' insistence upon a principle of doctrinal
authority although they violate it by arbitrary personal
choices, so far from showing it to be alien to them, shows it
so much theirs that they must insist on it even at the
expense of self-contradiction.[6]

Newman also argues that the rule of law throughout
the universe does not make miracles improbable, but
confirms their likelihood. It does so, of course, only to
those who believe that some miracles are beyond question ;
but for them, the very regularity of the universe argues for
more miracles at later times and in other places. Here,
once again, a principle which seems at first sight to weaken
Newman's conclusion is made to confirm it, but this time
only for a restricted class of people. And this introduces
a new point : arranging arguments not in a general form,
but so as to appeal only to a particular group, is very
common in Newman's work, and its effect must be traced.

(b) The 'argumentum ad hominem'.—This form of
argument is naturally common to all religious controversy,
and it is so frequent in Newman, and so easily identified,
that only the specially interesting examples will be quoted.
In the well-known satirical passage in the first lecture on
the *Present Position of Catholics*, a Russian Count, in 'a

Church appears as a grandiose superstition ; but, then as now, from within
it is a continuing authority, constantly assailed by heresy, as constantly
destroying it, and alone even in *claiming* genuine Catholicity, much more in
possessing it.

[1] DCD. 96.   [2] DA. i. 271.   [3] LDN. (DA. ii. 214).
[4] DCD. 372.   [5] DCD. 408.   [6] DA. i. 123.

great meeting held . . . at Moscow' after the model of meetings in England that attack Catholicism, gives a gross caricature of the British Constitution, and makes it appear the incarnation of tyranny and senseless superstition.[1] This *argumentum ad hominem* is interesting for its multi-farious development. Britain is at one extremity of Europe, and meddles officiously in the affairs of the Continent; its constitution, full of mystical nonsense like 'the King can do no wrong', is a crazy anachronism (this part of the argument is based on Blackstone's *Commentaries*); the Book of Revelation points out Queen Victoria as having the number of the beast, for at 18 she came to the throne in 1837, and $18 \times 37 = 666$ which is that number; English Kings have all murdered their relations and wives (of whom Henry VIII murdered six hundred); they indulged in black magic and died of gluttony; *sculls* may be seen floating daily on the Thames. One of the more cautious of the Count's listeners, examining his copy of Blackstone, glances only at the quotations, the title-page and the binding. The more choleric burn John Bull in effigy. Each time, if you think that what Newman describes would be ignorant and foolish, so you must the parallel real instances of slander against Catholics.

The *argumentum ad hominem* which Newman offers in defence of adoration of the Virgin is interesting, because here he also transfers the negative evidence into positive. Adoration of the Virgin is no more nor less a 'development' than the doctrine of the Trinity; Protestants accept one, and should therefore accept both. The doctrine of the Trinity is not, he maintains, to be found in the earlier Christian fathers; and indeed their partial statements of the doctrine are really heresies. The full doctrine of the Trinity is a complex of dogmas, any selection from which is not the true doctrine at all, but Sabellianism or Arianism or whatever it may be.[2] The references to the Trinity in

[1] PPC. 27-41.
[2] DCD. 14-15. Cf. DA. i. 345. For other examples of the *argumentum ad hominem* see DA. i. 321 (those who believe God's promise that there shall always be a church are committed to the Roman Church, the only candidate — cf. LDN. (DA. ii. 225-7), and *Loss and Gain*, 198); DCD. 81

the Early Fathers thus, in an unexpected way, actually suggest one further proof of Newman's theory of the *Development of Christian Doctrine.*

It was natural for Newman to rely on the *argumentum ad hominem*, because his first principles were neither self-evident nor easily proved, and indeed he considered them beyond proof. But he makes this virtual necessity a positive strength. Arguments of this kind are possible because religion is a system; and dependence on the system comes to look like positive confirmation of it. This shows most clearly in Newman's plea for consistency with regard to doctrinal developments. 'Nor do those separate developments stand independent of each other, but by cross relations they are connected, and grow together while they grow from one . . . you must accept the whole or reject the whole . . . it is trifling to receive all but something which is as integral as any other portion ; and, on the other hand, it is a solemn thing to accept any part, for, before you know where you are, you may be carried on by a stern logical necessity to accept the whole.' [1] Newman's own words hint here at some of the psychological effects of encountering and accepting these arguments. Not to accept them is to behave frivolously in face of the ordered system of truth ; their validity reminds us both of that system, and of its solemnity.

The *argumentum ad hominem* (besides of course performing its specific function in any given case) contributes in another way to the general impact of Newman's system : it recalls the essentially personal nature of any religious argument and thereby the irrelevance of logic, and the fact that blindness to religious truth is in a way culpable.

(those who would deny that certain arguments disproved Apostolic infallibility are committed not to use the same arguments to disprove Papal infallibility) ; DA. i. 301-2 (those who believe the Goths and Nestorians, despite magnitude or antiquity, to have been heretical, are committed to believe the same of the Greek Church) ; DA. ii. 231-2 (those who believe that being under a doctor's orders, though these may extend to any activity of life, is not an impossible tyranny, are committed not to believe that Papal authority is such a tyranny), etc., etc. This last case is of some interest as suggesting how the *argumentum ad hominem* may merge into argument by analogy.   [1] DCD. 94.

'Multitudes indeed I ought to succeed in persuading . . .
because they and I start from the same principles . . . but
if any one starts from other principles but ours, I have not
the power to change his principles . . . any more than I
can make a crooked man straight.' [1] This analogy of
the crooked man has an unmistakable meaning; had
Newman written 'any more than I can twist an iron bar',
the result would have been different.[2] The *argumentum
ad hominem* often recalls how a knowledge of truth in
fundamentals is the reward of virtue; and Newman's
insistence on the contrast between those to whom it is
addressed and those to whom it is not can bring before
the reader not only the shortcomings, but also the ultimate
fate, of those who reject his basic premisses. 'The primary
question, with every serious enquiry, is the question of
salvation. I am speaking to those who feel this to be so;
not to those who make religion a sort of literature or
philosophy, but to those who desire . . . to approve themselves to their Maker, and to save their souls.' [3] Those
whose first principles clash with his own are 'on the best
terms with Queen and statesmen, and practical men, and
country gentlemen, and respectable tradesmen, fathers and
mothers, schoolmasters, church-wardens, vestries, public
societies, newspapers, and their readers in the lower
classes'.[4] They may indeed have ability; but Newman
is ready for this. He concedes that it was 'a thought of
genius' to attack the Roman church by certain methods,
and merely adds 'as I think, *preternatural* genius'.[5]

(*c*) '*Tu quoque*' *Arguments, and rejecting the Burden
of Proof.*—Both of these modes of argument contribute
something to the quality of Newman's work. The first
rebuts an accusation by turning it upon the accuser, and

[1] GA. 413.
[2] Analogy is discussed below, p. 181 ff.; the sequel to this passage,
where the hint is developed, was discussed above, p. 162.
[3] DA. i. 271.   [4] DA. i. 13.
[5] PPC. 224 (my italics). For other instances see PPC. 179 (Protestants
demand a unity of secular and religious education just like Catholics),
180 (Protestants act as superstitiously when, by an image, they burn the
Pope in effigy, as Catholics when they use images in their ritual) and 184
(Protestant religious persecutions).

the second argues that one's opinion must be accepted
unless there are unanswered objections to it. *Tu quoque*
arguments seem always to have an *argumentum ad hominem*
implicit in them; as for example with Newman's contention that just as Catholics actually prevented a Protestant
Church in Rome, so Protestants would have liked to
prevent Catholic Churches in England,[1] or his argument
that if the Roman Church has occasional difficulties with
a celibate clergy, so have Protestant Churches with one
that is married.[2] To some extent, therefore, these modes
of argument have the same effect on a book's whole quality
as those we have just been discussing. Moreover, both
tu quoque arguments, and rejecting the burden of proof,
emphasize the concept of knowledge as a vast integrated
system where one opinion commits, or sometimes does not
commit, a man to others; and both, because they seem
circumspect and thoughtful, do something to sustain
Newman's tone.

At one point he makes this clear himself. The Papal
Encyclical of 1864, he argues, makes much less ambitious
claims than has been supposed. It does not condemn
liberty out and out, but merely denies that liberty of expression and worship of any and every kind is always and everywhere good. 'All that the Pope has done is to deny a
universal.' Then comes the point. The burden of proof
rests upon those who wish to maintain this universal. Of
these on the one hand, and the Pope on the other, he asks
'which of the two is peremptory and sweeping in his
utterance?'[3] The wrong tone goes with the wrong view;
and recalling that this tone is in fact wrong recalls what
view is right. Matthew Arnold will prove later to make use
of a similar mode of argument.

In conclusion, the full contribution of these modes of
argument is only seen when their dimensions are remem-
bered. They are often long enough for a single argument,
merely by its form, to change the quality of a whole
chapter. The *argumentum ad hominem* by which Newman

[1] DA. ii. 271.   [2] PPC. 134 ff.   [3] DA. ii. 274.

attempts to discredit the rule of Vincent of Lerins [1] occupies seventeen pages — rather over half of his Introduction. The *tu quoque* argument on Protestant persecution in *The Present Position of Catholics* occupies, with intermissions, forty pages, virtually the whole of one lecture.[2] The final result is like transposing one whole part of a work of music into a new key; and one should remember, if it seems over-ingenious to put much weight on what kinds of argument Newman relies on, that no other device of exposition can be prolonged like this.

(v) *Illustrations: the Church and the World*

But although the form of Newman's argument is important, it is the facts and examples with which he fills it that give his work its life and richness and movement, and these facts and examples all emphasize a single corollary of the view that the universe is one system.[3] This corollary is that the true Church, the Roman Church, is itself a system, and a microcosm of the created universe. Naturally the doctrines of Christianity itself are a system, if only because knowledge is a system. They have a 'harmonious order'; they 'are members of one family, and suggestive, or correlative, or confirmatory, or illustrative of each other'.[4] 'It may be a hard iron system, but it is consistent.' [5] When the Roman Church condemns a book, calling it 'scandalous, rash, false, schismatical, injurious . . . impious and heretical', this is not merely abuse. It follows systematically from a developed science of controversy; the different terms are used 'each with its definite meaning'.[6] But Christianity is more than a system of dogmas or knowledge. 'Prophets

---

[1] That 'revealed in Apostolic doctrine is "*quod semper, quod ubique, quod ab omnibus*"'. DCD. 10-27.

[2] PPC. 182-222.

[3] See *e.g.* UE. 124, 'the exuberant riches and resources, yet the orderly course, of the Universe'.

[4] DCD. 93. The conjunction here of words that refer to proof and those that refer to exposition is in exact accord with the general thesis of this book.

[5] *Loss and Gain*, 199-200. The earlier part of the sentence represents a character in the novel who is merely on the road to conversion.

[6] DA. ii. 284.

or Doctors . . . their teaching is a vast system . . . not to
be embodied in one code or treatise, but consisting of a
certain body of Truth, pervading the Church like an
atmosphere.' [1] The true religion is made up of facts that
constitute a Church; and it is on these facts, not on
doctrines, that Newman tries always to place the chief stress,
as we should expect him to do, from his conviction that
'Real Assent' requires not abstract argument but vivid
particular images. Expounding Christianity thus tends
always and naturally, for Newman, to turn into showing
that the Church is a system of persons and rituals and
customs, a single real thing, not an abstract theory; and
this he tends to do in two stages. First, a vivid impression
of the multifariousness, energy, and incessant changes
of human life everywhere on earth runs through most of
his work, and is so distinctive and so deeply felt that to
minds that are not religious it may well seem the most
profound and valuable of his insights. Then in contrast,
he suggests how in the Catholic Church this variety and
energy are not curtailed, but effortlessly and beautifully
co-ordinated, until every aspect of human life finds its place
there in an incomparable order.

   This impression of the crowded world, rich with
numbers, change, energy, variety, contributes to his
impression of the Church both by contrast, and (since the
Church is the same world, organized but not mechanically
regimented) also by analogy. Yet to Newman the contrast
is never simple and complete, except when the natural
world is positively corrupted. Thus over against the early
Catholic Church, he writes, stood an effete confusion of
pre-Christian sects and early heresies, 'with the Oriental
Mysteries, flitting wildly to and fro like spectres; with the
Gnostics . . . with the Neo-Platonists, men of literature,
pedants, visionaries, or courtiers . . . the Manichees . . .
the fluctuating teachers of the school of Antioch, the time-
serving Eusebians, and the reckless versatile Arians . . .
the fanatic Montanists and the harsh Novatians'.[2] At the
present time it is the same: 'There is no antagonist system.

[1] DCD. 76.   [2] DCD. 358.

Criticisms, objections, protests, there are in plenty', but
attempts to systematize them only reveal the chaos beneath :
'an incurable contrariety . . . a war of principles . . .
authorities keeping silence . . . the people plainly intimating
that they think both doctrine and usage . . . of very little
matter at all . . . the evident despair of even the better
sort of men'.[1] Several times Newman does all he can to
depict a Protestant chaos. He likens Protestant attacks
upon Rome to riotously clanging bells : 'A movement is
in birth which has no natural crisis or resolution. Spon-
taneously the bells of the steeples begin to sound . . . by
a sort of mechanical impulse, bishop and dean, archdeacon
and canon, rector and curate, one after another, *each on
his high tower*, off they set, swinging and booming, tolling
and chiming, with nervous intenseness, and thickening
emotion . . . the old ding dong . . . jingling and clamouring
. . . to the extent of their compass.'[2] He quotes a contemporary account of an uproar in a Protestant church when
the clergyman tried to preach in a surplice — and he makes
the incident seem typical. '"A young woman went off in
a fit of hysterics, uttering loud shrieks . . . a cry of 'fire'
was raised . . . a rush was made . . . whistling, cat-calls,
hurrahing, and such cries as are heard in theatres . . . the
row increased, some of the congregation waving their hats,
standing on the seats, jumping over them, bawling, roaring, and gesticulating, like a mob at an election."' His
final comment is 'here, at length, certainly are signs of
life, but it is not the life of the Catholic Church'.[3] The
tradition of hostility to Catholics in England is 'a tradition
of nursery stories, school-stories, . . . platform-stories,
pulpit-stories ; — a tradition of newspapers . . . pamphlets
. . . novels . . . light literature of all kind . . . selections from
the English classics, bits of poetry . . . chance essays . . .
a tradition floating in the air ; which we found in being
. . . which has been borne in upon us by all we saw, heard,
or read, in high life, in parliament, in law courts, in general
society. . .'.[4]

The world of Nature does not display this riotous and

[1] DCD. 95.   [2] PPC. 76-7 (my italics).   [3] DA. i. 56-7.   [4] PPC. 88.

sinister disorder. Admittedly, it suffers change and decay. 'Events move in cycles; all things come round; "the sun ariseth and goeth down, and hasteth to his place where he arose". Flowers first bloom, and then fade; fruit ripens and decays . . . the grace of spring, the richness of autumn, are but for a moment.'[1] But the changes are themselves transient, and the vicissitudes manifest a deeper order planned by the world's Divine creator. The theme is taken up again in one of Newman's two most famous sermons, *The Second Spring*: 'Frail and transitory as is every part of it, restless and migratory as are its elements, never-ceasing as are its changes, still it abides . . . though it is ever dying, it is ever coming to life again . . . one death is the parent of a thousand lives . . . spring passes . . . through summer and autumn into winter, only the more surely, by its own ultimate return, to triumph over that grave, towards which it resolutely hastened from its first hour . . . this material world, so vigorous, so reproductive amid all its changes'. But man himself lacks this inexhaustible revivifying power. Without help somehow from beyond him, 'man . . . tends to dissolution from the moment he begins to be . . . he is . . . as a bubble that breaks, and as water poured out upon the earth . . . as night follows day . . . so surely are failure, and overthrow, and annihilation, the issue of this natural virtue'.[2]

The crucial argument of *The Second Spring*, however, is that the Catholic Church — he is celebrating its return to England in an authentic form — breaks into this course of human dissolution. 'It is the coming in of a Second Spring; it is a restoration in the moral world, such as that which yearly takes place in the physical.'[3] When Newman describes particular events in the Roman Church, wild enthusiasm is hardly mentioned. There he sees significance in things like the calm confidence of an immense congregation, shut into a church by soldiery, remaining there for

---

[1] DCD. 199.

[2] This sermon was preached in July 1851, to mark the restoration of a Catholic episcopal hierarchy in England. See *Sermons preached on Various Occasions* (1857 Edition), pp. 190–93.

[3] *Op. cit.* p. 197.

two days, singing psalms until their oppressors join them and the blockade melts away; or Ambrose overthrowing the military power by the mere threat of excommunication;[1] or Rome when a criminal is to be executed, the multitude thinking only of whether he has repented, and bursting forth into an instantaneous shout of joy 'one concordant act of thanksgiving' when they hear that he has;[2] or some Catholic multitude, in an imaginary town — an 'idle and dissipated throng', singing, jesting as at a great fair, blaspheming, greedily buying false relics, acting pageants, letting off fireworks, crowding into confession, thieving on the very church-threshold — yet permeated with a living religion that qualifies everything they do, real children of their priest, always in and out of church, always under its shadow; or, in another quarter of that same town, some secluded convent, where every moment of the day is given over to silent worship, and even a sister who fraudulently pretends to the stigmata is a witness to the true faith, although also to human weakness.[3]

These are the impressions that Newman gives of the Roman Church. They are clear, vivid, comprehensive images, elaborated and sharpened until they sometimes might have come from a novelist. The Church appears to have all the energy and variety of human life, and all the order and harmony of a Divine institution. Newman can also say this more abstractly: 'the Catholic Church is necessarily developed into a thousand various powers and functions; she has her Clergy and Laity; her seculars and regulars . . . her diversified orders, congregations, confraternities, communities, each indeed intimately one with the whole, yet with its own . . . traditions . . . there is the ever-varying action of the ten thousand influences, political, national, local, municipal, provincial, agrarian, scholastic . . .'. And yet 'her centre is one . . . sheltered, moreover, in consequence of the antiquated character of its traditions, the peculiarity of its modes of acting, the tranquillity and deliberateness of its operations . . . her course is consistent, determinate and simple'.[4] But this

[1] DA. i. 49-50.　　[2] DA. i. 225-7.　　[3] DA. i. 249-53.　　[4] DA. i. 156.

generalized description is what the details and illustrations
bring to life. They actually show, vividly and immediately, the fused multifariousness and system that this
passage describes.

(vi) *Imagery in Newman*

Newman also relies on metaphors and analogies to provide
vivid imagery in which we may see the life of the world and
of the Church. He often likens humanity outside the
Church to a boisterous, wild, dangerous sea — a metaphor
that Carlyle was fond of. The Anglican Church is a
'wreck' at sea; the masses are a 'giant ocean' that,
suddenly swelling and heaving, strands all smaller craft,
until only 'the boat of Peter' can ride the waves; the Oxford
Movement, at one point in its career, was seeking a refuge
from 'the troubled surge of human opinion'; the early
Church was a spirit rising from the 'troubled waters of the
Old World'; [1] the developing Catholic faith was like a
vessel at sea; [2] the Anglican Church may serve, though
not as a bulwark, yet as a breakwater for truth; [3] he himself
found that joining the Catholic Church was 'like coming
into port after a rough sea'.[4] In contrast to this, the true
faith resembles the land or above all the sky. Scripture,
though 'unsystematic and various', 'is an unexplored and
unsubdued land, with heights, and valleys, forests and
streams...full of concealed wonders and choice treasures'; [5]
the Church safeguards 'the territory of grace'; [6] true
accounts of the nature of God are like pictures of landscapes.[7] God's own nature is like 'the starry firmament',
too vast to be taken in all at once; [8] the central articles of
faith are 'the sun, moon, and stars of the spiritual heavens'.[9]

To see in a general way how these comparisons add
something to our understanding and acceptance of Newman
is easy enough. But it is less easy to see precisely what
they add, and to do this one must have in mind the sort of
distinction that Coleridge drew between a metaphor and

[1] DA. i. 4, 22, 132, 339.   [2] DCD. 437.   [3] *Letter to Dr. Pusey* (DA. ii. 11).
[4] AVS. 215.   [5] DCD. 71.   [6] DA. i. 219.   [7] GA. 315.
[8] GA. 131.   [9] DA. i. 313.

an analogy. This was mentioned in the Introduction. 'The Language is analogous', he writes, 'whenever a thing, power, or principle of a higher dignity is expressed by the same thing, power or principle in a lower but more known form.' [1] The 'higher' and 'lower' are perhaps tendentious, but Coleridge is at the heart of the matter in speaking not of the two parts of an analogy but of the single 'same' principle that appears in two forms. The point is that an analogy compares two things that do not only resemble, but resemble because they are both the products of a single tendency or principle which is operating at two different places or in two different ways. In contrast with this, it is of course possible to compare things which undoubtedly resemble, but resemble by chance. This is what Coleridge would call a metaphor; and 'metaphors', he goes on, 'are always allegorical, *i.e.* expressing a different subject but with a resemblance'.

But the fact which makes this distinction so valuable to anyone expressing a world view has not yet been mentioned : it is that our knowledge is usually limited, and we simply cannot tell whether or not a resemblance between two things exists because they both result from the operation of a single 'thing, power or principle' — or more precisely, whether it exists wholly because of this, or only because of this in part, and otherwise is a chance resemblance ; or whether it is wholly by chance. The philosopher or sage, though, can exploit this uncertainty, and can use figurative language either to suggest that two things result from a single power or principle when he could not prove that they do ; or to suggest that they are wholly the result of a single power or principle when he could only prove that they are in part ; or if he could prove this analogy in full, at least to cause his readers to accept it without proof. And all these may be useful, if only because of their effect on a writer's tone, and of their power to sustain a sense of his general outlook even while he is saying nothing about it.

Some of Newman's analogies make this quite clear.

---

[1] *Aids to Reflection*, Aphorism 102, para. 5.

On the one hand, for example, he likens faith to the moral sense,[1] and on the other, he likens the Roman Catholic Church to a tree, and schismatic Churches to branches lopped off from it.[2] The first of these is doubtless a more exact parallel; but it reads like a comparison merely between the natures of two things, and hardly directs the mind to what made them as they are. The second is the comparison which strikes us powerfully and seems like an illumination of the subject; and this is because it seems to convey a clear sense of why there is a resemblance between Church and tree, of what there is in how the world is arranged that makes the comparison apt. The true Church can grow, can put forth blossoms, can suffer mutilation and heal itself just as a tree does, because the same Creator fashioned both on the same principles. The analogy is not chance; it is there because the world is a system. And the comparison (Newman is quite conscious of what he is doing here and speaks explicitly of a 'metaphor') serves a double purpose. So far as we are convinced already that the world is a great unified system, it offers good evidence, drawn from a related field, for what Newman says of the Church; and so far as the comparison seems apt, it offers confirmation of that general hypothesis about the world which explains its aptness.

Newman's two favourite analogies in this connection are that the true Church is like the world of Nature,[3] and that it is like the human body.[4] Both of these have the double effect that was described in the last paragraph: if we accept Newman's general outlook, the analogies encourage us to accept what he says of the Church, and if we accept the analogies, they encourage us to see his general outlook behind them. But all these analogies are useful to Newman in yet another way, a way which is concerned not with what causes resemblances, but only with the resemblances themselves, and which is of no help in making his general beliefs carry conviction, but can help him to win acceptance for more detailed points. There may well

[1] DA. i. 237.   [2] DA. i. 148, 163-4.
[3] DA. i. 148, 163 ; DCD. 90, 171-3.   [4] DA. i. 149, 164 ; DCD. 52, 442.

be a resemblance between two objects, and yet no one be quite sure what are its exact limits; and it is very easy for a writer to use either an analogy or a metaphor (in Coleridge's sense of those words) to suggest that a resemblance is fuller — not perhaps than it is, but at least than he wishes for the moment to prove it is. Consequently a metaphor can covertly state, in a non-controversial way, much that is highly controversial. It is easy to see this tendency at work in Newman's comparison between the Christian Church and the lopped tree. That a limb should be lopped off a tree is something futile, disfiguring, sad; the limb must die, the tree is mutilated for good — though it would be restored, perhaps, if the limb were grafted on again. And as Newman employs the metaphor we need not wonder whether the tree can grieve for its loss, for each time he uses the double sense of the word 'limb' to move on to another comparison, likening the Church to a man whose body is mutilated. Elsewhere, Newman suggests that the Church in growing is like a flower, or animal, or butterfly, or child. These comparisons suggest more than a capacity for doctrinal development; they bring with them the idea of a growth that is predetermined, continuous, natural, beautiful, and from a lower to a higher beauty and perfection.

This second technique, whereby a resemblance seems fuller than it is proved to be, can often be traced when the resemblance is supposed to arise from the operation of a single principle. But essentially, it is quite independent of this, and can take effect even if the reader clearly recognizes that the two things being compared resemble each other by chance. Thus Newman says that the Anglo-Catholics remain in the Anglican Church 'as the shrivelled blossom about the formed fruit'.[1] It would be extravagant, and probably also impossible, to argue that any single principle underlies this comparison. But it does not, on the other hand, convey simply that, although Anglo-Catholics persist as a historical curiosity, they are no longer an integral part of the Anglican Church. It hints

[1] DA. i. 17.

too that they were once fine and splendid and are now ugly,
once full of promise, now pathetic and doomed to be cast
off. Sometimes the comparison is a particularly pregnant
one, because it is a fusion of several comparisons. This is
true of the statement that Anglo-Catholic doctrine is alien
to the Established Church, a foreign substance, 'like oil
upon the water'.[1] Clearly Newman does not suggest here
that the same principle underlies both parts of the comparison; but it is also not a quite innocent or trivial illustration of two substances that refuse to mix. There is also
present the idea of the more precious not losing itself in
the less precious; and probably, too, that of a factitious,
unnatural and impermanent calm. The unidiomatic 'upon
the water' also seems to have a point, for it seems to contain
a hint of Christ himself walking upon the water. Again,
in a passage referred to already, Newman says that one
vessel only can ride the 'giant ocean' of worldliness; 'it
is the boat of Peter, the ark of God'. Here are interwoven
three Biblical strands, so that the Roman Church is made
to seem like the real boat of the Apostles on the sea of
Galilee, the real ark that survived the flood, and the Ark of
the Covenant that was the permanent symbol of Divine favour.

The most elaborate example of fused metaphor in
Newman is one for which conglomerated metaphor might
be a better name; but it illustrates very clearly how metaphors can be used to make controversial statements in a
non-controversial way:

The preachers of these new ideas from Germany and
America are really . . . like Caiaphas, prophesying for us.
Surely they will find no resting-place anywhere for their
feet, and the feet of their disciples, but will be tumbled down
from one depth of blasphemy to another, until they arrive at
sheer and naked atheism, the *reductio ad absurdum* of their
principles. Logic is a stern master; they feel it, they protest
against it; they profess to hate it, and would fain dispense
with it; but it is the law of their intellectual nature. Struggling and shrieking, but in vain, will they make the inevitable
descent into that pit from which there is no return, except

[1] DA. i. 31.

through the almost miraculous grace of God, the grant of which in this life is never hopeless. And Israel, without a fight, will see their enemies dead upon the sea-shore.[1]

Here, all at once, Liberal theologians are likened to fallen angels, *tumbled down* from heaven into the depths, to lost souls, *struggling and shrieking* as they slip towards the *sheer and naked* sides of the bottomless pit of damnation (there is almost a pun on 'sheer'), and lastly to Egyptians, who set the chosen people in durance, and were their inveterate persecutors.[2]

In at least one place in Newman's work there can be traced a third effect of using figurative language. It is an effect that concerns the whole quality of a discussion rather than any point of detail within the discussion, and it arises from the fact that if comparisons are made sufficiently often with things that have a distinctive quality, then this quality tends to become suffused throughout a whole book or chapter. George Eliot achieved something like this in using metaphors that sustained the general atmosphere of a novel,[3] and there is also a resemblance with how Carlyle maintained a sense of his principle that the world was wider than it seemed, simply by a phrase here and there about the sky and the green earth; or indeed a sense of life and energy by his menagerie of animals.[4] There seems to be only one clear instance in Newman, the fourth discourse of *The Scope and Nature of University Education*. Here Newman argues that liberal culture is, if not all-sufficient, at least a real and positive good in itself. He needs to convince those who think a liberal culture frivolous or even dangerous (many of those present at the original lecture might have thought this) and also those who see no use in an education that is not useful (and a good many might have thought this too). He could be neither too austere and devout, nor too materialistic. He had to

---

[1] DA. i. 27-8.

[2] Exodus xiv. 30. Another example occurs in a passage quoted on p. 178, when the phrase 'each on his high tower' — strictly, of course, not altogether accurate — does much to suggest that each Protestant cleric is isolated, and perhaps also bigoted.

[3] See p. 151 above.   [4] See pp. 29 and 32 above.

make his audience view the subject, if only to some slight degree, in a genial light; and to this end every least touch of colour or liveliness in his discussion would make its contribution, however small.

This being so, it is difficult to believe that the constant allusions in this discourse to colours, flowers, music, things that happen in the open air, do not serve a wider purpose than that which they serve in their localized context. The first metaphor in the chapter, almost before a page has passed, is that knowledge may vary as 'red and green and white change their shades' [1] when colours are combined. Then Newman goes on to say that a university can create 'a pure and clear atmosphere of thought', where knowledge has 'its lights and its shades'.[2] He finds occasion to mention things like the palaestra, the Olympic games, horse-riding, cricket, even a fox-chase; [3] and almost immediately after says that useful knowledge loses its delicacy like 'the labourer's hand'; [4] later he suggests that the exaggerations of liberal knowledge are 'like some melodious air, or rather like those strong and transporting perfumes, which at first spread their sweetness over everything they touch'.[5] Bacon's materialist outlook, though fallacious, brings almost every day 'fresh and fresh shoots, and buds, and blossoms, which are to ripen into fruit, on that magical tree of Knowledge'.[6] Then he compares Fouqué's tale of the 'old mediciner' who 'went out singing into the meadows so gaily, that those who had seen him from afar might well have thought it was a youth gathering flowers for his beloved, instead of an old physician gathering healing herbs in the morning dew'; [7] and admits that, whatever its defects, Bacon's attitude to knowledge has brought 'the gifts of nature, in their most . . . luxurious profusion and diversity, from all quarters of the earth'.[8] Finally, he speaks of the beauty of liberal knowledge: 'Why do you take such pains with your garden or your park? You see to your walks and turf and shrubberies; to your trees and drives; not as if you meant to make an orchard of the one,

1 UE. 91.   2 UE. 92.   3 UE. 98-9.   4 UE. 100.
5 UE. 107.   6 UE. 109.   7 UE. 110.   8 UE. 111.

or corn or pasture land of the other, but because there is a special beauty in all that is goodly in wood, water, plain and slope, brought all together by art into one shape, and grouped into one whole. Your cities are beautiful, your palaces, your public buildings, your territorial mansions, your churches; and their beauty leads to nothing beyond itself.' [1] So should it be with knowledge, even though 'man, in all his functions, is but a flower which blossoms and fades'.[2]

Here, then, perhaps a dozen times in twice as many pages, light, fresh colour, visions of the life of the open air, somehow tinge the texture of the discourse. Its whole character is made fresher and more genial by these touches; they provide a context for liberal knowledge, and it is treated of within the range of their influence, it catches their reflection. They modify the reader's or the listener's consciousness rather as if he read or listened actually in the open, with the clear air and light, and the gifts of Nature in their luxurious profusion. Yet in well over half the instances Newman is not paralleling these vivid details with liberal knowledge, but with various things that contrast with it. He has not even the wish to liken it to changing red and green and white, or a blossoming tree, or a strong and transporting perfume, or a walk in the morning dew; and had he done these things outright, his account would have seemed like a caricature. But his subject takes a colouring from these details as they operate indirectly.

(vii) *Suggestive Example*

All Newman's uses of figurative language accord with his theory of how Real Assent should be created, because all of them provide the mind with vivid particulars instead of abstractions. Illustrating general or abstract statements by examples is of course a more obvious way of achieving the same result; and once again Newman refines the method until it is not simply a means of illustrating, but another method of making the controversial seem non-controversial.

[1] UE. 113.   [2] UE. 114.

When, for example, he argues that real certainty never changes, he naturally has to explain how what looks like certainty does change sometimes, as for example when a devout believer in one creed is converted to another. His answer is that many articles of faith are common to different creeds. If a man were certain only of those articles in his old faith present also in the new, he could easily shed the others that he has merely taken for granted, and conversion could simply mean adding to his stock of certainties. And then Newman gives as his example how a man might move from heathenism 'through Mahometanism, Judaism, Unitarianism, Protestantism, and Anglicanism', right through to Rome. There is nothing unfair in this example, but it reminds us that the ingenious theory makes possible just the kind of conversion which Newman has at heart.[1] Again, when he asserts that formal contradiction between two propositions need not throw our minds into doubt, he gives as examples the Biblical account of Adam, and the findings of geology.[2] He is scrupulous in saying only that if he believed the Biblical account to be of divine origin, he would then not abandon belief in it; but as we read, that 'if' has some of the force of a 'since' without needing the defence that 'since' would need.

The *Essay on Development* is full of examples like this. To illustrate the principle, universally accepted, that in the long run ideas and institutions change together, Newman refers to a universal belief 'that, in one or other direction, there will come a change in Ireland, with a population of one creed and a Church of another'.[3] We do not forget what church it is that has thus somehow been dispossessed. To illustrate how in these changes, 'often the practical process is detached from the intellectual, and anterior to it' (which in itself, he suggests, is perfectly innocuous), he quotes Hooker, justifying and explaining the Elizabethan settlement when it was all over and done with.[4] For the principle that in some developments 'the intellectual character is so prominent that they may even be called *logical*',[5] he instances 'the Anglican doctrine of the Royal

[1] GA. 251.   [2] GA. 256-7.   [3] DCD. 43.   [4] DCD. 44.   [5] DCD. 45.

Supremacy, which has been created in the courts of law';
and at once he finds himself free, in passing, to mention
the Bishops dominated by politicians, and the Prayer
Book, exalting the King above God or the Church and
making sedition a graver crime than heresy. He continues
in the same way : 'principles are popularly said to develop
when they are but exemplified',[1] the example is Protestantism with its fragmentary sects ; 'a development . . . must
retain both the doctrine and the principle with which it
started', or else be 'barren, if not lifeless, of which the
Greek church seems an instance'. Then comes 'if one of
two contrary alternatives be necessarily true on a certain
hypothesis, then the denial of the one leads, by mere
logical consistency, and without direct reasons, to a reception of the other'. Of this abstraction he gives two
examples : 'Thus the question between the Church of
Rome and Protestantism falls in some minds into the
proposition "Rome is either the pillar and ground of the
Truth or she is Antichrist"' ; in proportion, then, as they
revolt from considering her the latter they are compelled
to receive her as the former. Hence men may pass 'from
infidelity to Rome, and from Rome to infidelity, from a
conviction in both cases that there is no tangible intellectual
position between the two'.[2] The principle of a development, he continues, may be only some minor point of
discipline. With Wesley it was 'preaching early in the
morning. This was his principle. In Georgia, he began
preaching at five o'clock every day, winter and summer.
"Early preaching", he said, "is the Glory of the Method-
ists ; whenever this is dropt, they will dwindle away into
nothing."' Then, after all this, the end of the chapter
remarks only, 'these instances show, as has been incidentally observed of some of them, that the destruction of
the special laws or principles of a development is its
corruption'.

[1] Examples in the remainder of this paragraph are taken more or less
continuously from DCD. 180-84.
[2] Cf. DCD. 180, where the choice is between Rome and 'what, for
want of a better word, may be called Germanism'.

It may be thought that these, though clearly tendentious, are trivial. But they are not trivial, because they sustain a continuous sense in the reader of Newman's outlook and opinions; and they subtly reinforce these opinions even while the discussion seems detached and abstract. Newman never quite forgets the issues that he really cares about, and never lets his reader quite forget either.

Examples, however, can sometimes be used in just the opposite way: they seem conspicuously innocent, leading the attention entirely away from controversial issues, and creating a sense that the general truth they illustrate is entirely familiar. But then they do not come alone. When they have made a principle seem innocuous, the controversial issues, those that Newman has really at heart, take their place. Newman first illustrates how Notional Assent can turn into Real, by taking examples from boys at school, reform of the army, the slave trade, or understanding the classics: only at this point does he refer to the gradually richening comprehension of Scripture that is important for his main contention.

The example of Adam and geology was prepared for by another example, innocent and tendentious all in one, of what we should believe if told that a man whom we saw die was alive and at work. Later, as an example of inference too subtle and complex to be reduced to formulae, he cites predicting a European war, and then, saying, 'I take this example at random; now let me follow it up by more serious cases', turns to belief in God, in miracles, in immortality. Apparently innocent examples are as useful to Newman as those that are clearly tendentious, for they make the principle they illustrate seem clearly and straightforwardly true, and then afterwards, Newman can relate it to the issues that, to him, really matter.

(viii) *Control of Meaning in Newman*

Verbal or partly verbal argument plays a very significant part in Newman's work; among the writers studied here

it is more important only in Carlyle.   There seem to be
four chief varieties of it :

(1) Arguing that the sense of a word is really wider
    than, or different from, what it is usually thought
    to be ; and therefore that it may properly be used
    of something that at first it seemed not to apply to.
(2) Almost the opposite of this, namely tracing the
    narrower or stricter meaning of a word ; and
    thereby discovering the real nature or central
    quality of something for which everyone has agreed
    to use it.
(3) A development of the last : refuting the arguments
    of one's opponents by showing that they have
    ignored the strict or real meaning of the words
    they use.
(4) Gradually drawing out the full meaning of a word
    that means a great deal, so as to show how much is
    conceded in agreeing to use it of something —
    almost the opposite of (2).

The first of these is the usual form of verbal argument
in Carlyle, but it is much less important in Newman.
There is no difficulty in seeing why it is useful.   Writers
naturally want to show that a word aptly describes an
unexpected case when the word is a term of praise (or can
be made a term of praise) and they want to give praise.
Thus Newman argues that liberal knowledge, useless in
the popular sense of that word, is really useful after all ;
for 'what has its *end* in itself, has its *use* in itself also'.[1]
This is much more simple and elegant and in harmony
with the whole quality of his work than to admit that liberal
knowledge is useless, then to explain the meaning of
'useless' which makes this admission necessary, and finally
to show that if this is its meaning not every useless thing,
and in particular not liberal knowledge, is worthless.   Elsewhere he argues that Anglo-Catholics ought not to obey
the Anglican church, but convert it to Rome ; yet this is
their real duty to the Anglican church, not a denial of

[1] UE. 155.

duty.[1] The logic of language, as we saw early in this chapter, must be supplemented by the 'more subtle and elastic' logic of thought.[2] 'Logic' is a term of praise, and qualifying it in this way enables Newman to retain its advantages and avoid its inconveniences.

One rather complex instance of explicitly finding a special sense for a word is interesting not only for its own sake, but also because it shows Newman saying very much the same thing as Carlyle. 'It is possible', he writes, 'to give an interpretation to the course of things, by which every event or occurrence in its order becomes providential.'[3] We can, it is true, give the course of things this interpretation only if we regard it from a distinctive viewpoint — though it is one natural and proper to mankind. This viewpoint offers us 'the unsophisticated apprehension of the many'; and what, Newman feels, can lead us to this apprehension and show us its truth is a distinctive sense for the word 'miraculous'. With this sense in men's minds, they can see that 'the successive passages of life . . . are so many miracles, *if that is to be accounted miraculous which brings before them the immediate Divine Presence*'. What Newman has done is first to suggest that there is some sense in which a paradoxical statement is true, and then to suggest that a certain quite distinctive sense is the sense in question; and the word 'apprehension' is enough by itself to show how here he is writing like a typical sage, trying to make us see where before we were blind. This apprehension has led us to a truth, and it was meant to do so, he adds, that is its part in the scheme of things; if it is illogical, 'so much the worse for logic'. In this sequence the effect of controlling what one's words mean is very clear. A distinctive sense for 'miraculous' can prompt us to see 'the course of things' in a new way; an adjustment in vocabulary opens our eyes and, unexpectedly enough, leads to a kind of increment in knowledge.

[1] DA. i. 57-8.   [2] GA. 359.
[3] GA. 401-3 (my italics). Cf. DCD. 112. 'If it is reasonable to consider medicine, or architecture, or engineering, in a certain sense, divine arts, as being divinely ordained means of our receiving divine benefits, much more may ethics be termed divine.'

But what Newman does most often is not to change the sense of a word in this way, and give it a new sense, but to restrict its sense within definite limits. Thus 'A University . . . by its very name, professes to teach universal knowledge . . . the very name is inconsistent with restrictions of any kind' in the range of teaching.[1] 'What is really meant by the word ?' he asks in beginning the discussion of liberal pursuits.[2] 'Knowledge . . . as it tends more and more to be particular, ceases to be Knowledge . . . when I speak of Knowledge I mean something intellectual . . . it is of the nature of science from the first, *and in this consists its dignity.*'[3] It is this kind of knowledge, and no other, that Education means. 'All I say is, call things by their right names, and do not confuse together ideas which are essentially different. . . . Do not say, the people must be educated, when, after all, you only mean amused, refreshed . . . or kept from vicious excesses. I do not say that such . . . are not a great gain; but they are not education . . . education is a high word.'[4] Another example is 'you do not bear in mind that a movement is a thing that moves; you cannot be true to it and remain still'.[5] That something is aptly described by the word 'movement' is enough to establish its essential character, the guiding principle of its existence. These arguments are easy to recognize, because they seem to invite one to add 'strictly speaking' or 'in essence', or 'true' or 'real' to the vital word in them; whereas arguments of the previous kind seemed to invite one to add 'in a sense'.

Insistence on the strict sense of words is one of Newman's chief weapons of attack; he constantly maintains that his opponents are using words loosely and wrongly. In these arguments the vital word, as they misuse it, seems to invite the damning 'so-called' as an addition to it; and Newman's attack culminates either in satirizing how his opponents travesty the word's meaning, or in contempt-

[1] UE. 11.   [2] UE. 97.
[3] UE. 104 (my italics; they show clearly how restricting the sense is what makes the word a term of praise).
[4] UE. 136-7.   [5] DA. i. 114.

uously offering them an alternative word which has quite
opposite associations, and asks to be qualified by 'mere'.
For example he argues that there are no religious developments 'of prominence and permanence sufficient to deserve
the name', except 'those which have possession of Christendom' (*i.e.* are Roman); it is false that Greek orthodoxy
deserves the name, for '. . . I am not aware that the Greeks
present more than a negative opposition to the Latins'.[1]
Elsewhere the argument is generalized : 'we must be aware
of the great error of making changes on no more definite
basis than their abstract fitness, alleged scripturalness, or
adoption by the ancients'.[2] These are not true developments at all : 'such changes are rightly called innovations'.
'Pagans may have, heretics cannot have, the same principles as Catholics ; if the latter have the same, they are
not real heretics, but in ignorance.'[3] The Church of
England, he says, 'has no love for its members, or what are
sometimes called its children, nor any instinct whatever,
unless attachment to its master, or love of its place, may be
so called'.[4] This is a double instance :. there are no real
children, only mere members, and no real instincts, only
mere attachment to place and master.

Sometimes the arguments are more elaborate. In
discussing certitude, Newman claims — this has already
been mentioned — that no one who is genuinely certain
ever changes his opinion : [5] mutable convictions, however
confident, are 'imaginations' or 'false certitude'.[6] Certitude and false certitude, he concedes, are not immediately
distinguishable ; but 'indefectibility' is at least a negative
test of the former, 'so that whoever loses his conviction on
a given point is thereby proved not to have been certain
of it'.[7] It is the 'very office', the 'very lot'[8] of certitude to
resist everything which threatens to dislodge it. There
may indeed be an assent which is both indefectible and
erroneous, and Newman has a name ready for it ; but that
name is 'prejudice'.[9]

---

[1] DCD. 95.   [2] DA. i. 119.   [3] DCD. 181.
[4] DA. i. 6-7.   [5] GA. 221 ff.   [6] GA. 255.
[7] GA. 255.   [8] GA. 256.   [9] GA. 258.

This is especially interesting because here, in asserting
that no mutable conviction can possibly be certitude, Newman reveals and indeed emphasizes how his statements
are actually made true by being made to approximate to
truisms. The view he rejects is proved to be false by
being shown to be the logical contrary of one which follows
from definitions. 'Prominence and permanence' amount-
ing to the possession of Christendom becomes part of the
meaning of 'true development'; a heretic is defined as
one whose principles are anti-Catholic. This tendency
towards truism shows again when Newman argues that
there are no quarrels of faith within the Catholic Church : [1]
it follows by definition that if the quarrel is one of faith,
one party to it stands outside the Church. But although
these statements of Newman's are not really statements of
fact, they are not mere verbal sleight-of-hand either. They
really do draw our attention to certain facts and make
these more vividly present than plain statement of them
could do. Thus it remains true that a certain mental
state — unshakable conviction — can sometimes have
truth as its object, or that there have really been developments which possess Christendom, or that when every
split through disagreement on matters of faith is allowed
for there still remains a great united body called the
Roman Church. A glance at Newman's assertion may have
made us think that he was telling us other facts ; but these
are facts all the same, and surely very important ones too.

In the next variety of verbal argument, the reader is
first brought to accept some quite innocent-seeming statement, and then, bit by bit, Newman unfolds all that has
been conceded by accepting, without a fight, one of the
words in it. This may occur in a single phrase, and then
at first sight it looks rather like the second variety. But
really it is quite different. Essentially it is a going-further,
not a narrowing-down, and the words that such an argument invites one to add are not 'strictly speaking' at all,
but 'indeed' or 'more than this'. Two clear examples of
this kind of argument, compressed into one sentence, are

[1] DA. i. 272.

'Christ set up a visible society, *or rather Kingdom*, for . . . His religion;'[1] and 'it is the law, *or the permission*, given to our whole race'.[2] Newman here is bringing out the full meaning of a word as he uses it; but bringing out that full meaning stage by stage may help us to grasp all that it comprises — and once again the sage can be seen opening his reader's eyes to something not easy to see unaided. Often the argument is more extended: it spreads out through a whole range of ideas. Thus Newman speaks at first, quite simply, of the system of Knowledge and its 'different aspects';[3] these, however, become not merely aspects, but 'partial views or abstractions'. Next, these 'views' prove to be none other than the 'particular sciences'. They are useful, but 'they never tell us all that can be said'; they stand to complete knowledge only as a craftsman's knowledge stands in its turn to scientific knowledge. The scientist is like 'the maker of a bridle or an epaulet'. These sciences 'converge upon the whole of knowledge' and 'contribute' to it; they each 'need external assistance . . . by reason of their incompleteness'. At first, they merely 'afford' this assistance to each other; though each, now, gives only a 'defective apprehension'. But affording this assistance, it appears in the sequel, means nothing less than that one science is 'applied, corrected and adapted' by another. Then comes yet another step. There is one science whose special function is to comprehend the mutual relations of others, and to adjust and duly appreciate them all one with another; 'which is my own conception of what is meant by Philosophy, *in the true sense of the word*'.[4] How much we find we conceded, in conceding simply that knowledge is composed of parts which make up a whole !

Consider another example.[5] The only argument for Anglicanism, Newman claims, is that it is a *via media*. How much do we admit in admitting that this is the ground of its claim ? The *via media* 'appeals to the good sense of mankind'. So far so good. 'It is very moderate

---

[1] LDN (DA. ii. 207; my italics).   [2] GA. 405 (my italics).   [3] UE. 36-42.
    [4] UE. 42 (my italics).   [5] DA. i. 327-42.

and liberal; it can tolerate either extreme with great patience . . . it is comprehensive'; and 'dispassionateness, forbearance, indulgence, toleration and comprehension' are all its attributes. The account still seems harmless enough. But in essence it is 'Protestant'; it is tied to 'the mutilated canon, the defective Rule of Faith'; its only aim is to moderate the extremes of Luther, so as to keep them out of harm's way, to 'keep them from shocking the feelings of human nature'; it is now not merely tolerant but 'cautious', and 'having an eye to the necessities of controversy'. There was another *via media*, the heresy of Eusebius, a form of Arianism arranged so as '. . . to evade enquiry . . .'; and Eusebius 'sided with those who blasphemed . . . sanctioned and shared their deeds of violence'; Constantius, who 'embraced the *via media* of Eusebianism . . . on conviction as well as from expediency', 'tortured and put to death the adherents to the Nicene Creed'. The seventeenth-century English divines in their turn spoke out in favour of these Eastern sectaries, Jeremy Taylor calling Eusebius 'the wisest of them all'. The school of Laud ultimately gave rise to the Latitudinarians. In short, then, we may say of the *via media*, 'its tendency in theory is towards Latitudinarianism; its position historically is one of heresy'; and in the Anglican church both have appeared. So much for rashly admitting that one is prepared to stand or fall by the *via media*.

Perhaps the most interesting examples of this technique are those where Newman practises it on several expressions at once, and thus claims to reveal the true and full nature of a choice. He argues in *The Difficulties of Anglicans*, for example, that Anglo-Catholics will be inconsistent if they retain their doctrinal principles and remain in the Anglican Church; though of course, there would be no inconsistency if they gave up the principles on seeing where they led. Here, apparently, is a plain choice; it proves by no means plain in the sequel.[1] Those who give up 'think that the movement has come to an end . . . it was a mere phantom, or deceit . . . which has taken you in' — 'I have

[1] DA. i. 108-11.

not a word to say'. As for accepting the inconsistency, it is to perpetuate what is now revealed as having been, all the time, an 'imposture'. The third course is to leave the Establishment; and this is to be guided by Divine grace, to be 'under a destiny'. But this sharpening of the contrast is not at an end. The inconsistency is 'preposterous'; [1] 'it is pride, or vanity, or self-reliance, or fulness of bread'; [2] as for renouncing the principle, it is the act of those who 'took up some fancy-religion, retailed the Fathers, and jobbed theology'; [3] but those who leave the Establishment, though at first the scorn and wonder of the world, will begin life anew and find glory and peace.[4]

Earlier in this book there is another interesting example.[5] Newman quotes an opponent's assertion that the Anglican Church, although it does not actively condemn heterodoxy, is not suffering from 'a decay of Christian life'. No doubt, Newman replies; no doubt it has life, but of what sort? Is it the so-called 'life' of religion in England or in Prussia — or is it Catholic life? 'If then "life" means strength, activity, energy, and well-being of any kind whatever, in that case doubtless the national religion is alive. It is a great power in the midst of us . . . it conducts a hundred undertakings . . . it opposes the Catholic church . . . bribes the world against her . . . apes her authority . . . in all parts of the world it is the religion of gentlemen . . . of men of substance, and men of no personal faith at all. If this be life, — if it be life to impart a tone to the court and houses of parliament . . . to be a principle of order . . . and an organ of benevolence . . . to make men decent, respectable, and sensible . . . to shed a gloss over avarice and ambition, — if indeed it is the life of religion to be the first jewel in the Queen's crown, and the highest step of her throne, then doubtless the National Church is replete, it overflows with life; but . . . Life of what kind?' [6] Catholic life, on the

---

[1] DA. i. 141.   [2] DA. i. 143.   [3] DA. i. 134.
[4] DA. i. 111.   [5] DA. i. 38 ff.
[6] Perhaps, if these statements about what 'life' means when the word is used ironically were translated into the direct statements about the Anglican Church that they suggest, the result would be more controversial than usual.

other hand, is 'supernatural'; it proceeds from the principles of Apostles and Martyrs. This is the true, the full
contrast before us.[1]

That all these arguments are 'about words' does not
make them either deceptive on the one hand, or trivial on
the other. The discussion has already shown how, as it
were behind them, there are usually (perhaps always in
Newman's case) plain statements about facts, even if only
statements that certain things like unshakable faith or a
large and united Roman Church really do exist. But these
plain statements, even if we find them surprising or thought-
provoking when we reflect on them, can easily seem dull
or trite at first glance. Something has to be done to awaken
a sense of all that they really mean, to put them in the most
striking way possible. Verbal arguments do this. The
last example shows particularly well how verbal arguments
can redirect our attention to a large and complex variety of
particular facts, and make us tend to see a new significance
in them. But these arguments do something else too. The
likelihood is that these plain factual statements would seem
controversial; or if not, that their relevance, their importance, would seem controversial. This the verbal argument,
with its air of detached enquiry, tends to conceal; and the
effect, as always, is that the reader tends, one item at a
time, to adopt the writer's viewpoint, and thereby takes
one step more towards entering into his outlook as a whole,
towards seeing that complete picture of converging lines
of thought which alone is to lead to Real Assent — to
conversion, in short. Moreover, verbal argument, seeming
as it does to replace controversial argument by non-controversial explanations about meanings, is invaluable to
Newman in sustaining both the conciliatory and the
imperturbable tones of his work. Finally, it lends support
to the idea that, at least for an enquirer in a natural con-

But Newman seems to have provided for this. Instead of saying simply
'"life" as used here means . . .', his argument is in the indirect form,
'*if* "life" as used here means . . . , then there is no doubt that one is
entitled to use it here'.

[1] Compare with this Carlyle's assertion, 'We have sumptuous garnitures
for our Life, but have forgotten how to *live*', referred to on p. 50.

dition of mind, truth is simple; [1] since, if we really understand what we are saying (and no one is ready to confess
that he does not), we already have within ourselves the
answers we seek.

Very briefly, Newman's work deserves now to be reviewed as a whole. He had a comprehensive doctrine
about the world, man's place in it, and how he ought to
live. This took the religious form of Roman Catholic
Christianity, and its metaphysical form was that the whole
universe was one integrated system. In making us accept
that view of life, particular doctrines and distinctive
methods of presentation or argument stand, as we have
seen, essentially related; each encourages the reader to
accept the other. As for the methods themselves, the
central point of this whole enquiry is that they do not
merely state Newman's outlook, but they display it. They
fuse together to be a picture with the qualities that he
wants us to see in the world. All the time, a variety of
techniques — metaphor and analogy, discussions of meaning, carefully chosen examples — steadily tend to make
the controversial non-controversial, so that we are not
coerced by any 'smart syllogism' into accepting Newman's
conclusions in the abstract, but brought imperceptibly to
a living understanding of his creed. The continuous
texture of his work modifies our receptivity until we find
ourselves seeing the world as he sees it. To this end all
the parts of his work act in conjunction. Tone, forms of
argument, illustration and example, imagery and manipulating senses integrate to make something which has a single
unified impact on the reader; and the impact is not that of
a formal argument, but in its fullness and vividness more resembles that of a work of art, something which can make the
reader find more in his experience, see it with new eyes,
because for a while it constitutes his whole experience.

[1] Cf. GA. 490: 'Christianity is addressed . . . to minds which are in the
normal condition of human nature'. For a good example of Newman's
insistence that truth is fundamentally simple, see UE. 113 : 'Surely we are
not driven to theories of this kind . . . surely the real grounds . . . are not so
very subtle or abstruse, so very strange or improbable. *Everything has its
own perfection, be it higher or lower in the scale of things'* (my italics).

CHAPTER VII

MATTHEW ARNOLD

(i) *Arnold's Doctrine and Temper*

'ONE at last has a chance of *getting at* the English public. Such a public as it is, and such a work as one wants to do with it! . . . Partly nature, partly time and study have also by this time taught me thoroughly the precious truth that everything turns upon one's exercising the power of *persuasion*, of charm; that without this all fury, energy, reasoning power, acquirement are thrown away.'[1] These few words lay bare the very core of Arnold's 'criticism of life', because there was one thing that he never allowed himself to forget. This was that to be successful, the moralist must do what success requires, and that success in this field requires, above all things, patience and self-control. 'Where shall we find language innocent enough, how shall we make the spotless purity of our intentions evident enough, to enable us to say . . . that the British Constitution itself' is 'a colossal machine for the manufacture of Philistines? . . . how is Mr. Carlyle to say it and not be misunderstood, after his furious raid into this field with his *Latter-Day Pamphlets*?'[2] By the fullness and care and circumspection with which he moulds and adjusts his work to the persuasive task, Arnold sets an entirely new standard — goes further here even than Newman. Yet his work does not tempt us to acquiesce in his outlook ignorant of what we are doing;

---

[1] Letter to Arnold's mother, 29th October 1863 (*Works*, xiii. 266). References in this Chapter are given to the volume and page of Arnold's collected works; and when one book or essay is quoted from several times in succession, its title is indicated only in the first of the corresponding footnotes.

[2] *The Function of Criticism*: EC. i. (iii. 28-9).

it is persuasive through being a memorable specimen of what that outlook produces, a specimen powerful in illuminating his position and helping his readers to see its attraction and strength. It is what distinguishes art in literature that Arnold directs to the necessities of persuasion : he aims to transform the reader's outlook, and he makes a call upon every part of his nature.

Arnold's polemics were less irresponsible than those of Carlyle, because his effort to persuade was much more sustained and planned ; and his task was a more elusive one than Newman's, because he had no rigid doctrines to argue for, only attitudes. His work inculcates not a set of ultimate beliefs — a 'Life-Philosophy' — but simply certain habits and a certain temper of mind. He limits his ambitions ; he advocates not so much any definite view, as the mental prerequisites of forming views. 'The old recipe, to think a little more and bustle a little less' ; [1] '. . . between all these there is indeed much necessity for methods of insight and moderation' ; [2] 'the free spontaneous play of consciousness with which culture tries to float our stock habits of thinking and acting . . . to *float* them, to prevent their being stiff and stark pieces of petrifaction any longer . . . our main business at the present moment is not so much to work away at certain crude reforms . . . as to create . . . a frame of mind out of which the schemes of really fruitful reforms may with time grow'. [3] It is the frame of mind that is crucial ; to what conclusions it will lead, once adopted, is for Arnold a secondary matter. Much of his work is negative : he wants to deprecate what is crude and exaggerated, to leave questions open where they have been precipitately closed. He seldom rejects an opposing view outright ; all he does is to regret its undue haste or narrowness, or see in it an excess of something by no means intrinsically bad. 'There is a catchword which, I know, will be used against me . . . cries and catchwords . . . are very apt to receive an application,

[1] *My Countrymen* (vi. 388).
[2] Letter to Arnold's mother, 9th November 1870 (xiv. 241).
[3] CA. (vi. 212-13).

or to be used with an absoluteness, which does not belong to them . . . and . . . narrow our spirit and . . . hurt our practice.' [1] In this sentence Arnold condemns his opponents' frame of mind, and suggests a better, all in one.

If he ever advances a more positive doctrine, it is usually of a kind by now familiar : the vital but essentially simple truths that seem to be the sage's peculiar province. What he says of his defence of a classical education is, 'I put this forward on the strength of some facts not at all recondite, very far from it; facts capable of being stated in the simplest possible fashion' — the facts are simply those of 'the constitution of human nature'.[2] Like other moralists, he regards his important function as that merely of bringing familiar knowledge alive. 'The larger the scale on which the violation of reason's law is practised . . . the greater must be the confusion and final trouble. Surely no laudations of free-trade . . . can tell us anything . . . which it more concerns us to know than that ! and not only to know, but to have the knowledge present. . . . But we all know it already ! some one will say, it is the simplest law of prudence. But how little reality must there be in our knowledge.' [3]

Clearly then, Arnold rigorously circumscribes his work. It suggests an approach ; or it is deliberately negative and inconclusive, or where positive its statements are deliberately commonplace and familiar. These restrictions greatly affect that element of Arnold's work which comes nearest to the speculative or metaphysical; for although he disclaims all ability for subtle philosophizing, yet, like Carlyle, like Newman, he too has a philosophy of history, a bedrock *credo*. He too writes of 'the natural current there is in human affairs, and . . . its continual working'; [4] and the fault of his opponents, like theirs, is that 'they cannot see the way the world is going, and the future does not belong to them'.[5] Further than this, he goes on occasionally to make success a test or sign of rightness : 'sure loss and defeat at last . . . ought to govern . . . action',[6] he writes,

---

[1] FE. (xii. 49).   [2] DA. (iv. 330).   [3] CA. (vi. 208-9).
[4] vi. 37.   [5] *My Countrymen* (vi. 376).   [6] ME. (x. 127-8).

or even 'that providential order which forbids the final supremacy of imperfect things'.[1] But this line of thought is not prominent in his work; and moreover, its development is entirely different in Arnold and in, say, Carlyle.

That difference becomes immediately plain if we complete the last quotation but one: 'sure loss and defeat at last, *from coming into conflict with truth and nature*'; or take such a remark as 'this contravention of the natural order has produced, as such contravention always must produce, a certain confusion and false movement, of which we are beginning to feel, in almost every direction, the inconvenience'.[2] The contrast is inescapable. All the apocalyptic quality of Carlyle's historical determinism is gone; the trend of events is governed not by some ever-ready and apocalyptic Hand, but by a gentle Platonic harmony between virtue, reason, and reality. The course of history is not grand, simple and mysterious, but neat and orderly, now one thing and now another, according to time and place. There are epochs of 'expansion' and of 'concentration'.[3] Hellenism, the urgent need in Arnold's own time, would have been in the Dark Ages 'unsound at that particular moment of man's development . . . premature'.[4] Different virtues and different measures require to be insisted on in different countries.[5] France may lack political freedom, England may rely on it to excess; England's chief need is greater amenity, France's greater purity, America's, a more elevated seriousness. Each may benefit by addition even of what is harmful elsewhere. One can now see the place in Arnold's work of how he grossly simplifies in writing of national characteristics. It helps him to modify optimistic determinism, as a philosophy of history, so that it seems reasonable and unmysterious, multiple in its aspects — as indeed every unmysterious thing is — yet simple to grasp, having no surprises for the calm, enlightened, unprejudiced observer.

---

[1] FE. (xii. 76). [2] CA. (vi. 139-40).
[3] See *e.g.* CA. (vi. 59-62) and *The Function of Criticism* (iii. 14-15).
[4] CA. (vi. 130).
[5] See *A Courteous Explanation* (vi. 398) and *Numbers* (iv. 283), *passim*.

Arnold has a doctrine of man which is the counterpart of this doctrine of history. It too contains nothing paradoxical or mysterious or not readily acceptable. Man, like the world itself and its history, is a complex of different elements which are readily brought together into a simple and natural unity. These are the 'facts not at all recondite, very far from it', touched upon above. 'We set ourselves to enumerate the powers which go to the building of human life, and say that they are the power of conduct, the power of intellect and knowledge, the power of beauty, and the power of social life and manners . . . this scheme, though drawn in rough and plain lines enough . . . does yet give a fairly true representation . . . Human nature is built up by these powers; we have the need for them all . . . the several powers . . . are not isolated, but there is . . . a perpetual tendency to relate them one to another in divers ways.' [1] Humanity is a 'composite thing', its elements so 'intertwined' that one can temporarily do duty for another; but ultimately there must be 'mutual understanding and balance', there must be genuine and organic integration, if the 'true and smooth order of humanity's development' is not to be arrested.[2] The 'natural rational life' — the juxtaposition, virtual equivalence of the adjectives, has significance — is one with 'body, intelligence, and soul all taken care of'.[3] These may be commonplaces; but for the present enquiry that is their interest.

This is so, because such a view offers, as it were, a minimum target to the critic; its quality of platitude enables Arnold largely to escape the burden of proof — or rather, to use an apter word, the business of justifying or arguing for a metaphysics, which constrains the other authors we have examined to a style of rhetoric, eloquence, exaltation or mystery. And such a style would inevitably have clashed with Arnold's central concern — to advocate a gentle critical reasonableness of mind. With such essentially simple and commonplace premisses, he could avoid a kind of writing which it would certainly have been hard

[1] DA. (iv. 331).   [2] CA. (vi. 143-4).
[3] *My Countrymen* (vi. 374).

to unite with the temper of mind he admired. Thus in Arnold there are little or no rhetorical fireworks. Metaphor and imagery are (except very occasionally for certain quite new uses) absent to a degree nothing short of extraordinary by comparison with Newman or Carlyle or George Eliot; and although definitions of words, in a sense at least, are not uncommon, they occur for purposes much more restricted than elsewhere, and are such that the element of prestidigitation — which would have been the alien element — is almost entirely lacking from them. Yet at the same time, Arnold's premisses are important for their substance : they offer a real justification for his method of compromise — that is, of seeing more than one side to any problem, and stressing or adding just what the given case requires, even though intrinsically this may be subordinate. But they do not dictate anything in the details of his approach. Others could start with the same premisses and probably reach any detailed conclusions they liked. What significance they had for Arnold is determined in the whole texture of his writing. If he offers anything of wisdom or sanity or mental poise, it is to be found in the whole experience of reading him, in a sense of what intellectual urbanity is that transpires rather from his handling of problems than from his answers to them. He mediates not a view of the world, but a habit of mind. Let us see how this is done.

To a degree quite unusual among polemical writers, Arnold's persuasive energy goes to build up, little by little, an intimate and a favourable impression of his own personality as an author, and an unfavourable impression, equally clear if less intimate and more generalized, of the personalities of his opponents. Over and over again one finds the discussion taking shape between these two poles ; and this is natural, because Arnold's chief purpose is to recommend one temper of mind, and condemn another, and such things are more readily sensed through contact than understood through description. No author, of course, can give a favourable impression of his own temper of mind, except obliquely and discreetly. When Arnold writes of himself at length, it is usually in a depreciatory vein ; but he causes us to glimpse his personality through various devices, and of these, as with Newman, perhaps the most conspicuous is tone. Indeed he adopts a tone not unlike Newman's, save that it is usually less grave and calm, more whimsical and apologetic. Newman, after all, thought he had a powerful silent ally as Arnold did not.

Thus in the first few lines of the Preface to *Essays in Criticism*, Series I, we find 'indeed, it is not in my nature — some of my critics would rather say, not in my power — to dispute on behalf of any opinion, even my own, very obstinately. To try and approach truth on one side after another, not to strive or cry, nor to persist in pressing forward, on any one side, with violence and self-will — it is only thus, it seems to me, that mortals may hope to gain any vision' of truth.[1] Here the opinion is mediated to us through becoming acquainted with the author ; and the second sentence, though not the first, reveals how close is the link with Newman.[2] 'No, we are all seekers still!' Arnold writes later in the same Preface.[3] This tone is frequent elsewhere : 'in differing from them, however, I wish to proceed with the utmost caution and diffidence . . . the tone of tentative enquiry . . . is the tone I would wish to take and not to depart from' ; [4] 'at present I neither praise it nor blame it ; I simply count it as one of the votes' ; [5] 'I have no pet scheme to press, no crochet to gratify, no fanatical zeal. . . . All I say is . . .'; [6] 'the line I am going to follow is . . . so extremely simple, that perhaps it may be followed without failure even by one who for a more ambitious line of discussion would be quite incompetent' ; [7] 'even though to a certain extent I am disposed to agree with Mr. Frederic Harrison . . . I am not sure that I do not think. . . . Therefore I propose now to try and enquire, in the simple unsystematic way which best suits both my taste and my powers. . . .' [8] Such phrases as these, running throughout the fabric of his work, create

---

[1] iii, p. v. [2] See above, p. 161. [3] iii, p. xi.
[4] DA. (iv. 330). [5] ME. (x. 55). [6] FE. (xii. 44).
[7] DA. (iv. 321-2). [8] CA. (vi. 4).

an image for us of the intelligent, modest, urbane Arnold who *is* what he advocates.

But he controls more than his own tone — he foists a contrasting tone on his opponents. He puts imaginary speeches into their mouths. 'I criticized Bishop Colenso's speculative confusion. Immediately there was a cry raised : "What is this ? here is a liberal attacking a liberal. Do you not belong to the movement ? Are you not a friend of truth ? . . . Why make these invidious differences ? both books are excellent, admirable, liberal ; Bishop Colenso's perhaps the most so, because it is the boldest. . . . Be silent therefore ; or rather speak, speak as loud as you can ! and go into ecstasies."' And, as if the contrast were not by now sharp enough, he concludes tersely 'but criticism cannot follow this coarse and indiscriminate method'.[1] It is the tone of the expression that shows the coarseness of the method ; and similarly it is the tone of his opponents he points to and condemns in such remarks as 'Surely, if they knew this, those friends of progress, who have confidently pronounced the remains of the ancient world to be so much lumber . . . might be inclined to reconsider their sentence'.[2] But the inclination to reconsider, or even much to consider, is rather what they lack. It will be necessary to return to this point in examining the very distinctive contribution made to our impression of Arnold and of his opponents by irony.

(ii) *Forms of Argument*

Arnold is also like Newman, and unlike Carlyle (and George Eliot in her discursive works), in developing our sense of his temper of mind, and of the kind of thinking he is doing, through the distinctive forms of his argument. Newman and Arnold both employ the *argumentum ad hominem*. In Newman this form is common, it is constantly employed on points of detail, and the effect of its frequency is to amplify our sense of the great integrated system of reality, as the author conceives it. Arnold uses

[1] *The Function of Criticism* (iii. 32).   [2] ME. (x. 37).

the argument much less often, and then in respect only of some fundamental issue. 'I speak to an audience with a high standard of civilization. If I say that certain things . . . do not come up to a high standard . . . I need not prove how and why they do not; you will feel instinctively . . . I need not prove that a high standard of civilization is desirable; you will instinctively feel that it is.'[1] *God and the Bible* is 'meant for those who, won by the modern spirit to habits of intellectual seriousness, cannot receive what sets those habits at naught'.[2] In *Literature and Dogma*[3] he writes approvingly of how Newman relies on this form of argument. But in his own case its oblique contribution is less to give the impression of system and precision than of circumspection in argument and modesty on the part of the author.

Again, like Newman, Arnold enlists the negative evidence. Scientists are likely to have an incomplete understanding of human nature not through their limitations, but actually through their special talents and interests.[4] Frederic Harrison may be right in arguing that men of culture are just the class who cannot be trusted with power in modern society; but this confirms, not his own attack on men of culture, but Arnold's on the society that cannot use them.[5] As for the Nonconformists, 'the very example (America) that they bring forward to help their case makes against them';[6] their knowledge of the Bible, which they make their infallible stay, is a typical specimen of knowledge and ignorance muddled together;[7] and when they rely on a 'fetish or mechanical maxim' to bring about an improvement in the state of affairs, they only succeed in adding slightly to the 'confusion and hostility'.[8] The administration of Athens under Eubulus, which at the time it would have seemed 'very impertinent' to condemn, was exactly what led to the collapse of the city.[9] Burke, bitterest enemy of the French Revolution, can yet at the very end of his work return upon himself to explain how a

[1] ME. (x. 58).　　　　[2] viii, p. xxxiv.　　　[3] vii. 318.
[4] DA. (iv. 336-7).　　[5] CA. (vi. 3).　　　　[6] vi, p. xxx.
[7] vi. 153-4.　　　　　[8] vi. 172-3.　　　　　[9] DA. (iv. 288-9).

great change in human affairs might under certain circumstances be proper and inevitable.[1] The general tendency
of these arguments is not to suggest any grand system, but
a polite irony in things that sooner or later makes cocksure
people look silly.[2]

The appendage to *Friendship's Garland* called 'A
Courteous Explanation' is especially interesting here. First,
it is an argument that finds support for Arnold's case where
one would least expect it. 'Horace', siding with the complacent English journals, has attacked him for depreciating
the value of free speech in England; Arnold quietly
observes that at all events this new opponent readily follows
his own lead in criticizing compatriots. 'How "Horace"
does give it to his poor countrymen . . . ! So did Monsieur
de Tocqueville, so does Monsieur Renan. I lay up the
example for my own edification, and I commend it to the
editor of the *Morning Star* for his.'[3] Second, Arnold
discredits his opponent, in the same unruffled style, by a
tu quoque argument. 'This brings me to the one little
point of difference (for there is just one) between "Horace"
and me.'[4] 'Horace' has accused him of giving no thought
to the needs of foreign countries. But does he give any
thought to it himself ? — far from it : he wants the English
to be told not what they, but what the French need to hear.
'"Horace" and his friends are evidently Orleanists, and I
have always observed that Orleanists are rather sly.'[5]
When Arnold has finished, 'Horace' looks less sly than
silly — or at least, one more opponent of the abrupt, unreflecting, unsubtle kind that Arnold seems so often to be
dealing with.

Perhaps the two forms of argument most distinctive of

---

[1] *The Function of Criticism* (iii. 16).
[2] The example of Burke is different. (*a*) In this respect he is an *example*
of the temper of mind Arnold wishes to recommend. (*b*) Arnold recommends his *own* temper of mind by taking a virtual opponent as a praiseworthy
example. (*c*) Burke's concession shows all the same how Arnold's opponents
are (if intelligent enough) constrained by the nature of events to introduce
exceptions and thereby accept Arnold's view. Burke is the opponent who
is wise, and retreats ; Frederic Harrison and the Nonconformists blunder
obstinately on.
[3] FG. (vi. 397).   [4] vi. 398.   [5] *Ibid.*

Arnold are *distinguo* arguments which keep the reader sensitized to his unrelaxing circumspection, and concessive arguments which emphasize his modesty. '"Let us distinguish", replied the envious foreigners' (who here are speaking for Arnold himself) 'let us distinguish. We named three powers . . . which go to spread . . . rational humane life. . . . Your middle class, we agreed, has the first. . . . But this only brings us a certain way. . . .'[1] Or again, 'It is not State-action in itself which the middle and lower classes of a nation ought to deprecate; it is State-action exercised by a hostile class'.[2] 'Just as France owes her fearful troubles to other things and her civilizedness to equality, so we owe our immunity from fearful troubles to other things, and our uncivilizedness to inequality.'[3] In *A French Eton* [4] he distinguishes the quite contrasting needs of schools providing for the different classes of society: those for the aristocracy need 'the notion of a sort of republican fellowship, the practice of a plain life in common, the habit of self-help'; while those for the middle classes need training in 'largeness of soul and personal dignity', and those for the lower, in 'feeling, gentleness, humanity'.[5] The same form of argument underlies a passage quoted earlier, Arnold's version of the attacks on him for his attack on Bishop Colenso: [6] the method of his opponents is coarse and indiscriminate just because they think that all 'differences' are 'invidious'. 'The practical man is not apt for fine distinctions, and yet in these distinctions truth and the highest culture greatly find their account.' [7] Arnold finds his account in them, because they not only lead him to the conclusions he desires, but give his thought and writing a distinctive temper in the process.

Concession in argument necessarily does little to advance the proof for one's own case; and for Arnold (believing as he did that there were many propositions true in the abstract but not needing stress in his own

---

[1] FG. (vi. 376-7).   [2] ME. (x. 34).
[3] ME. (x. 83).   [4] FE. (xii. 40).
[5] *I.e.* distinctions which would not confirm class distinctions, but mitigate them.
[6] See above, p. 209.   [7] *The Function of Criticism* (iii. 28).

times) it must necessarily have had little value, save obliquely in mitigating the tone of his work, or helping to create an impression of his personality. Its comparative frequency is thus a clear sign how these oblique functions are important. 'We ought to have no difficulty in conceding to Mr. Sidgwick that . . . fire and strength . . . has its high value as well as culture'; [1] 'Hellenism . . . has its dangers, as has been fully granted'; [2] 'there are many things to be said on behalf of this exclusive attention of ours to liberty'.[3] Sometimes the concession is 'placed' as it were, by a subsequent *distinguo* argument : 'the final aim of both Hellenism and Hebraism . . . is no doubt the same: man's perfection or salvation . . . still, they pursue this aim by very different courses . . . so long as we do not forget that both . . . are profound and admirable . . . we can hardly insist too strongly on the divergence of line and of operation by which they proceed'.[4] Sometimes, too, Arnold does something explicit to relate the concession he makes to his tone, and to our conception of himself : 'it is impossible that all these remonstrances and reproofs should not affect me, and I shall try my very best . . . to profit by the objections I have heard and read'.[5] One might say here that the substantial significance of the concession is virtually nil — Arnold gives no hint of what it is he is disposed to agree with — but just for that reason, perhaps, the oblique contribution is at its most direct and powerful. There is, of course, in that last remark, a hint also of something quite other than penitent humility.

The reader must have noticed that through the forms of his arguments Arnold does something to develop our notion of his opponents, as well as of himself. The abiding consciousness of those with whom he disagrees — it is something quite distinctive in Arnold's work — finds remarkable expression in *Friendship's Garland*. This is very largely a work discrediting the opinions of others ; and in the main it proceeds by methods of irony, which will be examined below. One cannot help noticing that

[1] CA. (vi. 146).   [2] vi. 155.   [3] vi. 54.
[4] vi. 121-5.   [5] vi. 45-6.

Arnold offers almost no objections of substance to the practical measures he most clearly condemns. But three times — coloured and half-concealed, certainly, by his satirical flashes — an argument does appear. This is how he takes up the case made out for the Deceased Wife's Sisters Bill: 'Let us pursue his fine regenerating idea . . . let us deal with this question as a whole . . . this is not enough . . . for my part, my resolve is formed . . . as a sop to those toothless old Cerberuses, the bishops . . . we will accord the continuance of the prohibition which forbids a man to marry his grandmother. But in other directions there shall be freedom.' [1] Then he attacks the 'gospel of liberty' in the same way. '. . . have we ever given liberty . . . a full trial ? The Lord Chancellor has, indeed, provided for Mr. Beales . . . *but why is Mr. Bradlaugh not yet a Dean?* These, Sir, are the omissions, these the failures to carry into full effect our own great principles which drive earnest Liberals to despair !' [2] Finally he turns, with this same weapon, to the nostrum of publicity: it is true that the government and the courts have recently refused to have sordid divorce and other cases heard *in camera.* 'All this was as it should be; so far, so good. But was the publicity thus secured for these cases perfectly full and entire ? Were there some places which the details did not reach ? There were few, but there were some . . . I say, make the price of the *London Gazette* a halfpenny; change its name to the *London Gazette and Divorce Intelligencer*; . . . distribute it *gratis* to mechanics' institutes, workmen's halls, seminaries for the young . . . and then you will be giving the principle of publicity a full trial.' [3] All these arguments take the form of the *reductio ad absurdum*; and above all, what they contribute to is our sense of the personality and the intellectual temper of those with whom Arnold disagrees. Caricature of the arguments is done in a style that indicates the true nature of the authors: it is

[1] FG. (vi. 307-9). The quotation abridges to the point of destruction a very entertaining piece of satire, though Arnold was sailing too near the wind to give his climax its real point.

[2] vi. 336. Mr. Bradlaugh was the well-known atheist and champion of birth-control.　　　[3] vi. 337-8.

Arnold's opponents, ultimately, who are being reduced to the absurd.

(iii) *The Value Frame*

Arnold's preoccupation, as we have seen, is with what states of mind and what attitudes are desirable in human society, and more particularly with what is the desirable temper of mind in which to conduct an enquiry. Apart from a rationalist historical determinism, which plays a minor rôle in his thought, he had no metaphysics which might form apparent premises for the moral principles he wished to assert. But because a certain temper of mind — the characteristic urbanity and amenity of Arnold — is so pervasively recommended to the reader by the whole texture of his writing, he had a quite distinctive means for both making and justifying value-judgements in other fields. He could praise and justify praise, or condemn and justify condemnation, by suggesting that the topic or the belief under discussion would appeal, or fail to appeal, to the frame of mind which appears throughout his work as the fundamental good.

This distinctive method is to preface or envelop the main assertion in clauses which invite the reader to view it with favour or disfavour, and suggest grounds for the attitude he is to adopt. These *value frames*, as they might be called, serve several different purposes in Arnold's work, and are sometimes very elaborate. Although by their nature they do not obtrude on the casual reader's notice, yet their influence on the texture of argument is great. It should perhaps be said that when they are quoted, one feels at first that the mere trimmings of a sentence have been given and its substantial part omitted: but this impression rapidly fades. Consider an example first: 'The aspirations of culture, which is the study of perfection, are not satisfied unless [what men say when they may say what they like, is worth saying]'.[1] Here the two

---

[1] CA. (vi. 15). In the following quotations the assertion itself, by contrast with the value frame for it, is put in square brackets or indicated by them.

elements, first praise, second the grounds for praise, are
fairly clear : first, a condition such as the assertion describes
would satisfy one whose concern was for *perfection*, and
this is as much as to call it *good*; second, it would satisfy
the *cultured*, *aspiring* and *studious*, and these qualities —
which *Culture and Anarchy* from beginning to end has
endeared to us — are here the grounds of goodness.
Compare 'the flexibility which sweetness and light give,
and which is one of the rewards of culture pursued in
good faith, enables a man to see that . . .'.[1] Here one
senses that the praise itself lies in 'rewards', the grounds of
praise in 'flexibility', 'sweetness', 'light', 'culture' and
'good faith': these are the qualities of mind to which
the assertion recommends itself.

Another interesting example of this device is, 'Surely,
now, it is no inconsiderable boon which culture confers on
us if in embarrassed times like the present it enables us to
[look at the ins and outs of things in this way] without
hatred and without partiality and with a disposition to see
the good in everybody all round'[2] — here not only can
both praise and grounds of praise be located easily, but
two further features appear : the first few words, and the
reference to embarrassed times like the present, distinguish
the author's tone and hint his personality; and the whole
sentence not only puts Arnold's key word 'culture' to use,
but also enriches its meaning, so that it can be employed
more compendiously elsewhere. Sometimes it proves
vitally important to control the exact significance of these
key-words: thus 'essential in Hellenism is [the impulse
to the development of the whole man, to connecting
and harmonizing all parts of him, perfecting him]'[3]
recommends a certain impulse, gives grounds for the
recommendation through the word 'Hellenism', whose
import is already fairly well determined, and thirdly,
amplifies this import itself. And this constant amplification of the import, or rather, constantly bringing it afresh
to the reader's notice, allows Arnold to take liberties. He
does so with 'Hellenism' on the very next page: 'that

[1] vi. 28.   [2] vi. 64.   [3] vi. 154.

[. . .], — this it is abhorrent to the nature of Hellenism to concede' — the reader can keep in mind, though, that Hellenism even *abhors* with amenity.

It is easy to see how much these value frames do, not only to recommend assertions and offer grounds for them, but also to elucidate and recommend the temper of mind to which they seem true, and above all to show that their strength lies in their appeal to such a temper. 'Do not let us fail to see clearly that [. . .]';[1] 'when [our religious organizations . . . land us in no better result than this], it is high time to examine carefully their idea of perfection';[2] '[this] is so evident, that no one in Great Britain with clear and calm political judgement, or with fine perception, or with high cultivation, or with large knowledge of the world, doubts it'.[3] On the other hand, there are negative instances that show equally clearly how some false proposition is born of the mental temper which Arnold condemns: 'Well, then, what an unsound habit of mind it must be which makes us [talk of . . . as . . .]'.[4] In either case it is clear that in cultivating this sense of a right 'habit of mind' throughout his argument, Arnold equipped himself with a precise and powerful instrument for giving effect to judgements of value.

Some of these examples influence us less because they describe than because they exemplify the right habit of mind; that is to say, they affect the reader less through their meaning than through their tone. 'Surely culture is useful in reminding us that [. . .]'[5] illustrates this tendency. But the significant point, for a comprehensive appreciation of Arnold, is how directly and openly this control of tone develops our sense of the author himself. 'Keeping this in view, I have in my own mind often indulged myself with the fancy of [. . .]';[6] 'to me few things are more pathetic than to see [. . .]';[7] 'the philosophers and the prophets, whom I at any rate am disposed to believe . . . will tell us that [. . .]'[8] — above all, 'now does anyone, if he simply

[1] vi. 25.   [2] vi. 27.   [3] ME. (x. 122).
[4] CA. (vi. 16).   [5] vi. 59.   [6] vi. 84.
[7] vi. 22.   [8] DA. (iv. 314).

and naturally reads his consciousness, discover that [. . .] ?
For my part, the deeper I go into my own consciousness,
and the more simply I abandon myself to it, the more it
seems to tell me that [. . .]' ; [1] — Arnold is using forms of
words that recommend his assertion and that develop our
sense of himself, all in one. And because the value frame
serves this purpose, it is naturally adapted to serve the
complementary purpose : it also, often enough, adds to our
impression of his opponents.

These three functions may be performed together
through simple antithesis. One example quoted above
was incomplete : Arnold wrote, 'So when Mr. Carlyle, a
man of genius to whom we have all at one time or another
been indebted for refreshment and stimulus, says [. . .]
surely culture is useful in reminding us that [. . .]'. Here,
words like 'refreshment' and 'stimulus', and the blunt
'says', give a tone to Carlyle's assertion, and the whole
phrase controls our impression of Carlyle himself ; but
Arnold's 'culture' is *useful* in *reminding* (it does not simply
say) ; and Arnold hopes to do something more significant
than refresh and stimulate. This is very similar to 'Mr.
Roebuck is never weary of reiterating . . . "May not every
man in England say what he likes ?" — Mr. Roebuck perpetually asks ; and that, he thinks, is quite sufficient. . . .
But the aspirations of culture . . . are not satisfied unless,
[. . .] culture indefatigably tries . . . to draw ever nearer to
a sense of [. . .].' [2] The contrast is clear ; Mr. Roebuck
is too satisfied too easily. In the sentence 'When Protestantism . . . *gives the law* to criticism *too magisterially*,
criticism *may* and *must remind* it that [its pretensions, in
this respect, are illusive and do it harm]', [3] Arnold's opponents are in the end described explicitly, by the words here
printed in brackets ; but they, and their critic, and the
quality of their respective assertions, are already distinguished plainly by the value frame, as the italics make
plain. The complex manner in which 'its pretensions . . .
do *it* harm' illustrates what was said above about forms of

---

[1] CA. (vi. 181).   [2] vi. 15.
[3] *The Function of Criticism* (iii. 38) ; my italics.

argument should not, by the way, be overlooked.

Arnold is able to endow even the simplest negative with significant and contrasting tone: for example, 'And, therefore, when Mr. White asks the same sort of question about America that he has asked about England, and wants to know whether [. . .] we answer in the same way as we did before, that [as much is not done]'.[1] Here there is a subtly suggestive difference in the sameness — White's pestering is monotonous and stupid, Arnold is urbane and patient. Almost exactly this construction comes again: 'And if statesmen, either with their tongue in their cheek or with a fine impulsiveness, tell people that [. . .], there is the more need to tell them the contrary'.[2] Sometimes the denial is fuller: 'When Mr. Gladstone invites us to call [. . .] we must surely answer that all this mystical eloquence is not in the least necessary to explain so simple a matter'.[3] And while foisting one tone on his opponents, Arnold can provide himself with quite another merely by changing the mood of his verb: 'Who, that is not manacled and hoodwinked by his Hebraism, can believe that [. . .]'; [4] 'When Mr. Sidgwick says so broadly, that [. . .] is he not carried away by a turn for broad generalization? does he not forget [. . .]?' [5] — the question-form itself is all that conveys Arnold's presence, but it is enough.

This quite distinctive device bears both inwards, as it were, and outwards: it suggests an attitude (and grounds for it too) that the reader should take up towards the assertion that it introduces; and through modulations of tone, it can do much to expand and sustain our notion of the writer's personality, and of that of his adversaries. In doing so it is one of the more important techniques creating that bipolarity between himself and them which runs like an axis through Arnold's work.

(iv) *Definitions*

It transpired above that the value frame might not only put one of Arnold's keywords, like 'culture', to use, but that

[1] CA. (vi, p. xxix).   [2] vi, p. xliii.   [3] ME. (x. 90).
[4] CA. (vi. 193).   [5] vi. 147.

it could also control its meaning; and this is to say that the value frame may be inverted in function (or have, as is more likely, two simultaneous functions), and serve as a kind of defining formula. Since definitions proved to be so important a persuasive device in Carlyle, George Eliot and Newman, it is high time to trace the contribution they make in Arnold. But we find that it is surprisingly small. This is not so, of course, in the works of Biblical exegesis — *Literature and Dogma*, *St. Paul and Protestantism* or *God and the Bible*. Here Arnold's central purpose is to reinterpret some of the essential concepts of Christianity: he is, in consequence, quite explicit in giving fresh meanings to the key terms of Scripture, and his argument is full of expressions like 'and the sense which this will give us for their words is at least solid',[1] 'a plain solid experimental sense',[2] 'what they really do at bottom mean by God is . . .'.[3] He even, at one stage, thinks of using re-defining arguments based on the etymologies of words, and mentions how this method is extremely common in Ruskin's social criticism — but in the end he decides not to use 'fanciful helps'.[4] These books, however, are not really of the type that concerns our enquiry. They do not seek to convince a reader that the world-view they express is true, so much as to convince him that it is the real world-view of the Old and New Testaments. Arnold's theology is not what Carlyle would have called 'Life-Philosophy'; it is a sustained *argumentum ad hominem*, addressed to those already sure that the Bible is true if rightly interpreted. When we turn to Arnold's independent work, we find that re-defining arguments virtually disappear; and at first sight this seems a very strange thing.

They are to be found, doubtless, from time to time — it would be inconceivably odd if Arnold were never to define a term anywhere. But by comparison they are certainly few in number, and what is more important, they lack the characteristic quality of such arguments, because they are trite. The typical re-definition seems to transform the import of a word, giving it a more pointed, provocative,

---

[1] LD. (vii. 58).   [2] vii. 62.   [3] vii. 327.   [4] St. P. (ix. 42).

pregnant, influential meaning by seeming to draw on some insight of unusual keenness. By contrast, Arnold's definitions are often textbook definitions; they are dull; they are diaphanous. It is not merely that they cannot facilitate interesting inferences; they preclude them, and this is their job.

Three examples will be sufficient: Arnold's accounts of the *State*, of *Civilization* and of *Human Nature*. If he wishes to be tendentious anywhere, surely it will pay to be tendentious here. But all we find is (1) '*The State — but what* is the *State?* cry many. . . . The full force of the term, *the State* . . . no one will master without going a little deeply . . .' So far all is like Carlyle; not, however, for long. '. . . but it is possible to give in very plain language an account of it sufficient for all practical purposes. The State is properly just what Burke called it — *the nation in its collective and corporate character*. The State is the representative acting-power of the nation . . .'.[1] (2) 'What do we mean by *civilized?* . . . we will try to answer. Civilization is the humanization of man in society. To be humanized is to comply with the true law of our human nature . . . says Lucan "to keep our measure, and to hold fast our end, and to follow Nature" . . . to make progress towards this, our true and full humanity. And to be civilized is to make progress towards this in civil society.'[2] Nothing could seem less pointed than this. (3) 'When we talk of . . . full humanity, we think of an advance, not along one line only, but several. . . . The power of intellect and science, the power of beauty, the power of social life and manners . . . the power of conduct is another great element.'[3] This may be true and useful, but it is not new.

The reason for this apparent lack of enterprise is clear. Unlike Carlyle and the rest, Arnold has no wish to draw controversial or unexpected conclusions from his definitions. On the contrary, it was partisanship or legerdemain of this kind that he was resisting. He defines the State,

[1] ME. (x. 40). [2] x. 61.
[3] x. 62-3. These same four powers are listed in almost identical words in *Literature and Science* (DA., iv. 330-31) as 'the powers which go to the building up of human life', or 'the constitution of human nature'.

only to rebut the view that States cannot be active except
harmfully (far from this, the state is good or bad as we
make it, he argues — it all depends upon the details); he
defines civilization to rebut a paradoxical conclusion about
France by Erskine May; in *Literature and Science* he gives
the same account of human nature in its various aspects,
so as to rebut the narrow and exclusive pretensions of the
scientist. Arnold is using a pattern of argument contrary
to the third pattern we distinguished in Newman's work:
he is arguing that his opponents use words in unduly
narrow and tendentious senses, and demanding that we
adopt unsuggestive, everyday senses instead. In short,
these passages are true definitions, not re-definitions; the
re-definition is a persuasive technique which it is their
purpose to reject and discredit.[1]

To be sure, the more usual type of tendentious re-
definition is not unknown in Arnold's work — or at least
one supposes oneself to have located it from time to time —
but here the position is still stranger, for Arnold appears to
use the technique for only one word, or rather one pair of
synonyms. These synonyms are 'culture', and 'criticism'. It has not been clearly recognized, perhaps, that
he distinguishes these two by nothing substantial; but
this is surely true. Culture, in its simpler sense, is grounded
on 'a desire after the things of the mind simply for their
own sakes and for the pleasure of seeing them as they are'; [2]
criticism's rule 'may be summed up on one word — *dis-
interestedness*',[3] and it works against obstacles in that 'the
mass of mankind will never have any ardent zeal for seeing
things as they are'.[4] True, 'there is of culture another
view . . .' where, though not itself active, it is a ground of
action — '. . . it is *a study of perfection*'; [5] but there is
another view of criticism too, and this time 'it obeys an
instinct prompting it to try to know the *best* that is known

---

[1] Arnold occasionally uses re-definitions of the normal type — for
example, 'What is freedom but machinery? What is population but
machinery? . . .' (CA., vi. 14). But for the most part (though scarcely here
in respect of freedom) they are trivial or incidental.

[2] CA. (vi. 6).   [3] *The Function of Criticism* (iii. 20).   [4] iii. 27.
[5] CA. (vi. 7).

and thought in the world'.[1] Most remarkable of all,
perhaps, is the fact that Arnold controls the value-implica-
tions of both words by giving a particular sense to the single
word 'curiosity'. Each time he shows that this word 'in
the terms of which may lie a real ambiguity'[2] has, as well
as its usual bad sense, a less usual but more important good
sense: and then writes, in one place, 'this is the true
ground to assign for the genuine scientific passion, however
manifested, and for culture, viewed simply as a fruit of
this passion';[3] and in the other, 'criticism, real criticism,
is essentially the exercise of this quality'. When one
remembers that, after all, each of these words is being
used as what Arnold would have called 'not a term of
science, but . . . a term of common speech, of poetry and
eloquence, *thrown out* at a vast object of consciousness not
fully covered by it',[4] their substantial identity is apparent,
and that it has not been more emphasized is remarkable.

There is no need to reproduce the argument whereby,
especially in *Culture and Anarchy*, Arnold develops this
concept — by whichever of the two words we think of it;
like the other Victorian prophets, he has been paraphrased
often enough. But the form of this development is significant. Earlier, we mentioned how Newman had a
pattern of argument which gradually unfolded the full
sense of a word;[5] but his method and Arnold's are
entirely different. Newman first *used* his word in an apparently non-controversial way, then strove to show that in
allowing him to use it like this the reader had conceded
more than he knew. But Arnold is explicit that his definitions are *analyses* of concepts. He announces[6] that he
will proceed to enquire 'what culture really is'; and
further, he does not confine attention to what we must call
its alleged essence, and say that this is really something
that usually goes by another name (and the essence of this
by a third, and so on through a whole series of 'charged'
expressions, which in Carlyle is frequent). Arnold's
method simply takes the reader through subordinate

¹ *Op. cit.* (iii. 18).   ² CA. (vi. 5).   ³ vi. 7.
⁴ LD. (vii. 191).   ⁵ See above, p. 196.   ⁶ CA. (vi. 4).

notions that comprise the meaning of his key term. He analyses, he does not reinterpret; and only when the analysis is complete does he claim that the key-term stands for something good — recapitulating the analysis to show why, and emphasizing that this *is* why. For example, 'If culture, then, is a study of perfection, and of harmonious perfection, general perfection, and perfection which consists in becoming something rather than having something . . . it is clear that culture . . . has a very important function to fulfil for mankind'; [1] '. . . well, then, how salutary a friend is culture . . . culture begets a satisfaction which is of the highest possible value . . .'.[2] We can see how the tone becomes gradually firmer, as a positive value is set more and more confidently on what 'culture' refers to. But Arnold makes it plain that the word carries this favourable tone explicitly because of the sense he gives it — and even admits openly that one may not necessarily be in error to give it another sense. 'I must remark . . . that whoever calls anything else culture, may, indeed, call it so if he likes, but then he talks of something quite different'.[3] And there is just such a *caveat* in the essay which defines criticism: 'But stop, someone will say . . . this criticism of yours is not what we have in our minds when we speak of criticism . . . I am sorry for it . . . I am bound by my own definition of criticism: *a disinterested endeavour to . . .*' [4] — and so on.

Arnold's way of manipulating senses is thus different in kind from that of Newman or Carlyle. His discussions do not suggest, as theirs did, that investigating senses is a kind of discovery. He is really finding a single convenient *name* for a complex of features plainly listed. And this precedes argument in Arnold, whereas the typical re-definition either *is* the crucial stage of an argument, or comes just after it, and shows that what seemed innocent was in fact crucial. Arnold is at no pains to conceal how the definition he adopts is in a sense arbitrary: for him it is an arbitrary but convenient first move. We have seen

[1] CA. (vi. 12-13).   [2] vi. 16, 17.   [3] vi. 67.
[4] *The Function of Criticism* (iii. 41-2).

how the real argument, when it begins, may also control the sense of a key word like 'culture' — sometimes, for example, through its use in a value frame. Yet this control does less to give the word a new sense, than simply to keep the established sense clearly before the reader. It emphasizes, indeed, that Arnold defines 'culture' first and then uses it with a constant meaning. Re-definition proper depends on ambiguities.

(v) *Articulating the Argument: Arnold and his Opponents*

The desire to have distinctive names for whatever he is discussing is a feature of much of Arnold's work. In chapter IV of *Culture and Anarchy*, writing of the 'energy driving at practice' and the 'intelligence driving at those ideas which are . . . the basis of right practice', he says 'to give these forces names . . . we may call them . . . Hebraism and Hellenism'.[1] Elsewhere we find 'these favourite doctrines of theirs I call . . . a peculiarly British form of Atheism . . . a peculiarly British form of Quietism';[2] or 'I may call them the ways of Jacobinism'.[3] How Arnold introduces the terms 'sweetness and light', or 'Barbarians, Philistines, Populace',[4] is perhaps too well known to need further remark. The effect of some of these is clear enough — they are what may simply be called *hangdog* names. But Arnold gives a reason for using the last three which indicates how they can contribute to the general texture of his prose. 'The same desire for clearness', he writes, '. . . prompts me also to improve my nomenclature . . . a little, with a view to making it thereby more manageable.'[5] This is important. To be clear and manageable are not new concepts in Arnold's work. They were the distinctive qualities of his tone, because he made this represent his temper of mind. By providing convenient names for his main topics, he not only influences our attitude through the nuance of those names, but articulates his argument with nodal points that soon become familiar, and easy to trace again. The kind of argument that is his at

[1] CA. (vi. 121).   [2] vi. 109-10.   [3] vi. 36.   [4] vi. 20, 79 ff.   [5] vi. 82.

his most typical, an argument that moves gently forward with a smooth, unruffled urbanity, owes not a little to the familiarity of these coinages, as they so contantly reappear. They do not affect the logic of his discussion, but they transform its quality.

The same principle of style also operates more widely. Sometimes he organizes the whole movement of his thought round a single concept denoted by a single constantly recurring word : an example is the essay *Numbers*, through all the earlier part of which runs the idea of a tiny *élite* which is gradually to leaven the whole of society, and for which Arnold borrows the word 'remnant'. Much more frequently, a whole essay or a whole book is permeated by certain phrases for ideas which have an abiding place of trust in his mind. 'Choose equality', 'sweetness and light', 'our best self', 'spontaneity of consciousness', 'a free play of the mind', 'a full and harmonious development', 'perfection at all points', 'the best that is known and thought in the world' — these phrases return constantly, and contribute not only through their meaning, but also by their recurrence. They bring the argument nearer to that easy limpidity which its author wishes to recommend. By being careful to repeat himself verbally, Arnold brings into a bright light the essential simplicity of his thought. He orders his argument with familiar landmarks. By this means he can hope to attune the reader to his message, just as the rich verbal confusion of Carlyle attunes a reader to an outlook which is quite different.

And the key phrases work to Arnold's advantage not only by their recurrence, but also by their origin. The first three in the list above are all borrowed — from Swift, Menander and Plato respectively. That they are borrowed in this way may add to the weight they carry, or it may not. But quoting authorities is so common in Arnold that it adds something quite distinctive to our impression of him as we read. Through it we see his modesty, his circumspection, and, oddly enough, his independence — not of mind, but of prejudice or strong emotion such as might provoke personal, precipitate, passionate comment.

His use of authorities is a contrast to that of Carlyle. Carlyle overwhelmingly gives the impression of willingness to form and express opinions; his 'quotations' are incidental and subordinate. The reader recognizes them as a game, an expression of the author's exuberance, his intellectual self-confidence and high spirits. Arnold really quotes, he does not invent authorities; and time and again his quotation is introduced at the crucial stage, and his authority constitutes the rock of his argument.

Consider some examples. The discourse *Literature and Science* begins by drawing entirely from Plato, and the fact that Arnold by no means expects his audience to defer to Plato's authority only emphasizes the very aspect of using an authority that we are discussing. Later, however, at a really crucial point in the argument, Arnold reverts to Plato. He has been arguing that men have in their nature four 'powers' or tendencies, intellectual, moral, aesthetic and social; and that just as they have a need to relate the points of their knowledge into a system, so they have a need to relate these four powers into a system. How is he to suggest that this need is worthy to be given free play? At this point Arnold withdraws from his argument, and makes a quite fresh start to introduce the authority of Diotima in the *Symposium*. All desire, says Diotima, is at bottom desire for the good; 'and therefore this fundamental desire it is, I suppose . . . which acts in us when we feel the impulse for relating our knowledge to our sense for conduct and our sense for beauty. At any rate, with men in general the instinct exists . . . and . . . it will be admitted, is innocent, and human nature is preserved by our following the lead of its innocent instincts.' [1] In the address on *Equality* [2] Arnold goes even further. He begins by asserting that in the Burial Service is to be found the maxim 'evil communications corrupt good manners'; but this is quite irrelevant and is never referred to again. Its only significance is to have been quoted from Menander; from whom another maxim (not already quoted anywhere) is 'choose equality and flee greed'.[3] With that the argument

[1] DA. (iv. 333).   [2] ME. (x. 46).   [3] x. 47.

can begin; but as it proceeds, George Sand, Turgot, Voltaire, Burke, M. de Lavelaye, Hamerton, Bossuet, the Book of Proverbs, Pepys and Charles Sumner come one after another, if not to confirm an opinion, at least to provide one which can be discussed and examined. At every turn Arnold seems to avoid taking the initiative, or forcing on the reader something which is merely his own. He even makes his method explicit on one issue: 'now the interesting point for us is . . . to know how far other European communities, left in the same situation with us . . . have dealt with these inequalities'.[1] All the time he is building up our sense of an author who thinks others' opinions more important than his own.

Perhaps it is also worth mentioning, as examples of some special importance, the first paragraphs of the discourse *Numbers*, deriving as they do from one of Johnson's sayings; and the authority of Burke appealed to at a crucial stage in the essay on 'The Function of Criticism'; [2] and the works of Biblical exegesis, which constitute one sustained appeal to authority. But the method is so common with Arnold that it cannot be overlooked. Nor can we overlook its significance, if only because Arnold at one point states it: 'I am grown so cowed by all the rebuke my original speculations have drawn upon me that I find myself more and more filling the part of a mere listener'.[3] Arnold quotes the views of others, rather than express his own, because this modifies our sense of his argument and our view of him. This is not simply to say that he conciliates the reader by refusing to disagree with him, or instruct him directly. Had Carlyle attempted to conciliate in this way he would have had to be at special pains to prevent its being a quite false note, thoroughly discordant with his argument. Once again, our concern is not with a superficial trick of persuasion, but with some modulation of style which is a genuine aid because, through developing our sense of the writer's personality, it genuinely mediates his point of view. That Arnold sometimes uses this method to excess is undeniable; the problem is to sense its point, where it is used aptly.

[1] ME. (x. 52).   See above, pp. 210-11.   [3] FG. (vi. 391).

Quotation, however, is something which Arnold is fonder of inflicting on his opponents than on his models. *My Countrymen*, for example, opens with a grand review of those who have disagreed with him: the *Saturday Review*, Mr. Bazley (M.P. for Manchester), Mr. Miall, the *Daily Telegraph*, the *Daily News*, Mr. Lowe, John Bright, the *Morning Star*, they are all there, marshalled against Arnold, by himself. *Culture and Anarchy* begins similarly — with Bright, the *Daily Telegraph*, and Frederic Harrison; so does *The Function of Criticism*. In *Equality*, Arnold begins with his opponents — Disraeli, Erskine May, Gladstone, Froude, Lowe, Sir William Molesworth — the moment he has done with Menander. The modest, fair, urbane Arnold shows in what seems like an attempt to do justice to the other side. But Arnold uses his opponents further. He quotes from them, and uses these quotations over and over again; wanting his readers to notice less their meaning (which is often uncertain) than their general tenor and their tone. He thus equips himself with a set of — let us say catch-phrases rather than key phrases — that crystallize the views he is resisting in the same simple and recurrent form as his most favoured expressions crystallize his own views. Both the false and the true are presented with the same urbane simplicity; and while we see Arnold's personality behind his selection and presentation of these phrases, and behind their calm and genial reiteration, we see his opponents in the catch-phrases themselves, a little more clearly and a little more disastrously each time. His own account of these phrases was 'profligate expenditure of claptrap'.[1]

Certainly, he collected some gems. Frederic Harrison was unfortunate enough to 'seek vainly in Mr. A. a system of philosophy with principles coherent, interdependent, subordinate, and derivative'.[2] Arnold never really let him forget it subsequently. Harrison it was too who told the working class that 'theirs are the brightest powers of sympathy and the readiest powers of action'.[3] Under Arnold's reiteration, the readiness takes on a fresh colour, the

<hr>

[1] vi. 258.   [2] vi. 299.   [3] CA. (vi. 101).

brightness gets a little rubbed. Arnold also lets us savour
Frederic Harrison's account of the middle classes, 'their
earnest good sense which penetrates through sophisms,
ignores commonplaces, and gives to conventional illusions
their true value'; [1] and John Bright's 'thoughtfulness and
intelligence of the people of the great towns'; [2] and *The
Times'* comment on East End children, 'Now their brief
spring is over. There is no one to blame for this; it is
the result of Nature's simplest laws!'; [3] and Robert
Buchanan's account in the same context of 'that divine
philoprogenitiveness. . . . He would *swarm* the earth with
beings . . .' [4] and his 'line of poetry':

'Tis the old story of the fig-leaf time.

The newspaper account of why a certain Mr. Smith committed suicide, that he 'laboured under the apprehension
that he would come to poverty, and that he was eternally
lost' [5] does service too; so does Roebuck's 'I look around
me and ask what is the state of England? Is not every man
able to say what he likes? I ask you whether the world
over, or in past history, there is anything like it? Nothing.
I pray that our unrivalled happiness may last' [6] — which is
a recurrent theme in *The Function of Criticism*, and reappears in *Culture and Anarchy*.[7] 'The Dissidence of
Dissent and the Protestantism of the Protestant religion',
which began life as a motto on the *Nonconformist*, is resur-
rected in both *Culture and Anarchy* and the *Discourses in
America*.[8] *The Times'* instruction to the British Government to speak out 'with promptitude and energy' enlivens
Friendship's Garland,[9] where Lowe's fatuous 'the destiny
of England is in the great heart of England' also rears its
empty head.[10] The desire of the Bishops of Winchester
and Gloucester to 'do something for the honour of the
Eternal Godhead' is saluted every so often throughout
Literature and Dogma; [11] and choicest of all perhaps, the

[1] CA. (vi. 101).   [2] vi, p. xxiv.   [3] vi. 201.
[4] vi. 202-3.   [5] vi. 157.   [6] iii. 23-5.
[7] vi. 110.   [8] vi. 23, and DA. (iv. 375).
[9] FG. (vi. 322).   [10] vi. 321, 371.
[11] *E.g.* vii. 4, 6-7, 33, 162, 183, 237, 239, 273, 288, 304, 364.

'great sexual insurrection of our Anglo-Teutonic race',[1]
product of a disciple of Hepworth Dixon, is one of Arnold's
most treasured literary possessions.

Now clearly, to introduce or reiterate so many phrases
of this kind does not in itself render the texture of Arnold's
argument simpler and more urbane : their straightforward
effect is to make it more variegated and less urbane, and it
will be necessary to see how he so 'places' them in their
context that this direct tendency is overruled, and the tone
of the quotation is prevented from interfering with the tone
of the main text. But what these quotations simplify for
us is our conception of Arnold's opponents and their shortcomings. Time and again, always in the same way, they
epitomize for us the defect of temper which is what above
all Arnold is condemning. In one simple, natural perception, we see what this defect is ; and every time
they are repeated, the flaw they reveal shows a little more
clearly.

The defective temper of mind which Arnold makes
plain in what his opponents say, is also plain in what they
do. He has no need of rhetoric or eloquence or complex
argumentation : the simple facts are silently eloquent by
themselves. For this purpose, inventions are as good as
realities. *Friendship's Garland* is almost a series of fictitious anecdotes of invented revealing incidents — the
Philistine Bottles giving Arnold's hero Arminius a jingoistic
number of *Punch* in the train, or sitting in all the Deceased-
Wife's-Sisters-Bill glory of his suburban residence ; the
Honourable Charles Clifford addressing the crowd from
the footboard of his hansom ; Dr. Russell of *The Times*
vainly striving to get astride his warhorse ; Cole's Truss
Manufactory in Trafalgar Square — 'the finest site in
Europe' ; [2] Lord Elcho's hat — 'to my mind the mere
cock of his lordship's hat is one of the most aristocratic
things we have'.[3] The technique reappears in *The Function
of Criticism* : trying to indicate the fault of temper in a
whole series of writings, Arnold again takes a single striking

[1] CA. (vi. 190 and 191) ; FG. (vi. 306 and 307).
[2] vi. 249.   [3] vi. 262.

case. 'Their fault is . . . one which they have in common with the British College of Health in the New Road . . . with the lion and the statue of the Goddess Hygeia . . . the grand name without the grand thing.' [1]

'The grand name without the grand thing' — Arnold is not unaware that, if he selects his opponents astutely, their names alone will be enough to expose their defects; and the method is ingenious, for although it says little explicitly, it makes one unable even to think of Arnold's victim without automatically seeing him in an unfavourable light. Beside the British College of Health we have 'Cole's Truss Manufactory', [2] and the *British Banner* : [3] Arnold adds 'I am not quite sure it was the *British Banner*, but it was some newspaper of the same stamp', which seems to show that he knew how the name, if only he could bring it in, would argue for him. It is not, however, only the sham pomposity of names that he enlists in his argument. 'Has anyone reflected', he writes 'what a touch of grossness in our race . . . is shown by the natural growth amongst us of such hideous names — Higginbottom, Stiggins, Bugg !' [4] In *Friendship's Garland* Arnold hints at the ludicrous, and also at the ugly, in his opponents, by invented names like 'Viscount Lumpington', 'the Reverend Esau Hittall', and 'Bottles Esquire'. [5] Elsewhere, for the same purpose, he selects from the material available. The result is Mr. Bazley, Mr. Blewitt, Mr. Bradlaugh, Mr. Blowitz (perhaps Arnold saw something banausic in the initial *B*), Miss Cobbes and Mr. Murphy. There are other names, too, which might be added to this list; and if any doubt remains whether the method genuinely colours Arnold's argument, a passage in *Culture and Anarchy* shows him somersaulting an opponent's argument of an exactly opposite kind : '"Well, but," says Mr. Hepworth Dixon, "a theory which has been accepted by men like Judge Edmonds, Dr. Hare, Elder Frederick and Professor Bush !" . . . Such are, in brief, the bases of what Newman Weeks, Sarah Horton, Deborah Butler, and the associated brethren,

---

[1] *The Function of Criticism* (iii. 36).   [2] *Loc. cit.*   [3] CA. (vi. 96).
[4] *The Function of Criticism* (iii. 26).   [5] FG. (vi. 286).

proclaimed in Rolt's Hall as the New Covenant!' Evidently, Arnold hints, 'Mr. Hepworth Dixon' is taken in by *not* the grand name without the grand thing. He goes on, 'If he was summing up an account of the doctrine of Plato, or of St. Paul . . . Mr. Hepworth Dixon could not be more earnestly reverential'. And now Arnold replies with his own selection of names: 'But the question is, Have personages like Judge Edmonds, and Newman Weeks, and Elderess Polly and Elderess Antoinette, and the rest of Mr. Hepworth Dixon's heroes and heroines, anything of the weight and significance . . . that Plato and St. Paul have?' [1] Here the first parade of names is enough to reveal the intellectual defects of Arnold's opponent, and the second is enough to conclude the discussion.

Arnold's comment on the ugliness of English names occurs in a passage when he is more serious, and is using a judiciously chosen example in another way, less to epitomize an outlook, than to reveal what it omits. It is of particular interest, not only because Arnold is using quotation, authority, the value frame, and example in a single integrated argument, but also because the contrast between the tone of the text itself and that of the inserted passages is particularly vivid. First, he quotes Sir Charles Adderley, 'the old Anglo-Saxon race . . . the best breed in the world', and Mr. Roebuck, 'the world over or in past history, is there anything like it? Nothing.' Against this comes a simple quotation from Goethe, framed or 'placed' by the phrase 'clearly this is a better line of reflection' — we see at once how the counter-move is directed against a certain mental temper, and recommends its opposite. Then Arnold returns to his opponents. They would not contradict Goethe, it is simply that they 'lose sight' of what he saw: they are carried away by controversy, they 'go a little beyond the point and say stoutly—'; so long as they are countered in the same spirit, 'so long will the strain swell louder and louder'. Instead of this, Arnold proposes another spirit, which he sees in simply giving, without comment, one example, one simple fact. 'Let criticism

[1] CA (vi. 97-9).

. . . in the most candid spirit . . . confront with our dithyramb *this . . .'* (my italics) :

> A shocking child murder has just been committed at Nottingham. A girl named Wragg left the workhouse there on Saturday morning with her young illegitimate child. The child was soon afterwards found dead on Mapperly Hills, having been strangled. Wragg is in custody.

'Nothing but that,' he goes on, 'but in juxtaposition with the absolute eulogies . . . how eloquent, how suggestive are those few lines . . . there is profit for the spirit in such contrasts. . . . Mr. Roebuck will have a poor opinion of an adversary who replies to his defiant songs of triumph only by murmuring under his breath, *Wragg is in custody* ; but in no other way will these songs of triumph be induced gradually to moderate themselves, to get rid of what in them is excessive and offensive, and to fall into a softer and truer key.' [1]

(vi) *Irony*

In that passage the sustained contrast between two tempers of mind, one which Arnold seeks to recommend or maintain, and one which he detects in his opponents, is so clear that the problem of how he maintains this duality is now inescapable ; and his chief method, beyond question, is irony. It is widely agreed that by irony an author can seem to the casual or uninformed reader to say one thing, but really say something quite different, clear only to the reader who is initiated or more attentive. But why should such a roundabout method of communication ever be employed ? Usually it is hard enough, one would suppose, to convey one's meaning straightforwardly — why, not content with one difficulty, does an author invent another ? Sometimes, perhaps, because irony can be like a sophisticated intellectual game, which writer and reader alike may enjoy for its own sake. But there may be a more substantial reason. Irony is a powerful and genuine instrument of persuasion. The meaning of a statement —

[1] *The Function of Criticism* (iii. 25-7).

especially one praising or blaming what is being spoken of, or doing anything of a similar kind — usually determines a characteristic tone in which it is reasonable to write or utter that statement. Outright condemnation of essentials tends to sound indignant, partial condemnation of details to sound mildly disapproving, plain description to sound detached, praise to sound admiring. These are no more than tendencies, but they are tendencies strong enough to be inconvenient to writers who, for example, particularly desire not to sound indignant or benignant; and irony is a means whereby a writer may say something in a tone that normally would be inappropriate to it. How easily that will influence the impression he gives the reader of himself, need not be laboured.

Quintilian says that to write ironically is to praise by blaming, or to blame by praising; of which two the last, of course, is the commoner. This is a method which Arnold uses fairly often. But, more than Quintilian's formula suggests, Arnold adapts the nuance of his blame, and of his praise too, so that it serves the general impression he wishes to give. The blame behind his seeming-innocent praise is relatively constant in kind; the praise itself is such that the uncomprehending complacence with which one fancies his opponents would receive it is enough to condemn them; there is no random hitting, because Arnold's irony is adapted so as to be exactly right for the general tenor of his work. Mr. Gladstone is

that attractive and ever-victorious rhetorician [1]

who

concludes in his copious and eloquent way.[2]

Other examples of this lethal innocence are

the ingenious and inexhaustible Mr. Blowitz, of our great London *Times* [3]

a hundred vigorous and influential writers [4]

the newspapers . . . who have that trenchant authoritative style [5]

[1] DA. (iv. 280).   [2] ME. (x. 49).   [3] DA. (iv. 311).
[4] FG. (vi. 368-9).   [5] vi. 353.

> this brisk and flourishing movement [1]
>
> our great orator, Mr. Bright . . . never weary of telling us [2]
>
> my nostrums of State Schools for those much too wise to want them, and of an Academy for people who have an inimitable style already [3]
>
> before I called Dixon's style lithe and sinewy [4]
>
> Mr. Lowe's powerful and much admired speech against Reform.[5]

There is no mistaking the trend of these passages. At first glance, they constitute just that genial, deferential praise which we might expect the urbane Arnold genuinely to give to his more forceful colleagues; but when the second meaning comes home, they are seen to diagnose just the smug, busy over-confidence that Arnold has made his inveterate enemy.

In this way Arnold makes his irony show both what he is like, and what his opponents are like. Images can do this as well as descriptions. In *A Courteous Explanation* he finds occasion to write: '(Horace) and his friends have lost their tails, and want to get them back'.[6] The tail here is a symbol of political liberty. But it is not long before Arnold is utilizing its ironic possibilities:

> I think our 'true political Liberty' a beautiful bushy object . . . it struck me there was a danger of our trading too extensively upon our tails, and, in fact, running to tail altogether. . . . Our highest class, besides having of course true political liberty, — that regulation tail that every Briton of us is blessed with, — is altogether so beautiful and splendid (and above all, as Mr. Carlyle says, polite) that for my part I hardly presume to enquire what it has or has not in the way of heads.[7]

Clearly, this beautiful bushy tail is — may one say it? — a two-edged weapon. There is a very similar passage at the end of *Friendship's Garland*, in the letter alleged to have been written by 'A Young Lion' from Paris; the hand

---

[1] DA. (iv. 321).   [2] iv. 285.   [3] FG. (vi. 353-4).   [4] vi. 306.
     [5] vi. 369.   [6] vi. 400.   [7] vi. 400-401.

is the hand of a lithe disciple of Hepworth Dixon, but of course the voice is the voice of Arnold :

> While Sala was speaking, a group had formed before the hotel near us, and our attention was drawn to its central figure. Dr. Russell, of the *Times*, was preparing to mount his war-horse. You know the sort of thing, — he has described it himself over and over again. Bismarck at his horse's head, the Crown Prince holding his stirrup, and the old King of Prussia hoisting Russell into the saddle. When he was there, the distinguished public servant waved his hand in acknowledgement, and rode slowly down the street, accompanied by the *gamins* of Versailles, who even in their present dejection could not forbear a few involuntary cries of 'Quel homme !' [1]

— by now the exact nuance of the blame behind the praise is beginning to be apparent, the warhorse has become a hobby-horse, and Arnold, once more, is depicting in his opponents the perennial source of his dislike.

The ambivalency between praise and blame that makes this passage ironical depends very much upon Arnold's giving it to an alleged author doing duty for the real author whom we sense in the background. It is one of his favourite devices to invent figures to speak his opinions for him. In part its contribution is like that suggested above for quotations and authorities ; but in part too it sustains that divorce of tone and statement which is the office of irony. Thus, in *My Countrymen*, it is 'certain foreigners' who deliver the attack on English life — and a most forceful and outspoken attack it is. But Arnold appears only as their interlocutor in defence of England — an anxious, embarrassed, excessively reasonable defender perhaps (as Arnold was likely to be for any cause) but a defender all the same.

> I used often to think what a short and ready way one of our hardhitting English newspapers would take with these scorners . . . but being myself a mere seeker after truth, with nothing trenchant or authoritative about me, I could do no

more than look shocked and begin to ask questions. 'What!'
I said, 'you hold the England of today cheap . . .?' . . .
Though I could not bear without a shudder this insult to the
earnest good sense which, as the *Morning Star* says, may be
fairly set down as the general characteristic of England and
Englishmen everywhere. . . . I begged my acquaintances to
explain a little more fully. . . .

  '. . . and intelligence [they said] . . . your middle class
has absolutely none.' I was aghast. I thought of this
great class, every morning and evening extolled for its clear
manly intelligence by a hundred vigorous and influential
writers. . . .[1]

But he has just been sent a copy of a speech by Mr. Lowe,
telling how the English middle class has been performing
unrivalled exploits :

  I took it out of my pocket. 'Now,' said I to my envious,
carping foreigners, 'just listen to me . . . Mr. Lowe shall
answer you. . . .' What I had urged, or rather what I had
borrowed from Mr. Lowe, seemed to me exceedingly forcible,
and I looked anxiously for its effect on my hearers. They did
not appear so much disconcerted as I had hoped.[2]

  In *Friendship's Garland* Arnold uses the same device
to escape the awkward tone implied by what he wants to
say. Here it is the mythical Prussian, Arminius von
Thunder-den-Tronkh, who delivers Arnold's attack direct.
And Arnold, speaking in his own person, writes :

  In confidence I will own to you that he makes himself
intensely disagreeable. He has the harsh, arrogant Prussian
way of turning up his nose at things and laying down the law
about them ; and though, as a lover of intellect, I admire
him, and, as a seeker of truth, I value his frankness, yet, as
an Englishman, and a member of what the *Daily Telegraph*
calls 'the Imperial race', I feel so uncomfortable under it,
that I want, through your kindness, to call to my aid the
great British public, which never loses heart and has always
a bold front and a rough word ready for its assailants.[3]

---

  [1] FG. (vi. 363-9).   [2] vi. 369-71.   [3] vi. 243-4.

Arminius himself is a likeable figure, with his pink face and
blue eyes, his shaggy blond hair, his ancient blue pilot-coat,
and pipe belching interminable smoke. But although his
personality may be likeable, it is very different from
Arnold's, and he can do what would be disastrous for
Arnold himself. Arminius and his creator go down to
Reigate by rail, and in the carriage is, as Arnold calls him,
'one of our representative industrial men (something in
the bottle way)'. When the manufacturer begins to talk
politics, Arnold tries to soothe the conversation with 'a
few sentences taken from Mr. Gladstone's advice to the
Roumanians'. But — 'The dolt! The dunderhead! His
ignorance of the situation, his ignorance of Germany, his
ignorance of what makes nations great, his ignorance of
what makes life worth living, his ignorance of everything
except bottles — those infernal bottles!' — that is Arminius's comment.[1] On another occasion, Arnold 'runs' to
appease him with a 'powerful letter' by Mr. Goldwin
Smith, published in the *Daily News*, and 'pronouncing in
favour of the Prussian alliance . . . "At last I have got
what will please you"', cries he. But Arminius only gives a
sardonic smile, and puts it all down ungraciously to the
Prussian needle-gun.[2] 'Your precious *Telegraph*',[3] he says
bluntly; and of *The Times*, 'that astonishing paper'.[4]
Arnold contrasts Arminius and himself directly: '"You
make me look rather a fool, Arminius," I began, "by what
you primed me with . . . ." "I dare say you looked a fool,"
says my Prussian boor, "but what did I tell you?"'[5]
Even Arminius himself is made to emphasize just the
contrast Arnold wishes us to see. 'I have a regard for
this Mr. Matthew Arnold, but I have taken his measure.
. . . Again and again I have seen him anxiously ruminating
over what his adversary has happened to say against his
ideas; and when I tell him (if the idea were mine) that
his adversary is a *dummkopf*, and that he must stand up to
him firm and square, he begins to smile, and tells me that
what is probably passing through his adversary's mind is
so and so.'[6]

[1] vi. 245.   [2] vi. 246.   [3] vi. 235.   [4] vi. 275.   [5] vi. 274.   [6] vi. 252-3.

This example introduces one of Arnold's most characteristic manœuvres. Having introduced imaginary characters to speak for him, he recommends himself to the reader by interruptions that deny their excesses. Here he adds to Arminius's comment the footnote, 'A very ill-natured and exaggerated description of my (I hope) not unamiable candour'. In the Dedicatory Letter to *Friendship's Garland* he reports Arminius *verbatim* at length and then appears in his own person to retract : 'I doubt whether this is sound, Leo, and, at any rate, the D.T. [*Daily Telegraph*] should have been more respectfully mentioned'.[1] Arminius asserts dogmatically that Mr. Lowe is descended from Voltaire's insufferable optimist Pangloss : Arnold says that he believes there is no more than 'a kinship in the spirit' — Arminius, he fears, was suffering from a fixed idea.[2] Later, Arminius records an unbelievable interview with Lowe. Arnold observes gravely that since everything he makes Lowe say actually appeared in Lowe's printed speeches, there is reason to fear that the interview was only imaginary.[3] When Arminius tirades against the style of the *Daily Telegraph*, Arnold writes, 'though I do certainly think its prose a little full-bodied, yet I cannot bear to hear Arminius apply such a term to it as "incorrigibly lewd" ; and I always remonstrate with him. "No, Arminius," I always say, "I hope not *incorrigibly*."'[4] And Arnold has a delightful footnote to 'Young Lion's' account of Dr. Russell mounting on horseback, in which he confesses sadly to not having found, in Russell's correspondence, quite the confirmatory descriptions that 'Leo' spoke of. 'Repeatedly I have seemed to be on the trace of what my friend meant, but the particular description he alludes to I have never been lucky enough to light upon.'[5] Sometimes the retraction by Arnold is implicit in one word, as when, pretending to report Arminius's own words about his inventor, he writes 'the newspapers which you are stupid [*sic*] enough to quote with admiration'.[6]

The general effect of this device, however, might pos-

---

[1] FG. (vi. 237).   [2] vi. 260.   [3] vi. 272 n.
[4] vi. 284.   [5] vi. 347 n.   [6] vi. 235.

sibly be misunderstood. Only a child would see Arnold
in these disclaimers alone. To a reader acquainted with
the methods of irony the first rough impression of his
personality, coming perhaps from these by themselves, is
immediately corrected by a sense that he is author of the
whole tissue of assertion dramatized in character and dis-
claimer with an edge to it. The undercurrent of meaning
establishes that he is fully in earnest, has something he
thinks it important to say. But concern for his message
has not carried him away, and we see him still able to
select exactly the most telling mode in which to express it;
we are made to feel that there is no self-importance in a
man who can so depreciate himself, even in play. Arnold
develops both that first rough impression of himself, and
the more complete impression, by explicit means: 'for
posterity's sake, I keep out of harm's way as much as I
can. . . . I sit shivering in my garret, listening nervously
to the voices of indignant Philistines asking the way to
Grub Street. . . . I write with a bit of coal on the lining of
my hat.' [1] Here the reference to posterity reminds the
reader that it is all a game, though one, perhaps, that serves
a serious end. So it is when in *Culture and Anarchy*, he,
after some havering, offers himself as an example of the
Aristotelian extreme of *defect* in possessing the virtues of
his own class. 'Perhaps there might be a want of urbanity
in singling out this or that personage as the representative
of defect . . . but with oneself one may always, without
impropriety, deal quite freely; and, indeed, this sort of
plain dealing with oneself has in it, as all the moralists
tells us, something very wholesome. So I will venture to
humbly offer myself as an illustration of defect in those
forces and qualities which make our middle class what it
is.' [2] He has done nothing, he confesses, to help uproot
the evils of church-rates, for example. He quite lacks the
'perfect self-satisfaction' current among the Philistines.
'But these confessions', he concludes, 'though salutary,

[1] vi. 395-6.
[2] CA. (vi. 80-81). Cf. vi. 90, 'I again take myself as a sort of *corpus vile*
to serve for illustration in a matter where serving for illustration may not by
everyone be thought agreeable'.

are bitter and unpleasant.' Here again the effect is twofold : first, simply, of Arnold offering himself humbly as
an example of defect ; and second, less simply, of Arnold
being sufficiently at ease and in command of himself
(despite the unmistakable note of seriousness) to play a
nice, an elaborate game of self-apology that is also in a
way self-praise. But these impressions converge to make
a single effect : that if Arnold ever had, like Dr. Russell,
a warhorse, it had the same history as the Cheshire cat, and
there is nothing left of it but the grin.

This double sense in the reader of Arnold first as
simply a man in the situation he describes, and second as
a writer forming that situation, arises also when he contrasts
himself and his opponents. The *Saturday Review*, he
says,[1] maintains that we have 'found our philosophy';
but when obliged to travel almost daily on a branch line
close to the scene of a railway murder, Arnold found his
fellow-travellers so demoralized by fear that to begin with
he thought they disproved this. 'Myself a transcen-
dentalist' (the *Saturday Review* has accused him of it) 'I
escaped the infection ; and day after day, I used to ply
my fellow-travellers with . . . consolations . . . "suppose
the worst to happen", I said, addressing a portly jeweller
from Cheapside ; "suppose even yourself to be the victim ;
il n'y a pas d'homme necessaire" . . . All was of no avail.
Nothing could moderate . . . their passionate, absorbing,
almost bloodthirsty clinging to life . . . but the *Saturday
Review* suggests a touching explanation . . . the ardent
longing of a faithful Benthamite . . . to see his religion in the
full and final blaze of its triumph.' Here our impression
is in part of Arnold living through the experience, and in
part of him as its gleeful inventor ; and of his opponents,
partly in their fictitious guise of Arnold's jeweller, partly
in their real form, the *Saturday Review* that can write as
it does in a world of branch lines, railway murders, and fat
poltroons. Nor is it impossible for Arnold to modify his
effect by giving us a sense of himself as writer, even when
he is most serious. The passage from *The Times*, quoted

[1] EC. i (iii, pp. ix-x).

above,[1] about conditions in the East End, is fitted by
Arnold into a personal experience. 'This firm philosophy',
he writes, 'I seek to call to mind when I am in the East of
London . . . and indeed, to fortify myself against the
depressing sights . . . I have transcribed from the *Times*
one strain . . . full of the finest economical doctrine, and
always carry it about with me. . . .'[2] Then he continues
by quoting Buchanan on the Divine Philoprogenitiveness,
observes that this must be a *penchant* he shares with 'the
poorer class of Irish' and continues 'and these beautiful
words, too, I carry about with me in the East of London,
and often read them there'. Buchanan's 'fine line' of
poetry, too, 'naturally connects itself, when one is in the
East of London, with God's desire to *swarm* the earth with
beings'. There is no mistaking the bitterness, but our
sense of Arnold himself is largely a sense of the control
and the grim humour that give to that bitterness this
expression.

These more elaborate examples, then, confirm the view
that Arnold uses irony to widen his range of assertion, while
still remaining within the range of tone that his outlook
demands. It is one further method whereby he conveys a
certain temper of mind by example rather than description,
and it emphasizes once more that this temper is essentially
what his work strives to express. This explains, too, why
he is so prominent himself in his writings, why his personality is progressively revealed in a favourable light that the
hostile reader, revolting from Arnold's whole attempt to
persuade, labels complacency. Nothing will rigorously
prove this label mistaken; but we tend less, perhaps, to
call Arnold's method complacent, once we have equipped
ourselves with a proper knowledge of its detail, and its
function.

[1] See p. 230.   [2] CA. (vi. 201).

CHAPTER VIII

HARDY

(i) *Introduction*

HARDY presents in many ways this book's most interesting problem, though surely also one of its most difficult. The first difficulty is a very obvious one : he wrote so much that to illustrate his outlook and methods on a truly adequate scale would take far too long.[1] Another difficulty is more serious. He has probably been more written about than any other of the authors discussed here. His 'view of life' has been expounded, reinterpreted, and attacked many times over ; often so fully that a good deal has also been said of how plot, character, dialogue or setting enrich its expression. One is inclined to think that his view is already familiar, and that his method of exposition has already been examined. Can any purpose be served by one enquiry more ?

Yes ; because certain accidental or temporary factors have made many discussions of Hardy's work incomplete. This is partly his own fault, for saying that the books he called 'Novels of Character and Environment' expressed his outlook most fully,[2] and then including *Jude the Obscure* among them without further comment. As the last of his novels, and that which provoked most excitement when it was published, this book has consequently been seen as the most explicit, the typical expression of his views, and his other books as converging upon it. I hope

---

[1] Hardy's verse is not discussed in this chapter for reasons of space and uniformity ; though he makes clear himself (see *The Later Years of Thomas Hardy*, by Mrs. F. E. Hardy, p. 217) that one part of what he calls his 'philosophy of life' — that concerned with the 'Cause of Things' — finds in the verse its chief expression.

[2] General Preface to the Novels and Poems (TD, p. vii).

the present chapter will show that *Jude* is an anomaly among this group of novels rather than their norm. But there are other reasons why Hardy has often been discussed incompletely. In some sense or another, Hardy's outlook was clearly a rejection of Christianity; and this was enough to make many of the earlier critics feel obliged either to blame or justify him. Consequently they saw only that part of his thought which related to the *course* of Things, and to who or what governed that course. This narrowly theological interest has had a curious result: Hardy is familiar in two quite different rôles, as chronicling a ghastly world of planless and ironic Fate, and as recording all the interest and variety and even charm of rustic life; and it is left unnoticed that if these ever occur unintegrated in a single book, Hardy is probably ridiculous as an artist. Something important remains to be said of how he does integrate them, and it can only be said if we recognize one important fact. This fact is that Hardy has a good deal more to say about the quality of events, the feel of them, than about their course.

It may be that another omission has been even more significant. We saw how George Eliot and Disraeli (to say nothing of the authors who were not novelists) had views on two different subjects: what the world is like, and how men ought to behave in it. Hardy is also, though not in quite the same way, both a philosopher and a moralist. But this has often been quite ignored, except for one minor and at first sight paradoxical aspect of his work, his attack on contemporary marriage conventions. One can easily see how the omission came about. The notion that Hardy had deep and earnest convictions, of a quite general and systematic kind, about what was good and what bad in human life, hardly occurred to the many critics who thought him irreligious or scandalous. But a more important influence was also at work. Hardy does not, like George Eliot, exhort his readers to comply with what he admires and give up what he does not; about this he is fatalistic, and he rarely seems to suppose that men will or even can do much to reform their lives. But a definite though unobtrusive sense of values is clear almost throughout his work; and indeed, it is spread more widely through the novels than are his purely speculative notions. This sense of values is of direct concern here; for Hardy is like all the other writers discussed in this book, in that what he finds good or bad in life is a part or corollary of his whole view of life. And what he finds bad in the conventional view of marriage proves, incidentally, merely to follow from his general scheme of values.

A recent penetrating study of Hardy, A. J. Guerard's *Thomas Hardy, the Novels and Stories,* has suggested that much is lost through excessive interest in Hardy's philosophy. 'Academic schematizing . . . has . . . fastened on certain structural and didactic aspects of the major Wessex novels to the neglect of much else which remains readable and can even be useful to the novelist writing today.' One should not, Guerard continues, 'reduce . . . a novel's meaning to some philosophy of life . . . theorize oneself quite away from the living complex of the work of art, and the impression it actually makes'.[1] Hardy would have welcomed Guerard's approach. Several times he denies that he is advancing any general theory of things, anything that can be tested by its abstract consistency; and the word 'impression' is his own favourite term for whatever sense of life his novels convey. 'Like former productions of this pen', he writes, '*Jude the Obscure* is simply an endeavour to give shape and coherence to a series of seemings, or personal impressions, the question of their consistency or . . . their permanence . . . being regarded as not of the first moment';[2] or again, 'a novel is an impression, not an argument'.[3] But one can easily see that Hardy's attitude is not wholly clear; in the General Preface to the Wessex Edition of the novels he writes 'that these impressions have been condemned as "pessimistic" shows a curious muddle-headedness . . . it must be obvious that there is a higher characteristic of philosophy than pessimism, or . . . optimism . . . — which

---

[1] *Op. cit.* p. 2, pp. 6-7.   [2] JO, p. viii.
[3] TD, p. ix. (from the General Preface).

is truth'.¹ He writes elsewhere that since some 'philosophy of life' was necessary in an epic work like *The Dynasts*, he used that which he had 'denoted' in the early verse and also to some extent in the prose. *Naturam expelles furca, tamen usque recurret.* Plainly we must strike some sort of balance between Hardy's desire not to be seen as a theorizing philosopher, and his clear conception of himself as somehow giving expression to a 'philosophy' all the same.

This can be done. A Hardy novel is not an argument, because it *is* an impression : not idle romance, but the work 'in all sincerity of purpose' of one who though modestly 'a mere tale-teller' is nevertheless a thinker and a realist, and 'writes down how the things of the world strike him'.² Wessex was, for him, not a place simply of picturesque oddity, a colourful geographical freak. Its people 'were meant to be typically and essentially those of any and every place where

Thought's the slave of life, and life time's fool,

[that is, *every* place] — beings in whose hearts and minds that which is apparently local should be really universal'.³ It imposed no limitations on an author interested in the central realities of life ; its humble dramas could rise to 'a grandeur and unity truly Sophoclean'.⁴ Surely, in view of these assertions, Guerard's warning is not a discouragement but an encouragement to apply to Hardy our present method. If anything can do justice to its dual aspect, as embodying a considered view of the world, and as in essence remote from theorizing abstractions, it will be an attempt to recreate the author's 'idiosyncratic mode of regard'⁵ by studying the whole texture of his work. Hardy's emphasis on 'impression' is rather like the emphasis laid just now on the quality of things as he sees them rather than their course. His idiosyncratic mode of regard had usually to come to terms with making a livelihood by selling stories,

¹ TD, p. xii.   ² TD, pp. xv, xx (the General Preface).
³ TD, p. ix.   ⁴ W. 4.
⁵ A phrase Hardy uses himself (*Early Life*, p. 294, March–April 1890) to indicate what modifies the 'common events of life' when they appear in a work of art.

and in many of his books it is no more than fitfully or partially present. One problem will be to locate where it is conveyed with tolerable fullness. But there is little doubt that if we look in this sense for a view of things in Hardy's novels, we look for something he often put there, and put deliberately.

(ii) *The Course of Things*

Hardy's attitude here scarcely warrants much argument. Since neither the truth nor the consistency of his pronouncements is at present in question, all the general formulation we require was done by Hardy himself, and done very briefly. Of the philosophy of *The Dynasts* he writes, 'I quite agree . . . that the word "Will" does not perfectly fit the idea to be conveyed — a vague thrusting or urging internal force in no pre-destined direction'; [1] and later 'neither Chance nor Purpose governs the universe, but Necessity'.[2] These abstractions will not perfectly fit the idea to be conveyed, and nor will any others, because abstractions never do. What matters is how they are vivified; and that Hardy uses both the details and the general trend of his plots to vivify these abstractions is well known. So well known is it that illustration is hardly required : Tess's vital letter of confession that slips uselessly under the mat, the spouting gargoyle in *Far from the Madding Crowd* that washes the newly-planted flowers out of Fanny Robin's grave, Jude's son Little Father Time unexpectedly turning up and then hanging all his brothers and sisters — these mean something even to many who have not read the novels. At all events, it is a familiar criticism that Hardy's desire to illustrate this planless but necessitated thrusting led him into wild improbabilities which are perhaps the most serious blemish on his work.

At the risk of incompleteness I shall say little of these aspects of Hardy's novels. Some of the incidents and turns of plot are indisputably flaws. There is, though, a too

[1] To Edward Wright, 2nd June 1907 (*Later Years*, p. 124).
[2] *Ibid.* p. 128.

facile kind of criticism which, having noticed that blemishes in Hardy are often improbabilities, proceeds to catalogue all the improbabilities on the assumption that they must be blemishes. Hardy's critics do this at times with a confidence in deciding what can happen naturally in life and what cannot which to me seems preternatural. Yet the gift is not really germane. Literature often narrates (or dramatizes) the wildest improbabilities; and failure seems almost never to reside in an improbability *per se*, but in some defect of presentation, some crudity or casualness in writing, which makes the improbable unconvincing, but would make the probable unconvincing too.

This is true of Hardy, though his workmanship is not always faulty in the same way. In *A Pair of Blue Eyes*, for example, the heroine Elfride, as she walks home with her dissatisfied lover, quotes 'thou hast been my hope, and a strong tower for me against the enemy'; at that instant the tower of the village church (being demolished, but still standing before them as they walk) totters, falls and vanishes in a cloud of dust.[1] The incident, certainly, is ridiculous; not, though, through its improbability — towers are never demolished, one suspects, except at significant moments in some respect [2] — but through the self-betraying perfunctoriness with which it is introduced. The spouting gargoyle that washes out Troy's carefully planted flowers is unconvincing for another reason — that Hardy stresses a trivial incident at tedious length. Little Father Time hanging the family is an unparalleled literary disaster for other reasons again: perhaps because one always scents a trick in multiple tragedies (three dead infants for one), because Hardy is sentimentalizing (that unspeakable message — 'done because we were too menny'), and because the whole incident interrupts the novel almost like a digression, since it seems a far more elaborate disaster than any reader needs to prepare him for the only significant result, Sue's fit of remorse. In each case, the root of the trouble lies not in improbability but in callow artistry.

[1] PBE. 356-7.
[2] And never except at insignificant moments in others.

But the aim of this chapter is not to defend Hardy's improbabilities. It is to identify those pervasive aspects of his work with which they accord and harmonize — those aspects which, so far as anything does, help his novels to receive and assimilate improbabilities and show them convincingly within one 'idiosyncratic mode' of regarding the world. It should be recognized, in the first place, that Hardy's major novels rarely or perhaps never actually turn on their improbabilities. They develop through basic and abiding factors of character and environment; and it is usually clear that if the incident Hardy describes had not occurred, some other detail could soon enough have brought about the same ultimate result. There is no real feeling that had Angel Clare received Tess's letter and read it, he would have torn it up and cheerfully married her; [1] no real possibility that Clym and Eustacia would have lived happily ever after, had his mother's knocking at the door only wakened him as he slept; [2] no life of success for the Mayor of Casterbridge, had he not read his wife's last letter too soon because it had been faultily sealed.[3] It is a mistake to think that Hardy's novels move through arbitrary accidents to a sad end, in the way that for example the novels of Fielding or Dickens often move through accidents to a happy end. The potentialities of change are in the people, and Hardy merely waits until what in *The Dynasts* he calls the 'listless sequence' of events [4] produces something that moves the action a step further on.

There are, in Hardy, unexpected or apparently unlikely incidents of rather another kind. These are incidents which do not advance the story, but illustrate its significances more or less symbolically. In *The Woodlanders* Grace and Fitzpiers, on the brink of their disastrous affair, are chatting together by the woodman's fire in the forest, when two amorous pigeons flutter and tumble into the hot ashes and singe themselves.[5] When Tess leaves the dairy with her husband after the wedding, the cock crows although it is

---

[1] TD. 268.   [2] RN. 338.   [3] MC. 143.
[4] *Op. cit.* Part I, Act 5, Sc. 4 (Wessex Ed. p. 128).
[5] W. 168.

afternoon.[1] When Mrs. Yeobright, exhausted and at the
point of death, sits on the lonely Heath after her futile
visit to Clym, she sees a heron flying above her into the
sunset, gleaming like silver as his body catches the light,
and seeming to symbolize the happy release from earth to
heaven that she has begun to long for.[2] Incidents like
these raise a point of some interest. At first, they may seem
improbable : but on reflection, it seems likely that something of the kind could well have occurred each time,
provided only that we have regard, as Hardy has, to a
wider range of fact than most people normally consider.
And for these symbolic incidents not to seem vain and
artificial, Hardy must in some way persuade his readers
that this wider range of observation is not fanciful, but
justified seriously. He must, in the given cases, persuade
them that the lives of humans and of birds are related by
more than whimsical significances. Hardy's success or
failure in these incidents can only be judged against his
whole view of the quality of human life and the human
environment. Our response to the detail must be coloured
by our enduring sense of what is mediated all in all. On
these grounds it seems right to say no more of how Hardy
views and treats the course of things, but to turn to his
picture of the quality of things, the 'feel' of life and of its
locale.

(iii) *The System of Nature*

The very word 'Nature' can confuse Hardy's view of
things. A shallow and uncomprehending reading of
Wordsworth, for example — a reading which ignores the
deeper significance of his poetry — has by now made it
difficult to use this word except for scenery, for vistas and
panoramas that in one way or another can please the
observer's eye, and that may provide the novelist with a
picturesque static backcloth which his characters may
adorn, and ignore. 'Nature' for Hardy is scarcely picturesque, clearly not static, and above all not a backcloth.
It is the working and changing system of the whole world —

---

[1] TD. 274.   [2] RN. 343.

Nature in the older sense of Chaucer or Spenser or Pope
(for they had one sense in common), though with a detailed
knowledge of its operations which none of these displayed
or perhaps possessed. Nor is it a backcloth against which
to see human activity ; it is a system which includes that
activity, profoundly modifies it, and ultimately controls it.
But this impress of the system of Nature on man's life
must be seen as following from the life that Hardy sees in
nature itself. To explore this is therefore the next problem.

As always, this cannot be tidily expressed in a simple
formula, because it is a sense of something, an imaginative
insight. But in tracing how Hardy mediated his insight
to the reader, it may help to distinguish four of its most
distinctive and prominent aspects :

> *First*, Nature is an organic living whole, and its con-
> stituent parts, even the inanimate parts, have a life
> and personality of their own.
> *Second*, it is unified on a great scale through both time
> and space.
> *Third*, it is exceedingly complex and varied, full of
> unexpected details of many different kinds — details
> that are sometimes even quaint or bizarre.
> *Fourth*, for all that, these heterogeneous things are
> integrated, however obscurely, into a system of
> rigid and undeviating law.

All these aspects may to some extent be traced through
Hardy's account, in *The Woodlanders*, of Giles' and Marty's
special understanding of their native woodland country :

> The casual glimpses which the ordinary population
> bestowed upon that wondrous world of sap and leaves called
> the Hintock woods had been with those two . . . a clear
> gaze . . . to them the sights and sounds of night, winter, wind,
> storm, amid those dense boughs were simple occurrences
> whose origin, continuance and laws they foreknew . . .
> together they had, with the run of the years, mentally col-
> lected those remoter signs and symbols which seen in few
> were of runic obscurity, but all together made an alphabet.
> From the light lashing of the twigs on their faces when brush-

ing through them in the dark either could pronounce on the species of the tree whence they stretched; from the quality of the wind's murmur through a bough either could . . . name its sort afar off. They knew by a glance at a trunk if its heart were sound, or tainted with incipient decay, and by the state of its upper twigs the stratum that had been reached by its roots. The artifices of the seasons were seen by them from the conjurer's own point of view and not from that of the spectator.[1]

Had the whole argument of this section to stand or fall by one quotation, this would perhaps be enough to make it stand.

The personality in and behind nature is something that Hardy often stresses explicitly. When the wind sweeps over Egdon Heath (which is often called the chief character in *The Return of the Native*, though this obscures how Hardy's method here is typical of him through many novels) it makes three distinct sounds, of which one comes from the myriads of dead heath-bells as it blows through them. Now comes the salient point. Hardy adds that the sound is not like something simply from the florets themselves; it is 'the single person of something else speaking through each at once'.[2] When Henry Knight, in *A Pair of Blue Eyes*, was hanging precariously over the cliff-face, he 'felt himself in the presence of a personalized loneliness'; he begins to realize that to speak of the 'moods' of Nature is no idle metaphor, but a grim reality; the wind is 'a cosmic agency, active, lashing, eager for conquest . . . not . . . insensate'; the sea is like a living creature restlessly waiting for him below, the sun looks like a leering spectator.[3] The Isle of Slingers, in *The Well-Beloved*, has a presence and unity of its own, is like a great drowsing animal.[4] The great earth-work of Mai-Dun 'asserts itself through the night-gauzes as persistently as if it had a voice'.[5] The twilit Hintock woods on a summer evening seemed, as Grace Melbury walked through them, to be full of

[1] W. 399-400.   [2] RN. 60-61.   [3] PBE. 239-45.   [4] WB. 2, 12.
[5] 'A Tryst at an Ancient Earthwork' (*A Changed Man and Other Tales*, p. 172).

half-human forms: 'the smooth surfaces of glossy plants
came out like weak, lidless eyes: there were strange faces
and figures from expiring lights that had somehow wandered
into the canopied obscurity; while now and then low peeps
of the sky between the trunks were like sheeted shapes, and
on the tips of the boughs sat faint cloven tongues'.[1] These
are not figments of Grace's fancy, for she is preoccupied
and hardly notices; but what she scarcely notices is what
Hardy wants to point out: that in a somehow more than
fanciful sense the woods are alive.

The chief method, though, by which Hardy stresses
this aspect of Nature is something which makes his work
quite distinctive. What many writers see as a visual backcloth is to him a busy world of events and processes and
interrelations. This is how he sets the focal point of *Two
on a Tower*:

> the sob of the environing trees was here expressively manifest;
> and moved by the light breeze their thin straight stems
> rocked in seconds, like inverted pendulums, while some
> boughs and twigs rubbed the pillar's sides, or occasionally
> clicked in catching each other. Below the level of their
> summits the masonry was lichen-stained and mildewed, for
> the sun never pierced that moaning cloud of blue-black
> vegetation. Pads of moss grew in the joints of the stone-work,
> and here and there shade-loving insects had engraved on the
> mortar patterns of no human style or meaning. . . . The rarity
> of human intrusion was evidenced by the mazes of rabbit
> runs, the feathers of shy birds, the exuviae of reptiles . . .
> the well-worn paths of squirrels down the sides of trunks
> and thence horizontally away.[2]

The appearance of Nature simply *is* the elaborate complex
of interdependent processes which make up its system.
In *A Laodicean* he evokes the heat of noon by calling it
that time of day when forest birds prefer walking to flying,
and can be heard rustling over the dead leaves.[3] In the
same novel, describing a late autumn scene, he says at
first merely that the sky was lined with low clouds; but

[1] W. 360.   [2] TT. 3-4.   [3] L. 46.

turns immediately from the appearances to the events —
tempests are slowly fermenting, every now and again a
leaf spins to the ground and joins those fallen already, the
brook by the pavilion runs 'brown and thick and silent,
and enlarged to double size'.[1]

Perhaps it is natural enough to describe the breeze or
the wind by referring to what it moves; but Hardy does
so with unique detail and elaboration. There is a stormy
afternoon in *Under the Greenwood Tree*: Hardy notes how
far down the trees sway in the wind, how the flat branches
move vertically and the upright ones horizontally, how the
trees beat against each other, how far the leaves are blown,
how they come to rest at last.[2] He tells how the boughs of
a young tree being planted begin to sound in the breeze
the instant it is stood upright;[3] how rain on a windswept
cliff goes not downward but upward;[4] how (as we saw) the
wind makes three distinct sounds when it blows over the
open country; and exactly how a storm on Egdon Heath
moves and damages the leafy branches of trees.[5] In *Far from
the Madding Crowd* he portrays how a wind at night played
among trees, fallen leaves, hedges and field grass, and just
what was the difference in sound between gusts of different
force as they crossed the upland pastures.[6] He hints at
the different sounds made by the wind in plants of different
kinds;[7] and in a well-known passage he describes exactly
how the sound of the wind changes as it passes through one
kind of tree or another.[8] All these details accumulate
imperceptibly; and little by little they create in the reader's
mind a sense of the system of Nature which no general
description could conceivably evoke.

But perhaps the clearest and fullest example of how
Hardy sees Nature as what it *does* is in the account in
Far from the Madding Crowd of the great storm from which
Gabriel Oak saved Bathsheba's corn-ricks.[9] This is not
treated as a brief spectacular incident, but as an extended
and slow-changing complex of many natural processes

[1] L. 209.   [2] UGT. 165.   [3] W. 73.
[4] PBE. 243.   [5] RN. 60-1, 246-7.   [6] FMC. 7-8.
[7] *A Changed Man*, 174. [8] UGT. 1.   [9] FMC. 274-92.

great and small. Hardy writes first of the warm breeze all day, and the clouds moving athwart each other. There is something significant in how the sheep, the horses, and the birds behave; in a toad that Gabriel stumbles across as it makes its way over the footpath; even in what the snails and spiders do. The storm comes at last, but step by step: the wind changes, black clouds rise gradually above the horizon in a new direction, the other clouds are blown backwards, the moon goes out, the wind falls, and when the first lightning comes it is 'a light flapped over the scene as if reflected from phosphorescent wings crossing the sky'. Every flash of lightning is different, not simply in appearance, but in how it moves and what it does. One of them silhouettes Gabriel's figure against the ground; another frightens the cattle; another silhouettes a poplar tree on the wall of a barn; another strikes the makeshift lightning conductor he has set on the rick; and another when the thunder 'fell upon their ears with a dead, flat blow, without that reverberation that lends the tones of a drum to more distant thunder', splits the poplar from top to bottom. Then the lightning diminishes. After a time Gabriel hears the weather-vane grate round to a new direction; a strong cool breeze rises steadily, and the rain begins to fall. The mere spectacle of the storm is only hinted at through a chronicle of the events which made it part of the natural order.

The incessant animation of nature is brought out in another way, unobtrusive in itself, but important in the novels generally. This is the constant emphasis in his work on sounds; particularly the varying sounds of running water. Once, at least, Hardy makes the meaning of country noises explicit. This is how he begins *The Romantic Adventures of a Milkmaid*: 'It was half-past four o'clock . . . on a May morning in the eighteen forties. A dense white fog hung over the valley of the Exe. . . . But though nothing in the vale could be seen from the higher ground, notes of differing kinds *gave pretty clear indications that bustling life was going on there*.' [1] Here the bustling life is

---

[1] *A Changed Man*, 299 (my italics).

that of the dairy-folk, but very often it is that of the things
of Nature. A clear and explicit example comes in *Tess*:

> Returning from one of these dark walks they reached a
> great gravel-pit over the levels, where they stood still and
> listened. The water was now high in the streams, squirting
> through the weirs, and tinkling under culverts; the smallest
> gullies were all full. . . . From the whole extent of the invisible
> vale came a multitudinous intonation; it forced upon their
> fancy that a great city lay below them, and that the murmur
> was the vociferation of its populace.
>   'It seems like tens of thousands of them,' said Tess; 'hold-
> ing public-meetings in their market-places, arguing, preach-
> ing, quarrelling, sobbing, groaning, praying, and cursing.' [1]

This passage might be compared with part of the account
of Henry Knight hanging over the sheer edge: 'Pitiless
nature had then two voices, and two only. The nearer was
the voice of the wind in his ears rising and falling as it
mauled and thrust him hard or softly. The second and
distant one was the moan of that unplummetted ocean
below and afar — rubbing its restless flank against the
Cliff without a Name.' [2]

The last few paragraphs have been examining certain
favourite examples by which Hardy illustrates how Nature
is more animated than we normally realize. This significance is constantly heightened and stressed by another
means. If the reader turns back to the passage from *The
Woodlanders* quoted on page 252, he will find that it contains
no less than ten metaphors. All of them do something to
reinforce the impression that Nature has a quasi-human
life. Figurative language is common and varied and very
important in Hardy's work, and some of the most striking
examples help to convey that part of his outlook now under
discussion. Not every specimen can be pressed into
service. The river in *The Trumpet Major* that clucked like
a hen means no more than George Eliot's parish clerk who
talked like a hen; [3] and examples like the willow-trees that

[1] TD. 257.   [2] PBE. 245.
[3] See above, p. 146.

seemed to Tess like spiny-haired monsters, or the snow that licked the land, are perhaps too commonplace to be much worth examining. But when Hardy writes of trees in a storm over Egdon 'each stem was wrenched at the root, where it moved like a bone in the socket',[1] we seem to find something that both illustrates what was happening, and implicitly expresses a doctrine, assimilating trees to humans; for as illustration this is inaccurate, and Hardy must have known it was. And while Henry Knight was on the cliff the icy rain-drops 'struck into his flesh like cold needles' : [2] is there not a hint here of the malignancy of the old witchcraft custom, in which a wax model of the victim is jabbed everywhere with needles or pins — a custom to which Hardy devotes a whole scene in *The Return of the Native* ?

But perhaps the most interesting examples of figurative language conveying this part of Hardy's view are all variations on one theme. When it is bonfire night on Egdon Heath, the fires of twigs or timber are 'steady unaltering *eyes* like planets' ; [3] elsewhere, bonfires are 'like wounds in a black hide',[4] while in other books a grove of beech-trees can form 'a line over the crest, fringing its arched curve against the sky, like a mane',[5] and meadow-grass is 'the grey beard of the hill'.[6] These comparisons have little real basis in visual resemblance, and they operate chiefly to make us fancy a resemblance by conveying a doctrine which would justify and explain a closer resemblance than we can actually see. The doctrine — it is an old one — is simply that the earth itself is a great living creature. Hardy has one even bolder comparison of this sort : after having described the sky becoming overcast and foggy, he writes 'the air was as an eye suddenly struck blind'.[7] This only seems not forced if we incline a little to the implicit assertion at which it hints, but for which it is not evidence : an assertion which would account for a resemblance that is not, in fact, to be seen.

So much for how Hardy conveys that Nature is alive

<hr>

[1] RN. 247.   [2] PBE. 243.   [3] RN. 30 (my italics).   [4] RN. 4.
[5] FMC. 8.   [6] *A Changed Man*, 174.   [7] FMC. 323.

beyond our ordinary knowledge; but we could have very
different impressions of this life, and Hardy wants to
present one quite distinctive impression. For him, the
life of Nature is such that the smaller unity lies always
under the impress of the larger. Nothing is cosily self-
contained, nothing can be seen in isolation. Hardy's view
always quickly expands until it depicts something of a
whole landscape, of the varied integration of a region. For
him the proper expression of Nature's active principle
tends always to lie in geography, in an organization that
runs on mile after mile through a massive and abiding
English countryside. The passage quoted just now from
Tess illustrates how Hardy can begin to give this sense of
the spreading landscape through turning our attention to
the streams and rivers of a landscape. Elsewhere in the
same novel this is clearer still; and one thing which exemplifies the unity of Hardy's work is how he uses rivers to
evoke a sense of life, a sense of landscape, and a distinctive
emotional quality. Tess leaves her home in the Vale of
Blackmoor to start life afresh in the Froom Valley. Hardy
describes how she crosses the intervening upland to find
herself on a summit overlooking the whole new landscape :
'the world was drawn to a larger pattern here. The
enclosures numbered fifty acres instead of ten, the farm-
steads were more extended . . . these myriads of cows
stretching under her eyes from the far east to the far west
outnumbered any she had ever seen at one glance before
. . . the birdseye perspective before her was not so luxuri-
antly beautiful, perhaps . . . but it was more cheering. . . .
The river itself, which nourished the grass and cows of
those renowned dairies, flowed not like the streams in
Blackmoor. Those were slow, silent, often turbid; flowing
over beds of mud. . . . The Froom waters were clear . . .
rapid as the shadow of a cloud, with pretty shallows that
prattled to the sky all day.' [1]

Hardy is particularly careful to spread his scene to its
full extent towards the opening of a novel. Of this, Egdon
Heath — 'vast tract of unenclosed wild' — is the familiar

[1] TD. 132-3.

example.[1] But the method is the same elsewhere: Norcombe Hill in *Far from the Madding Crowd*, bare chalk and
soil, so open to the sky that the rotation of the earth makes
itself felt at night;[2] the forest and orchards of *The Woodlanders*;[3] the 'fertile and sheltered tract of country' within
its 'rim of blue hills' where Tess lived as a child;[4] and
the obscure nondescript road in the heart of the country —
'the scene ... might have been matched at almost any spot
in any county in England at this time of the year' — along
which go Henchard and his wife at the opening of *The
Mayor of Casterbridge*.[5] Nor is this Hardy's practice only
in these best-known novels which are veritably pervaded
by his sense of landscape. In the opening scene of *Two
on a Tower* 'the central feature of the middle distance ...
was a circular isolated hill ... with a wide acreage of surrounding arable';[6] almost the first event in *Desperate
Remedies* is the journey of Cytherea and Owen through
undulating corn-landscapes and hills of stone and clay;[7]
and the first event in *A Pair of Blue Eyes* is another journey
through a hilly twilight region where little is to be seen
except the scattered red points of the gorse-burners' fires.[8]
This sense of the spatial extent of nature, though, proves to
disappear in the course of all three novels, and Hardy's
initial hints of it here mean something to us only because
they confirm a tendency. It is sustained only in the 'Novels
of Character and Environment'; and not, as will prove
important later, in all of these.

But at least in *Far from the Madding Crowd*, *The
Return of the Native*, *The Woodlanders* and *Tess*, it clearly
is sustained; and indeed extended and amplified. There
is an interesting passage in the first of these novels when
Joseph Poorgrass the farm-hand is travelling through the
countryside and watches the sky clouding over: 'looking
to the right towards the sea as he walked beside the horse,
Poorgrass saw strange clouds and scrolls of mist rolling

[1] RN. 3-7.   [2] FMC. 8-9.   [3] W. 1.
[4] TD. 8-9. Both here and in *The Woodlanders* Hardy uses the idea of
what a traveller (on foot) would find as he entered this whole region.
[5] MC. 3.   [6] TT. 1.   [7] DR. 18-19.
[8] PBE. 5.

over the long ridges which girt the landscape in that
quarter. They . . . indolently crept across the intervening
valleys, and round the withered papery flags of the moor
and river brinks. It was a sudden overgrowth of atmo-
spheric fungi which had their roots in the neighbouring
sea . . . this being the first arrival of the autumn fogs, and
the first of the series.' [1] And Hardy hints at a wider-
spreading scene still when in *Tess*, describing winter on
the upland farm of Flintcomb-Ash, he records how in the
depths of the frost 'strange birds from behind the North
Pole began to arrive' and suggests that they still retained
the 'expression of feature' they had acquired in the Arctic
itself. [2]

Hardy's system of Nature not only spreads through
space, but is also vast in time. Clym looks over the ferny
valleys and hillocks of Egdon Heath, and the landscape
seems to belong to the world of the Carboniferous period ; [3]
to this the Heath goes back in a slow, obscure continuity,
through the Middle Ages, the Roman period, pre-historic
times. [4] Mrs. Yeobright, finding a colony of ants on the
Heath, recalls how they have been steadily there, generation
after generation, for many years. [5] Norcombe Hill, where
Far from the Madding Crowd opens, was 'a shape approaching the indestructible as nearly as any to be found on
earth'. [6] Henry Knight on the Cliff sees a tiny fossil in
the rock, and 'separated by millions of years in their lives,
Knight and this underling seemed to have met in their
place of death'. [7] The Earthwork at Casterbridge, Four-
ways the ancient cross-roads in *Jude the Obscure*, Bathsheba's medieval barn, the circles of Mai-Dun, [8] are all
examples of this age-long permanence and continuity of
things.

Two interesting examples of figurative language are
relevant here : each reveals how a simile or metaphor can
be almost indefinitely rich in implicit suggestions. The

[1] FMC. 323.   [2] TD. 367.   [3] RN. 241.
[4] RN. 6-7.   [5] RN. 343.   [6] FMC. 8.
[7] PBE. 20. The direct and also the ironical force of 'underling' should
not be overlooked.
[8] MC. 80 ; JO. 139 ; FMC. 164 ; *A Changed Man*, 171 f.

first is from Hardy's account of the Mai-Dun circles:
'The roar of the storm can be heard travelling the complete
circuit of the castle — a measured mile — coming round at
intervals like a circumambulating column of infantry'.[1]
This is a most inappropriate comparison, unless we see it
less as conveying the quality of the wind's movement
(which clearly it fails to do) than as bringing out the scale
of the whole scene, the distances involved, the fact that
even a high wind expends time and energy in traversing
a circular measured mile. Besides this, the comparison
also hints at the temporal permanence of Nature, since a
passing sense is created that winds and infantry are related
to the castle in the same way, and were once there together.
Another similar complex image occurs in *Tess*, when Hardy
writes of 'the irregular chalk table-land or plateau, bosomed
with semi-globular tumuli — as if Cybele the Many-
breasted were supinely extended there'.[2] This image, I
think, achieves no less than four things. It suggests, like
the eyes on Egdon Heath, that the whole landscape is
living; it makes possible a more integrated sense of the
spatial expanse; through personification it *states* that the
chalk-land is alive; and it hints also at the age and permanence of the scene — it is, we are made to feel, like the
landscapes which first suggested the notion of Cybele to
their early inhabitants.

It is Nature's expanse, as much as anything, which
gives Hardy opportunity for portraying Nature's variety.
He carefully drew attention to the profusion of different,
unexpected, and often oddly contrasted events occurring
simultaneously in the natural world. The varying reactions
of plants and animals, birds and even insects, all made their
contribution. Of this, the storm scenes in *Far from the
Madding Crowd* have already served as an excellent example.
Hardy points out specially how the 'creeping things'
seemed not to know of the coming thunderstorm, but did
know of the rain that would follow it, while the sheep
had the opposite knowledge and ignorance. As Tess
wanders through the garden at the Talbothays Dairy, and

[1] *A Changed Man*, 175.   [2] TD. 359.

listens to Angel playing on the harp, Hardy is careful to
amass the trivial and also the bizarre details of the scene:

> . . . the outskirt of the garden in which Tess found herself . . .
> was now damp and rank with juicy grass which sent up mists
> of pollen at the touch; with tall blooming weeds . . . whose
> red and yellow and purple hues formed a polychrome as
> dazzling and brilliant as that of cultivated flowers. She went
> stealthily as a cat through this profusion of growth, gathering
> cuckoo-spittle on her skirts, cracking snails that were under-
> foot, staining her hands with thistle-milk and slug-slime, and
> rubbing off upon her naked arms sticky blights which,
> though snow-white on the apple-tree trunks, made madder
> stains on her skin. . . .[1]

This passage is almost uniquely significant for understanding Hardy. The scene is centrally important in *Tess* itself,
and among the most intensely realized its author ever
wrote. One cannot possibly miss how distinctive was the
sense of man and Nature which, at such a crisis, relied
for point upon details so unexpected.

There is a similar scene in *A Pair of Blue Eyes*, when
Henry Knight and Elfride are in a summer-house at night,
and the rejected Stephen is watching them from the
garden. Henry strikes a match, and Stephen sees only
the lovers. But Hardy makes the reader see, at the same
time, the leaf-shadows and patterns 'of all imaginable
variety and transience', the waking gnats, the spiders'
webs, even the earthworms. The humans seem to be
blundering unconsciously through Nature; but these are
the details that show what Nature is really like.[2] In *Far
from the Madding Crowd* is a particularly vivid example of
how Hardy hints at this element of the bizarre: as he
portrays the newly married Troy leaning one morning
from Bathsheba's bedroom window, he makes a point of
noting that the beads of dew on the creepers distort what
is behind them like powerful lenses.[3] The same novel
contains an account of how the seasons change in an upland
landscape. Hardy suggests that the yearly round is less
conspicuous here than among woodland scenery, but that

[1] TD. 158.   [2] PBE. 273.   [3] FMC. 269.

winter's coming is still easily traced; and what it may be
traced in is 'the retreat of the snakes, the transformation
of the ferns, the filling of the pools, a rising of fogs, the
embrowning by frost, the collapse of the fungi, and an
obliteration by snow'.[1] Every example shows the same
thing — an unexpected variety in which the bizarre is
always present.

But this example also gives emphasis to the last of the
four points mentioned on page 252 : that all the variety of
Nature is integrated within a system of necessity and un-
deviating law.   This is something which the coming of
summer may illustrate as easily as the coming of winter :
'The season developed and matured.   Another year's
instalment of flowers, leaves, nightingales, thrushes, finches,
and such ephemeral creatures, took up their positions
where only a year ago others had stood in their place
when these were nothing more than germs and inorganic
particles.   Rays from the sunrise drew forth the buds and
stretched them into long stalks, lifted up sap in noiseless
streams, opened petals, and sucked out scents in invisible
jets and breathings.'[2] Here there is no general statement
about the processes of Nature ; but one is conveyed powerfully, through stress and selection in this account of a
single process.   And Hardy hints often enough at how the
system of necessity operates through space as well as
through time.   The account of how arctic birds come in
winter has already illustrated this.[3] But the best illustration is perhaps the statement that Marty and Giles were
'part of the pattern in the great web of human doings then
weaving in both hemispheres from the White Sea to Cape
Horn' ;[4] and as we watch them weaving through this
pattern, we become aware of the pattern itself.

(iv) *Man and the System of Nature*

It is not difficult to see, then, how Hardy creates a developed sense of what the world is like and how it functions ;
and that he does so much more vividly and sensitively

[1] FMC. 95.   [2] TD. 165.   [3] Quoted p. 261 above.   [4] W. 21.

through particular scenes and incidents than through the abstractions which from time to time accompany them. Hardy has a corresponding picture of human society; and this proves to show the life of mankind as, sometimes at least, a microcosm of Nature as a whole. The correspondence is integral to Hardy's work, for the former, in his opinion, is properly no more than a part of the latter, and moulded by it totally and without intermission.

That human life, and indeed human consciousness itself, is wholly subject to the control of Nature is something which the people in Hardy's novels illustrate everywhere. It is his constant care to make the reader visualize them encompassed by a landscape to which they are subordinate. Clym, in his furze-cutting days, is 'a brown spot in the midst of an expanse of olive-green, and nothing more'; [1] when Tess and her companions are out walking in the meadow, Hardy writes 'thus they all moved on, encompassed by the vast flat mead which extended to either slope of the valley — a level landscape compounded of old landscapes long forgotten'. [2] One cannot overlook his haste, even, to subdue the particular to its general context here, nor the distinctive quality which he gives the scene. The opening passages of his novels very often depict a solitary figure moving over a landscape or submerged in it: *Under the Greenwood Tree*, *A Pair of Blue Eyes* (the second scene), *The Return of the Native*, *Two on a Tower*, *The Mayor of Casterbridge*, *The Woodlanders*, all exemplify this. So does *Jude* in its second chapter, with Jude himself as a small boy scaring off the birds from the hill ploughland: 'the brown surface of the field went right up towards the sky all round, where it was lost by degrees in the mist that shut out the actual verge and accentuated the solitude'; [3] and a hint of the same thing lies in the numerous cases where a figure is silhouetted against a landscape — of which Eustacia motionless on the summit of the Rainbarrow is the obvious example. [4]

---

[1] RN. 298.   [2] TD. 140.   [3] JO. 10.
[4] RN. 13. Cf. W. 2 (the carrier's van 'in the notch of sky'), PBE. 5 two men, having at present the aspect of silhouettes'), the opening lines

But that Hardy shows people as merely situated within a wider and spreading landscape is not the full story. They are not simply in, but governed by and subdued to their environment. Tess has this quality always : 'on these lonely hills and dales her quiescent glide was of a piece with the element she moved in . . . became an integral part of the scene'.[1] When she works at Flintcomb-Ash, 'a figure which is part of the landscape',[2] Hardy goes on to show how everything about her, as she stands there, is subject to the system and operations of nature. She is 'a field-woman pure and simple, in winter guise; a grey serge cape . . . a stuff shirt . . . buff leather gloves. Every thread of that old attire has become faded and thin under the stroke of rain-drops, the burn of sun-beams, and the stress of winds.' Clym Yeobright was 'inwoven with the heath'; [3] he was 'permeated with its scenes, with its substance . . . his estimate of life had been coloured by it'.[4] The Heath limits Eustacia in the same way, though she is a newcomer to it.[5] Mrs. Yeobright, Clym's mother, is also 'limited by circumstances'.[6] But what brings these assertions to life and gives them their nuance is such a scene as Clym watching Eustacia while she goes away over Egdon on a sunny day. 'Clym watched her as she retired towards the sun. The luminous rays wrapped her up with her increasing distance. . . . As he watched, the dead flat of the scene overpowered him . . . there was something in its oppressive horizontality which too much reminded him of the arena of life; it gave him a sense of bare equality with, and no superiority to, a single living thing under the sun.' [7]   And later in the novel, as he crosses the Heath himself, this time passionately angry with Eustacia, his anger is silently frustrated and annulled by his environment; 'this overpowering of the fervid by the inanimate' is what Hardy calls it.[8]

Hardy also suggests the intimacy of the link between

of 'A Tryst at an Ancient Earthwork' (*A Changed Man*, 171), or TD. 400 (Alec reappears : 'far beyond the plough-teams, a black speck was seen').

[1] TD. 108. [2] TD. 357. [3] RN. 198.
[4] RN. 205. [5] RN. 77. [6] RN. 224.
[7] RN. 245. [8] RN. 384-5.

man and his environment by apparently quite trivial details
which rely for effect on symbolism. In the middle of the
scene where the future Mayor of Casterbridge is selling his
wife, a swallow flits into the fair-booth and passes to and
fro a while before it goes out again ; and the conversation
lags while the bird momentarily absorbs attention.¹ When
later on, having fallen into a drunken sleep, Henchard
wakes up there the next morning, the tent is empty save
for 'a single big blue fly buzzing musically round and
round it'.² Elsewhere Hardy traces something like this
within the pattern of man-in-landscape : Grace Melbury,
now Mrs. Fitzpiers, watches her philandering husband
riding away and disappearing among all the colourful profusion of an autumn landscape ; but she recalls how the
fruits of harvest-time, usually sound, are sometimes unsound, and we see that Fitzpiers has his analogues in the
scenic environment.³ The inter-connection shows again
in a passage from *The Melancholy Hussar*, where Hardy
describes the loneliness and peace of a country scene in
earlier days : what sounds like the brushing of a visitor's
skirt is only a leaf in the wind, the apparent sound of a
carriage is really someone sharpening a sickle to trim the
garden where at dusk yew bushes look like real people.⁴
The ultimate effect of deliberately confusing human and
natural in this way is to make them seem, in essence, one
and the same. And in Tess, where more even than elsewhere Hardy sustains our sense of how the characters
belong to their landscape, there is a description which
draws together several of the features traced already. Angel
and Tess go walking in the country. Hardy carefully
builds up the kind of image which makes these walks
reveal his general sense of things ; the paths that the lovers
take naturally follow the valley streams, the babble of
water mingles with their talking, Nature is near enough
for them to observe its hidden oddities (the little foggy
shadows under trees in bright sunlight) ; and their shadows
in the setting sun stretch a quarter-mile before them over

¹ MC. 9. ² MC. 15.
³ W. 245-6. ⁴ *Wessex Tales*, 46-7.

the meadows, pointing at the distant hills that hem them in all round.[1]

There is an interesting remark in *Under the Greenwood Tree* which suggests that Hardy, in thus relating his characters to their environment, is making explicit something more or less to be seen in them always. The Mellstock Choir, on their first appearance, trudging uphill in the dusk, had 'lost their rotundity with the daylight, and advanced against the sky in flat outlines, which suggested some processional design on Greek or Etruscan pottery'.[2] Of set purpose, Hardy's characters often lack rotundity in a literary, figurative sense. Tess is 'an almost standard woman'; [3] she herself declares earnestly that 'your nature and your past doings have been just like thousands' and thousands', and . . . your coming life and doings'll be like thousands' and thousands'' too.[4] This concept was with Hardy almost at the beginning of his literary career: it is just what the brother and sister in *Desperate Remedies* overlook, and yet at a critical moment Hardy tells us that it is exactly true of them.[5] At least once, moreover, Hardy stresses that this is a quality which humans have in common with the rest of Nature; in *The Mayor of Casterbridge* the wayside bird sings a 'trite song' which 'might doubtless have been heard on the hill . . . at any sunset at that season for centuries untold'.[6] That some of Hardy's characters, like Diggory Venn, Gabriel Oak or Giles Winterbourne have little personal vitality has often been noticed; and the same is true in another way of Troy or Fitzpiers or Angel Clare or Jude, and of others too. But however much this may reduce their interest in isolation, it increases the power of these novels to give a single unified effect. Hardy's world does not easily breed heroic figures or men of dominant personality; and if, as with Michael Henchard, one is to be found in it, his strength of character is frustrated or negated at every turn — a trouble to others, and his own undoing.

Figurative language does much to convey Hardy's sense

[1] TD. 247.   [2] UGT. 5.   [3] TD. 114.
[4] TD. 162.   [5] DR. 13-14 and 137.   [6] MC. 3.

of man set in Nature. As in George Eliot, the man-and-
tree comparison turns up often ; sometimes — for example
in the assertion that affection between Grace and Fitzpiers
'grew as imperceptibly as the twigs budded on the trees',[1]
it has regard to the 'decorum' of a whole book, and thereby
sustains its atmosphere. It also implies that human
affairs illustrate the same necessitated slowness as the
affairs of Nature. Another commonplace metaphor, the
man-river comparison, is used by Hardy (as it was by
George Eliot) to convey the same notion : Tess and Clare
were 'converging, under an irresistible law, as surely as
two streams in one vale'.[2] These well-known comparisons
are not all that Hardy uses. Again like George Eliot, he
has some apparently sentimental images that are not sentimental, because of the doctrines they imply covertly.
Tess listens to Angel's harp 'like a fascinated bird' ; [3]
later Hardy says that she 'had been caught during her days
of immaturity like a bird in a springe'.[4] This is no vague
sentimentality, but an exact and insistent image to remind
us that when Tess was seduced at night in the wood, her
experience really was like that of an animal caught in a
trap — as might have happened in the very same place.
That Hardy is not interested in the pretty-pretty aspects
of bird-life is clear from his account of Marty South at
work bark-ripping : 'there she stood encaged amid a mass
of twigs and buds like a great bird, running her ripping-
tool into the smallest branches'.[5] If Nature's life is half-
human, human life for Hardy is half like that of birds and
animals.

Some other comparisons reinforce this impression, and
confirm that sense of the unexpected and bizarre which
runs through Hardy's portrait of man as of Nature. Tess
'was yawning, and he saw the red interior of her mouth as
if it had been a snake's' ; 'having been lying down in her
clothes [she] was as warm as a sunned cat' ; she is 'like a
plant in too burning a sun'.[6] As Eustacia laughs, the sun
shines into her mouth 'as into a tulip, and lent it a similar

scarlet fire'.[1] Earlier in the same novel a group of country-men 'marched in tail, like a travelling flock of sheep ; that is to say, the strongest first, the weak and young behind'.[2] Clym says that his life 'creeps like a snail'.[3] Jude, after his first meeting with Arabella 'felt as a snake must feel who has sloughed off its winter skin'.[4] But several of these metaphors do more than suggest a continuity between man and Nature, or an element of the bizarre in human life. Some of them — Tess like a cat, Tess or Jude like a snake — are potent in signifying the ultimate result of the casual moment they describe. They are *proleptic* images ; they hint at the whole determined sequence of things. Two comparisons in Tess bring this out with surprising clarity. Angel's interest in Tess is first established when he finds her and her three companion dairymaids in difficulties with the flooded highway, and 'clinging to the roadside bank like pigeons on a roof-slope'.[5] Hardy, at this very point, reinforces the dove-symbol by a detail in the scene : as Angel approaches, his gaze is captured by the innumerable flies and butterflies caught and imprisoned in the girls' gauzy skirts, 'caged in the transparent tissue as in an aviary'. (Hardy makes us see how in different ways both Angel and Tess are victims, each of the other.) Later in the novel the bird-sacrifice comes again. Tess in her misfortunes spends another night out in a wood, this time alone ; she hears the pheasants that have been wounded by shot fall one by one from the branches, and in the morning she *breaks their necks*.[6] There is another proleptic metaphor in *Tess*: Crick the dairyman is listening to Tess herself describe how she can day-dream her mind out of her body : he 'turned to her with his mouth full, his eyes charged with enquiry, and his great knife and fork . . . *planted erect on the table like the beginning of a gallows*'.[7] On every reading after the first, this comparison is incandescent ; surely it does more than any volume of generalities to fix in us Hardy's sense of the unalterable sequence of things.

Three other of Hardy's images must be noticed here ;

[1] RN. 104.   [2] RN. 15.   [3] RN. 379.   [4] JO. 47.
[5] TD. 183.   [6] TD. 355 (my italics).   [7] TD. 154 (my italics).

all of them reveal his sense of the expanse of the human environment. There is something of this in his description of Elfride on her horse, 'upon which she sat, alternately rising and sinking gently, like a seabird upon a sea-wave'; [1] unless we recognize that this image reinforces our sense of space, it seems barely apt. But the description of Henchard staring at the letter which tells him he has no daughter is more significant; he 'regarded the paper as if it were a window through which he saw for miles'.[2] Visual resemblance is slight; what matters is the image of vast space in which Henchard is isolated, and the suggestion of continuity in time indicated by a second comparison (space is like the future) within the first. Finally, a strange and vivid passage describing Tess and her dairymaid friends out walking seems to convey this sense of space, to imply the animality of humans, and in its closing words to suggest the sort of confusion among the constituents of Nature which might prompt us to see it as an organic unity: 'The girls drew onward . . . advancing with the bold grace of wild animals — the reckless unchastened motion of women accustomed to unlimited space — in which they abandoned themselves to the air as a swimmer to the wave'.[3]

(v) *Society, a Microcosm of Nature*

Hardy has one portrait of a self-sufficient human society, the town of Casterbridge in *The Mayor of Casterbridge*, which is so extraordinarily vivid and detailed that it is without rival in illustrating this section. Characteristically, the first account is of the town as it appears to Mrs. Henchard and her daughter at the end of their journey to it on foot. Hardy at once uses a pointed metaphor — 'it is shut in by a square wall of trees, like a plot of *garden ground* by a box-edging' [4] — and proceeds to deepen our sense of how the town is rooted in a tract of countryside: 'To birds of a more soaring kind' it is a mosaic of subdued reds,

---

[1] PBE. 351.   [2] MC. 143.   [3] TD. 223.

[4] MC. 30 (my italics). The main accounts of Casterbridge are to be found in MC. 30-32, 65 and 105.

browns, greys and crystals, in a frame of green. To the human eye it is 'set in the midst of miles of rotund down and concave field'. This, though, is merely the superficial aspect of an essential, organic interfusion between the town and its surroundings. 'Casterbridge was the complement of the rural life around; not its urban opposite.' Butterflies take a natural course down the high-street to reach the meadows beyond, thistle-down and dead leaves, in their seasons, float and drift everywhere among the buildings. Reapers at their work nod to townsmen at the street corner, and the bleating of sheep is heard in the court-room. In one street the barn-doors stand every few yards among the houses, the wheat ricks lean against the church tower; tufts of stonecrop and grass grow everywhere up the tower of the main church, almost to the battlements, so much have time and weather nibbled at the stonework. Even the shop-windows reveal the interdependence of town and country, for they are filled with scythes, bee-hives, milking-stools, harnesses, hedging-gloves, rural clothes, every variety of unexpected oddment that belongs to the life of the rustic and the countryside.

That in this there is something bizarre is not thoughtlessly read into the picture by a townsman; it is integral to Hardy's vision of the richness and variety of his subject. He gives a hint of it in his very first description, when Casterbridge seen indistinctly at evening gradually assumes the shapes of towers, gables and the rest, each building 'shining bleared and bloodshot with the coppery fire' from the setting sun. Tile roofs are patched with slate, slate with tiles; the clocks chime the hour one after another, in their distinctive singular ways, for minutes on end; painted figures on an inn signpost have become 'a half-invisible film upon the reality of the grain'; [1] over Lucetta's front door is a carved stone mask, chipped and broken away till it is ghastly and ludicrous; [2] as one walks up the high-street one sees right through the open front door of the houses 'as through tunnels' to the gardens behind, blazing with bright flowers. [3] Some of these flowers Hardy calls by their

---

[1] MC. 46.   [2] MC. 161.   [3] MC. 68.

country name 'bloody warriors'; and this seems to add a significant touch. For does it not associate in the reader's mind with the skeletons of tall Roman soldiers, curled in an oval scoop in the chalk like a chicken lying in its shell, and turning up everywhere in the town fields and gardens, or with the gladiators who fought in the Ring earthwork above the town, and whose cells, it is said, can still be traced?

Behind those bright flowers, too, can be seen the 'crusted grey stone-work remaining from a yet remoter Casterbridge'; and here Hardy conveys not only the long continuity of the town in history, but also the slow-changing and systematic quality of that succession. The earthwork [1] that used to be an amphitheatre for gladiators cannot throw off its tradition of violence and passion. For long it was the place for the town gallows and for witch-burnings; it still is for meetings that belong rather to the tragic side of life. Lovers avoid it, boys playing cricket have given up its mournful isolation. Its quality is fixed. The same systematic nature of change reveals itself in the two town bridges.[2] 'Every projection in each was worn down to obtuseness, partly by weather, more by friction from generations of loungers . . . even the flat faces were worn into hollows by the same mixed mechanism. . . .' Like the earthworks, these two bridges are also invested by now with a permanent emotional quality, and have their fixed and allotted place in the town's life as the known resort of all who fail or are disappointed in life. Hardy hints that it may be because this height over the flowing water is a part of man's environment which can offer what such men ultimately need. It is grim enough, perhaps, but there is something in Nature even for them. Finally, there is at least one metaphor to suggest the naturalness of the town : the sordid area of Mixen Lane is 'this mildewed leaf in the sturdy and flourishing Casterbridge plant'.[3]

Thus Casterbridge has all the qualities most prominent in Hardy's notion of Nature itself. It is easily the most comprehensive portrait of a human society in his work. But some of his other pictures of human society show the

[1] MC. 80-82.   [2] MC. 257.   [3] MC. 295.

same thing more emphatically, though less elaborately.
He often hints at what might be called the geography of
human relations, their extension in a slow-changing system
over a wide area of country. Over part of the cider-making
country in *The Woodlanders*, each farm has its own apple-
mill ; Grace, married now to Fitzpiers, finds Giles in the
yard of her hotel because he works through 'the margin of
Pomona's plain', the 'debatable land neither orchard nor
sylvan exclusively',[1] where he goes from place to place with
a movable cider-press. To our sense of the characters in
their landscape is added a sense of their system and
society. Greenhill Fair is 'the Nijni Novgorod of South
Wessex'.[2] Hardy describes how the sheep-flocks slowly
come, for perhaps a week before the Fair begins, from all
parts of the country and from all directions ; he indicates
the events that occur on the road, the varieties of the
sheep ; and he integrates all these details ingeniously to
make one great image of extending space. 'When the
autumn sun slanted over Greenhill this morning and
lighted the dewy flat upon its crest, nebulous clouds of
dust were to be seen floating between the pairs of hedges
which streaked the wide prospect around in all directions.
These gradually converged upon the base of the hill, and
the flocks became individually visible, climbing the serpent-
ine ways which led to the top. There, in slow procession,
they entered the opening to which the roads tended, multitude upon multitude. . . .'

Both *The Woodlanders* and *Far from the Madding
Crowd* sustain, throughout, this sense that human society
and its doings are distributed over a landscape. But this
impression probably emerges most clearly from two other
books, *The Return of the Native* and *Tess*. In the former
of these, the manner in which the various human dwellings
are scattered insignificantly across the all-enveloping Heath
is really never lost ; the very obscurity of Hardy's geography in this book reinforces it. In *Tess*, the two Valleys
and their surrounding uplands, the village of Clare's father,
Alec D'Urberville's home, and even the little seaside town

<hr />

[1] W. 209.   [2] FMC. 386.

where at last he lives with Tess, make a single integrated
landscape : to and fro over which Tess herself is really
harried, at a slowly increasing pace as the book goes on.
But it is important to notice that this landscape is not mere
geography, not a mere cat's-cradle of roads and places, but
a unity of soil and scenery and occupations that we see in
all its varieties of related life.   Ultimately, that is, Hardy
shows us South Wessex in this novel as, from the standpoint
of human society, a single organism.

The continuity of human affairs through time is prominent in Hardy.   There are other examples of this much
like the two bridges in *The Mayor of Casterbridge* — for
instance Bathsheba's great shearing-barn, with porches
high enough for a loaded grain-wagon, great stone but-
tresses, a magnificent roof of chestnut beams : 'the eye
regarded its present usage, the mind dwelt upon its past
history, with a satisfied sense of functional continuity
throughout — a feeling almost of gratitude, and quite of
pride, at the permanence of the idea which had heaped it
up'.[1]   Tess at Talbothay's Dairy finds the posts of the
milking-shed worn smooth by generations of cows ;[2]
Winterbourne in *The Woodlanders* hesitates on the doorstep
of Grace's house, and his fingers mechanically trace the
'timeworn letters' carved by 'gone generations of house-
holders'.[3]

The sense that these bygone generations still live in the
main characters of the novels also runs through much of
Hardy's work.   For him — as for George Eliot — the
quality of life is to be traced partly in human kinship.
Between Clym and his mother there is a deep bond of this
kind ; and at one point she recognizes him as he walks
over the Heath because, unaccountably at first, his gait
reminded her of her long-dead husband.[4]   The whole
plot of *The Mayor of Casterbridge* turns on Henchard's
deep need for kinship, and his deprivation of it.   He recalls

[1] FMC. 164-5. Cf. TD. 299, where Hardy writes that while the Cister-
cian abbey near where Angel and Tess spent their wedding night had
perished, 'creeds being transient', the mill still worked on, 'food being a
perennial necessity'.

[2] TD. 136.   [3] W. 51.   [4] RN. 328.

the ancient superstition that the ancestry of sleeping people is revealed in their faces, and creeps into his supposed daughter's bedroom at night : 'in sleep there come to the surface buried genealogical facts, ancestral curves, dead men's traits',[1] Hardy writes. Henchard, finding a plain message on the sleeping face, knows that he has no child. In *The Woodlanders* it is largely Grace's father who pushes her on, first to atone for what he did as a young man, and then to ignore this debt that she was to pay on his behalf. The link between Tess and her remote kin, the dead knights and ladies of the D'Urbervilles, is never wholly put out of sight. We are not, of course, invited to share Angel's naïve and inconsistent attitude to it ; but though it does not mechanically determine Tess's whole person-ality, it roots her in the historical life of where she is. It is, in fact, a local trait ; the parson who first breaks the doubt-ful news to Tess's father tells him that other local families have passed from power to obscurity, and one of Tess's companion dairy-maids is an example.[2] In *Jude the Obscure* the continuity of kinship is perhaps even more prominent, as we watch Jude and Sue running constantly into trouble both through the unnoticed impress of their heredity, and their confused consciousness of it. In *The Well-Beloved*, the continuity and subtle change of kinship is the central fact, and it is more closely focused upon a locality than in any other of the novels.

That Hardy saw kinship as important is sometimes confirmed by novels where it cannot be said to lend sub-stance to an integrated view of life. In *A Laodicean*, for example, De Stancy's tangled relations with his illegitimate son produce a good deal of the action, and his desire to get back the ancestral home for his family produces most of the rest. In *Desperate Remedies*, the ultimate key to the action is Miss Aldclyffe's desire to marry her illegitimate son to the daughter of her first lover. In *A Pair of Blue Eyes* the salient fact is that Elfride cannot marry Stephen Smith because his father is an artisan in her own village. Hardy in this is rather unlike George Eliot, for he rarely

MC. 144.   [2] TD. 164.

suggests that these ties of kinship are the focal points of duty. That is not his interest. What matters is that they control the individual in fact, and show once more how human society is a microcosm of Nature.

The varied, the unexpected, the bizarre in human life has been often noticed in Hardy; it could scarcely have been overlooked. Much that in a cursory or light reading might please by its quaint charm is taken from the fanciful customs or superstitions of Wessex peasantry. But these fanciful incidents prove on more serious reading to have a deeper meaning. Hardy is not exploiting them as oddities pure and simple; each is odd if thought of by itself, but all together they are the kind of things which for him largely constitutes the day-to-day pattern of life. They are integral to Hardy's general picture, and they are analogous to that element of the bizarre which he traces outside human life in the complexity of nature. This well illustrates how the outlook of a writer is not the sum of his abstractions, but how he interprets them. The abstractions of George Eliot and Hardy about the general course of things are to some extent similar. But their picture of life is totally different. In one Necessity suggests a bracing drabness; in the other a sometimes dreamlike inconsequentiality.

In most of the 'Novels of Character and Environment', odd customs, occupations, superstitions and so on are common. In *The Return of the Native* there is the strange figure of the reddleman, the heath bonfires of 5th November and their scarcely human attendants, the mummers' play, Eustacia pricked with a needle in church as a witch, an eclipse of the moon, the extraordinary scene where Wildeve and the reddleman, surrounded by a ring of heath ponies, gamble at night on the heath by glow-worm-light, the village gipsying, the incident of the wax image and the pins, and the picturesque Maypole scene.[1] In *The Wood-landers* there is the strange reunion between Grace and Giles as he stands in the market-place with a grown apple-tree that he is selling upright in his hand, Grace's going to Fitzpiers to persuade him not to insist on taking Grammer

[1] RN. 9, 15 f., 141 f., 209, 229, 270 f., 306, 423, 459.

Oliver's dead body for dissection, and the superstitious festivities of Old Midsummer Eve.[1] There are one or two such things in *Far from the Madding Crowd* — Gabriel pricking the sheep distended from eating clover, or playing on his flute like a pastoral shepherd, or the Harvest Home festival.[2] In *The Mayor of Casterbridge* there is the wife-selling, and the vivid account of how Henchard seeks advice of the weather-prophet in his remote cottage.[3] *The Trumpet Major* has at least two such incidents, the Aeolian harp Bob makes for Anne, and the strange weather-beaten weather-vane, painted with the Miller's soldier son on one side and his sailor son on the other, that, as it spins round and round, symbolizes all that happens in the story.[4]

There are similar oddities in *Tess* — Tess herself pricking her finger on one of Alec's roses, the moonlight haloes that surround the heads of her fellow-workers as they walk home through the dew and darkness, the strange diabolical figure of the engine-man in the threshing-scene at Flintcomb-Ash.[5] Each of these, again, is a symbol. There is, too, the sleep-walking scene where Angel lays Tess in the stone coffin by the abbey (which no one, perhaps, finds very satisfactory), and Tess's final sleep, before her capture, upon the stone of sacrifice at Stonehenge.[6] It should perhaps be said, in justice to Hardy, that although this scene may fail, he did a good deal to make Tess, in her last days, a symbolic and archetypal figure — in the sleep-walking scene, in many details, several of which have been mentioned, and also when she swears on the stone not to be a temptation to Alec. He, indeed, thinks her vow is made on a wayside cross; but in fact it is on a prehistoric monolith or a memorial to a devil-worshipper who was executed there.[7] These are only a few examples of the kind of scene which Hardy introduces frequently; the problem is to see how they are integrated with, and profoundly qualify, his whole picture of what human affairs are like.

[1] W. 40, 114, 171.   [2] FMC. 156-61, 275-80.
[3] MC. 214-15.   [4] TM. 12.   [5] TD. 50, 84, 415.
[6] TD. 315-18, 503-5.   [7] TD. 396-8.

Quite frequently, though for the most part only in a passing phrase, Hardy suggests that all these events make up one great system of necessity. 'The next slight touch in the shaping of Clym's destiny occurred a few days later',[1] he writes. The troubles that threatened Tess while she was happy with Angel might, as she knew, 'be receding, or they might be approaching, one or the other, a little every day'.[2] When Tess is seduced, and when her family is evicted, Hardy reminds us that when her ancestors were landowners they were doubtless the oppressors often enough, and comments 'so do flux and reflux — the rhythm of change — alternate and persist in everything under the sky'.[3]

Hardy's figurative language reinforces this point : he often draws metaphors from science, sometimes very much like those of George Eliot. The little coil of Fanny Robin's hair that Troy carried in his watch is 'the fuse' that led to the explosion destroying his marriage.[4] Alec D'Urberville is 'the blood-red ray in the spectrum of Tess's life'.[5] The inhabitants of Talbothays dairy begin to differentiate themselves to Clare 'as in a chemical process'.[6] Boldwood's passionate inner nature might have been guessed from 'old floodmarks faintly visible',[7] though the high tides that made them have receded ; Tess and Clare come together 'like two streams in one vale' ;[8] Fitzpiers remarks that lonely people 'get charged with emotive fluid like a Leyden jar with electric'.[9] If it is not studied too much, there is also one quite complex metaphor which belongs to this class : if thought over with any care its chief effect is, I fear, delighted incredulity. It concerns the 'drops of logic' which Tess lets fall as 'crystallized phrases' into 'the sea of [Alec's] enthusiasm', and thereby 'chills' its 'effervescence' to 'stagnation'.[10] Not much, perhaps, can be claimed for this, as conveying system in human life or elsewhere.

The sense that human events move on slowly but irre-

[1] RN. 224. [2] TD. 249-50. [3] TD. 91, 448. [4] FMC. 378.
[5] TD. 47. [6] TD. 152. [7] FMC. 138. [8] TD. 165.
[9] W. 138. [10] TD. 413.

sistibly to their appointed conclusion is important in Hardy,
because it produces one of the two rather different kinds of
irony in things which he portrays. Ironical situations —
the faded weather-vane in the Miller's garden, Tess's vow
on the roadside stone, Fitzpiers happening to meet Suke
Damson's wedding procession, Tess wringing the necks of
the wounded pheasants [1] — are a reflection in Hardy's work
of the bizarre variety of things. But much more important,
because having to do with the whole span of one novel after
another, is the irony that lies in the long-term consequences
of human actions. For example, in *A Pair of Blue Eyes*
the crucial event is Elfride's jilting Stephen for Henry, and
this is brought about by her dutifully going to watch the
packet-boat as it brings Stephen back to her from India.
The Mayor of Casterbridge ultimately becomes a workman
to Farfrae through trying to tyrannize over Farfrae his
employee. Eustacia marries Clym to escape the Heath,
and finds that he is devoted to it; while Clym in part
marries her because he thinks she could help in his pro-
jected school, which is the last thing she would or could do.
In *The Woodlanders*, Melbury's ambition to have Grace
marry well only unites her to a wastrel; Felice Charmond,
exacting revenge on Giles for his rudeness, finds that by
making him a poor man she has thrown her own lover into
Grace's arms; and the horse that Giles gives Grace as a
present is ultimately the means both of saving Fitzpiers
his rival from a fatal accident, and of carrying him on his
adulterous visits to Felice. Tess's early misfortunes result
from her mother's ambitions to have her marry well;
Angel marries the fallen Tess in quest, we are told, of rural
innocence; and in confiding his sceptical opinions to her,
he ultimately makes possible her return to D'Urberville.
Avice Caro, in *The Well-Beloved*, thinks that she is being
broad-minded and modern in refusing to take part in the
betrothal ceremony traditional in the island, and by this
sets in motion the deep forces of loyalty to the island that
dominate her lover's whole life and persist long after her
own has ended. One novel after another, that is to say,

[1] TM. 12; TD. 396; W. 408; TD. 353.

testifies over its whole development to the existence, and to the quality, of a determined system of things which ultimately controls human affairs without regard for human wishes.

(vi) *The Human Deviation*

George Eliot and Disraeli were both novelists who in one form or another believed in heroic actions. For Hardy the heroic deed is barely possible; and since this is so, the moral outlook he expresses is a good deal less overt and emphatic than theirs. In his view, wise or right conduct can never be spectacular, and dramatic exhortations to pursue it simply fail to recognize life's major determinants. His values tend as a result not usually to be obtrusive in the novels; but all the same one book after another quietly embodies them. The single abstraction which does most to summarize Hardy's view is simple enough: *it is right to live naturally*. But this is the abstraction central to any number of moralities; Hardy glosses it by showing how to live naturally is to live in continuity with one's whole biological and geographical environment. The earlier parts of this chapter have shown what he thought this is like, and what human society is like when in continuity with it. The remaining problems are of what he sees as the significant kinds of unnatural behaviour, and whether his details add anything to our sense of what constitutes accepting our environment and living as part of it.

Accepting our environment is not, for Hardy, any grandiose, Carlylean gesture of *Entsagung*, and is also not passive submission. It is unobtrusive and unambitious like his whole scale of values, but it is not nothing; human choice can exert some influence at least on the course of things, simply by working with and not against it. Henchard's daughter 'had learnt the lesson of renunciation . . . yet her experience had consisted less in a series of pure disappointments than in a series of substitutions'. Ultimately her life is teaching others 'the secret . . . of making limited opportunities endurable; which she deemed to consist in the cunning enlargement, by a species of microscopic treatment, of those minute forms of satisfaction that offer themselves to everybody not in positive pain'.[1] Sue Bridehead's 'but self-abnegation is the higher road. We should mortify the flesh — the terrible flesh. . . . Self-renunciation — that's everything! I cannot humiliate myself too much'[2] is clearly 'placed' by Hardy as the latest aberration of an irredeemable neurotic. Had they used the same terms, Carlyle and Hardy would have seen 'somnambulism' in more or less opposite places.

Hardy does not portray any great range of admirable characters, and makes no attempt to portray what many people regard as the more complex or sophisticated kinds of excellence. There are plenty of approximations to Caleb Garth in his work, but no Maggies, no Dorotheas, no Ladislaws, no Felix Holts. Perhaps Hardy saw things in unrealistically simple terms; but it seems truer to say that he had the more formed (and controversial) view of what was basically the ideal mode of life for man, while George Eliot was more definite about the principles of moral choice valid within any life one happened to be leading. Hardy's admiration is really whole-hearted for one kind of life and one only. It is fairly clear that he saw intellectual culture as at root a trouble to human happiness (though he seems to have regarded its growth as inevitable in his own time). Clym Yeobright's features 'showed that thought is a disease of the flesh'.[3]

The people whom Hardy presents in an altogether sympathetic light are like Gabriel Oak, Diggory Venn and Giles Winterbourne — all solid sterling characters completely satisfied with their position in life and at one with it. Their only misfortunes are in love, and they endure them with resignation and calm. They all have a sense of humour and they all have simple country pleasures — Gabriel his flute, Diggory his practical jokes, Giles his little 'randy' for the Melburys. Marty South and Elizabeth-Jane Henchard are women rather of the same basic kind; Farfrae in *The Mayor of Casterbridge* is not dissimilar, though rendered more obtuse perhaps by his commercial life;

[1] MC. 205, 385.   [2] JO. 416-17.   [3] RN. 162.

Loveday and Crick the dairyman at Talbothays are men like Gabriel or Giles, but placed in more amenable circumstances so that we see less of their deeper nature. The minor rustic characters in what have been called Hardy's 'choruses' are the same too — genial, kindly, content with their station in life, resigned to disappointments, and never without a touch of humour. Hardy calls them 'the philosophic party'.[1] One of them is the only person entirely loyal to Henchard. Tess's dairymaid companions at Talbothays have the same good qualities, taking it for granted that Angel will not marry one of them, free of ill-feeling for Tess when he chooses her, and true to her through her later misfortunes. All these characters live in that continuity with their environment which for Hardy is the one root of a right life.

His whole concept of good and bad follows these lines, and is perfectly simple : people are to be admired as they have continuity with nature more or less completely, and those whom he stresses as on a false track in life are those who have lost it, and pursue some private self-generated dream instead. Among the latter is Henry Knight, who cannot abide the thought that his fiancée was kissed before he met her : 'the moral rightness of this man was worthy of all praise ; but . . . Knight had in him a modicum of that wrong-headedness which is most found in scrupulously honest people. With him, truth seemed too clean and pure an abstraction to be so hopelessly churned in with error as practical persons find it.' Elfride puts Hardy's own point of view when she says, 'I almost wish you were of a grosser nature, Harry . . . where the lover or husband is not fastidious, and refined, and of a deep nature, things seem to go on better'.[2] Angel Clare's susceptibilities, and his mistakes, were rather similar : 'some might risk the odd paradox that with more animalism he might have been the nobler man. We do not say it. Yet Clare's love was doubtless ethereal to a fault, imaginative to impracticability.'[3] Hardy, in effect, *was* 'saying it'. Clym Yeobright, Jude, and Jocelyn Pierston (*The Well-Beloved*) also

[1] MC. 355.   [2] PBE. 390, 343.   [3] TD. 312.

pursue impossible ideals. Clym's notion of a night-school to raise the heath-dwellers at one step to the heights of philosophical cultivation is the result of a 'disproportion' of mind. ''Tis good-hearted of the young man', a rustic neighbour observes, 'but, for my part, I think he had better mind his business.'[1] Jude, a village boy and a stone-mason's assistant, dreams of becoming an Oxford scholar; he and Clym make just the same mistake, one for others, and one for himself. At the end of the novel the now disillusioned Jude sees that he was trying to do in one generation something for which the natural course of things allots two or three;[2] and earlier on he briefly glimpses the truth. 'For a moment there fell on Jude a true illumination, that here in the stone-yard was a centre of effort as worthy as that dignified by the name of scholarly study. . . . But he lost it under stress of his old idea. . . . This was his form of the modern vice of unrest.'[3]

Examples of the wrong course of life among Hardy's women follow the same pattern. Sue Bridehead, Grace Melbury and Elfride, in their different ways, have a dream of the higher intellectual life; Eustacia and Felice Charmond dream of the higher passions; Fancy Day is a more venial offender, and dreams childishly for a moment of the higher income. Ultimately we see them learning of their error or sensing their false position. Ethelberta dreams of riches too, and 'My God, what a thing am I !', she exclaims in a moment of self-knowledge (induced, one is sorry to say, by a donkey's disapproving stare).[4] Grace Melbury says, 'I wish you had never thought of educating me. I wish I worked in the woods like Marty South ! I hate genteel life . . . cultivation has only brought me inconveniences and troubles . . . I have never got any happiness outside Hintock that I know of.'[5] Felice Charmond at one point exactly senses her deficiencies : 'I am the most inactive woman when I am here . . . I think sometimes I was born to do nothing, nothing but float about, as we

---

[1] RN. 202.   [2] JO. 393.   [3] JO. 98.
[4] HE. 264.   [5] W. 267.

fancy we do sometimes in dreams. But that cannot be my destiny.'[1]

Hardy always sees evil setting in at this very point. The great disaster for an individual is to be *déraciné*. Perhaps, if Tess has a weakness, it is what she has in common with the dreamers. At the vital moment in the novel when Angel first catches sight of her, she is telling how 'our souls can be made to go outside our bodies when we are alive' by staring at a bright star in the darkness. Hardy brings this 'fancy' up against the kindly dairyman's down-to-earth amazement; and Tess goes significantly on to say 'you will soon find that you are hundreds and hundreds o' miles from your body, which you don't seem to want at all',[2] reminding us for a moment of the price she will ultimately pay for her dream-world spirituality. But Hardy makes plain, on the other hand, where Tess is likely to be at her strongest: 'All the while she wondered if any strange good thing might come of her being in her ancestral land; and some spirit within her rose automatically as the sap in the twigs'.[3]

Angel, on the other hand is a *déraciné* who partially and temporarily takes root again. His religious scruples and the narrow tradition of his family cut him off from the university *milieu* relatively natural to a man of his type, and his life begins at that point to become disorganized and aimless. At the dairy he lives as a solitary at first; but he slowly joins in the life of the group and comes to belong to it. He begins to like outdoor life, to see the variety and richness of simple human nature, to shake off the 'chronic melancholy' of sceptical civilization. He finds that the creed of his own family is narrow and abstract and ignores the complexities of the real world; and in commenting upon his fuller insight into life Hardy makes an important juxtaposition. 'He grew away from old associations, and saw something new in life and humanity. Secondarily, he made close acquaintance with phenomena which he had before known but darkly — the seasons in their moods, night and noon . . . water and mists . . . and the voices of

[1] W. 68.   [2] TD. 154.   [3] TD. 127.

inanimate nature.' [1]   Angel is acquiring the kind of wisdom
that the sage can teach in part; but Hardy points also to
its ultimate source.

That the bad is essentially the rootless insinuates itself
sometimes into Hardy's scenes and descriptions. Tess, at
work in the reaping field has 'the charm which is acquired
by woman when she becomes part and parcel of outdoor
nature, and is not merely an object set down therein'.[2]
In contrast to this scene — or to the town of Casterbridge
— is the *parvenu* Alec D'Urberville's mansion: 'a country-
house built for enjoyment pure and simple . . . which rose
like a geranium against the subdued colours around . . .
everything on this snug property was bright, thriving, and
well kept'.[3]   And in the tragic scene of her confession to
Angel, Tess is deliberately placed in an alien and hostile
setting: she is surrounded by the portraits of her by now
irrelevant ancestors, she is wearing Angel's family jewels.
Hardy emphasizes how 'all material objects around an-
nounced their irresponsibility with terrible iteration'.[4]

Finally, it is true that the whole trend of one novel after
another portrays this same scale of values. To adapt one's
life to one's traditional situation is good, to uproot oneself
for material ends is bad, to do so for romantic passion or an
abstract ideal is if anything worse. *Under the Greenwood
Tree* has a happy conclusion along these lines. *Far from
the Madding Crowd* shows a return to stability after aban-
doning these values has brought tragedy. Throughout
The Well-Beloved, Jocelyn's right course is to return to
his island world; though this he can never do until at the
very end he marries Marcia — his infatuation for whom
in youth was what cut him off from home. Most of the
novels recount how tragedy sooner or later results from the
attempt to abandon the natural pattern of things in pursuit
of the dream. In *A Pair of Blue Eyes*, the disaster comes
because both Elfride and Henry are infatuated with empty
intellectual ideals; in *Two on a Tower* the tragic situation
is implicit in Swithin, the country lad who wants to be
Astronomer Royal. *The Return of the Native, The Wood-*

---

[1] TD. 150-3, 305.   [2] TD. 111.   [3] TD. 43.   [4] TD. 291.

landers, *Tess* and *Jude* are all novels where the catastrophe
comes through evading the established and natural order
for the sake of one illusion or another; and whatever is
saved from the wreck — the marriage of Thomasin and
Venn, for example, though contrary to Hardy's own
original plan, or Angel's union with Tess's sister, though
forced and hurried — is in one way or another a reversion
to that natural order.

There is one novel which actually illustrates this bias
in Hardy's work, though to begin with it seems plainly to
contravene it. This is *The Hand of Ethelberta*. The only
parts of this book which can in the least be taken seriously
are the hints that Ethelberta's social climbing is corrupting
her whole family ('O, this false position, it is ruining your
nature, my too thoughtful mother!' she melodramatically
exclaims herself at one point [1] — and her youngest brother
says, 'We be all Fashion's slave' to justify adopting the
vices of a fashionable servant [2]). That Ethelberta's course
is basically wrong shows plainly throughout. Her ultimate
marriage to Lord Montclere is just defaulting on Hardy's
part; but he makes a gesture to restore the integrity of
the book by recounting, in its last pages, how Ethelberta
has been transformed from upstart literary lioness to
improving territorial landlord. It is a travestied and Dis-
raelian solution, but noticing its direction is of interest,
for it confirms the general trend of the Hardy plot.

(vii) *Conclusion*

When Hardy's view of life is really seen in its full extent
and detail it appears at least as comprehensive and rich
in content as that of anyone else discussed in this book,
or perhaps any other English writer in the century. This
is not necessarily to say that it is true, or to deny that in
virtually dispensing with the higher life of the intellect or
emotion it was not defective; it is merely to say that Hardy
has an unusually detailed, developed, idiosyncratic picture
of what the world is like, how the human species is placed

[1] HE. 292.   [2] HE. 143.

in it, and how by consequence that species ought to live. But only a smallish minority of the novels actually display this picture more or less completely. Hardy's fourteen longer stories may be divided into two groups, the seven 'Novels of Character and Environment' and the seven other novels. Of these latter seven, none (except *A Pair of Blue Eyes* in the cliff scene, which stands quite by itself) has more than a glimpse of what might be called Hardy's cosmology, his view of the world and of man's situation; and only three do much to develop what might be called Hardy's 'rule of life'. These are *A Pair of Blue Eyes*, *The Hand of Ethelberta* and *The Well-Beloved*; and, as Hardy knew, all of them are slight and perfunctory to a greater or lesser degree.

There remain the seven better-known novels. But although all of these are serious and sustained works of literary art, it is important to see that not all of them mediate Hardy's view of things in anything like its fullness. *Under the Greenwood Tree*, clearly enough, is altogether more limited in scope than the others. But *The Mayor of Casterbridge* is rather distinctive too. It certainly creates and sustains Hardy's picture of nature, and especially man in nature; but his characteristic beliefs about what is good and bad in human life do not really appear. Except in a very strained sense, there are no intellectual or romantic dreamers, no conflicts between life in accordance with nature and the life of the *déraciné*, no thrusts at modernity. This is not, of course, in the least to condemn either novel; the poise and artistry of *Under the Greenwood Tree* is generally accepted, and it is probably what is absent from *The Mayor of Casterbridge* which gives it a power and economy and integration unique in Hardy, and makes it artistically his best work. But it simply remains true that his characteristic rule of life is not prominent in it.

In *Jude*, on the other hand, it is certainly prominent; but this novel too does not fully represent Hardy, because the other part of his outlook is almost entirely absent. There is in this book no background at all of nature or of a harmonious common life in accord with it. Hardy

portrays a whole world of *déracinés* — a neurotic woman
intellectual who paints ecclesiastical figures, an artisan who
aspires to learning, a barmaid, an eccentric schoolmaster —
who hurry from town to town in trains, or live isolated in
inns and extemporized lodgings. It is this very restriction
of scope which makes the book so much more agitated and
bitter than Hardy's others. All rectifying stabilities have
dropped out of sight; and nothing is left but a frustrated
aggregate of querulous and disorientated individuals. We
might say that this novel and *The Mayor of Casterbridge*
are complementary. Each gives expression only to half of
Hardy's whole view of life. It is in *Far from the Madding
Crowd*, *The Return of the Native*, *The Woodlanders*, and
Tess of the D'Urbervilles that the 'impression' must be
sought in its completeness; whether or not we prefer the
books, and whether or not we like the impression, this is
where it is.

CHAPTER IX

CONCLUSION

THIS chapter can be a short one. Its purpose is not to elicit, from the evidence supplied by the rest of the book, some ingenious single answer solving the whole problem of what 'the' sage is doing and how he does it. There is no such answer; rather as there is none which explains the ambitions or methods of 'the' poet. The seven previous chapters are not evidence for one theory. They are seven separate studies of writers who, though pursuing among other things the sage's own distinctive task, did so, all of them to a greater or lesser degree, by the essentially individualist methods of the artist. There is scarcely a need to do anything at this stage except, quite briefly, make certain points which may set their work in a clearer light.

Although it was mentioned earlier, one thing of general importance needs comment again. This is the danger that lies in accumulating a large body of evidence, consisting in part of small, detailed points, and taken sometimes from several quite different books, without thinking sufficiently of the fact that what ultimately counts is not each item seen alone, but the integrated effect of those which are fused into the unity of a particular discussion or a particular book. But this risk is run in every discussion of work where the meaning of the whole is more than that of the parts, or of any author where certain distinctive things recur from one book to another, but where in each book they have a separate and distinctive life. There are two reasons why, in the present case, it is a risk that is clearly worth running.

First, the material brought together here is not brought together very often. Philosophers glance at some of it, and critics select from the rest. Therefore anything which, by setting the individual pieces of evidence side by side, thereby shows the small but genuine impact of each, is worth doing. Second, it is probably true that while many of the novels which this book discusses (and also Carlyle's *French Revolution*) are closely integrated and sustained, and dominate their details by some clear and all-embracing quality, this is much less true of most of the discursive works. In these, the single argument which proceeds through control over meaning, the single vivid illustrative incident, the single character sketch or even metaphor, probably have something nearer to an independent existence. The sage's discursive essay has a loose and easy unity; and the risk that this book runs of filling the reader's mind with disorganized fragments in the place of a unified original, is at least less than that which critics regularly take with novels or poetry.

If the reader, with these two things in mind, wishes to see some particularly striking example of how the details in a discursive book can grow together to form a continuous tissue, one brief chapter in Newman may provide what he needs. This is the *General Answer to Mr. Kingsley*, at the end of the *Apologia pro Vita sua*. It is one of the few places where Newman gives anything like a comprehensive account of life and the world; and it is very striking that every fresh turn in the discussion displays one or other of the features examined in the chapter on Newman above. Every more personal touch helps to control the complex tone, every metaphor or example means more than one thinks at first glance, every piece of apparently negative evidence is transformed into positive, every detail of the argument is represented as naturally part of a great system of thought. Moreover, there is nothing else into which these turns of presentation have to fit. They are the staple of the argument; they make it; they create the homogeneity to which they belong.

This is important, and it applies to the other writers too. Within the details that the previous chapters have brought together there is already an organization whereby the smaller points depend on the larger ones. The luxuriant metaphors of Carlyle, for example, do not occur in a patternless profusion. Most of them are organized upon that single basic contrast between the sham and the true to which they largely give meaning, but from which they simultaneously draw a support for themselves. It is this same basic contrast, too, around which are grouped the arguments where Carlyle changes the meanings of words. Each of these employs the same underlying contrast: which the particular argument both depends on, and once again confirms. Carlyle himself put the word 'real' or 'sham' into many of these arguments, and all the rest seem ready to welcome either one of those terms or the other. Similarly, it is the whole optimistic trend of the typical Disraeli novel which permits the engaging sequence of events creating his motley sparkling world; and it is the ultimate trend of each novel towards stability when the hero becomes a territorial magnate, which strings together the various examples of traditionalism throughout the story. George Eliot's characters argue with each other in a language which controls the meanings of the terms they use; but this is not something fortuitous, for it grows out of their distinctive personalities as these develop throughout a whole novel.

Verbal argument in Newman, and the turns of sense that Arnold gives by means of his value frames, are the same. They flow naturally from the tone which both writers try to sustain from beginning to end of their books. They fall into place as the natural modes in which writers like these would hope to express themselves. And in Hardy it is the deep irony at the heart of the story, shown in the movement of the whole plot, which provides the frame for what is ironical or bizarre or unpredictable in the smaller points. These are only a few examples of how in part this book has already discussed what integrates the materials it has examined. There is not something beyond this material which unites it, so much as a relation between its parts whereby they depend on each other.

Though all six writers adopt the same kind of task, they do not all range equally widely. Carlyle cheerfully takes the whole cosmos for his subject. Newman in fact does the same, but his main emphasis falls only on the nature of human life and more still on how it may be organized socially in religious institutions. Hardy gives a somewhat wider picture: the life of man and the character of his immediate natural environment. The same might be said of George Eliot, though she rarely moves beyond strictly human matters; and Disraeli never does. Arnold's field is narrower still. He barely sketches a view of how men live in the world, and in the main he seeks to bring alive for his readers only one part of human behaviour, that which comprises the formation of opinion, and the actions which flow from opinion. And the moral preoccupations of these sages vary also. For all of them, some concept of how mankind should aim or hope to live is a consequence of what they think the world is like; and they insist more or less vehemently on their views, according to the quality of their whole philosophy. But Disraeli and Hardy insist much less than the others, the former partly because his work is all in all the least serious, but chiefly because his sanguine outlook makes him see less need to insist on virtue with passionate seriousness, and the latter because he is at the other extreme, and for him any great insistence on how man should live is likely to be wasted effort.

But in spite of such differences, there are similarities between these writers which confirm the view that they have a common basic intention. Some of these were mentioned in Chapter I, where the sages' common concern with their special task and their special modes of expression was discussed. It is interesting, for example, to notice how four of these six authors refer explicitly — the novelists in the manner appropriate to them — to that seeing more widely or more deeply into life which it is the sage's peculiar gift to give. Carlyle's assertion that we shall 'find ourselves in a world greatly widened' (see p. 21) is re-echoed when Tancred exclaims 'life is stranger than I deemed' (p. 88), or when for Gwendolen Harleth 'the world seemed getting larger' (p. 134), or when Angel Clare 'saw something new in life and humanity' (p. 285)

and Tess was 'viewing life from its inner side'.[1] Each
novelist opens the eyes of a character as a means of opening
those of his readers. It is also significant that both Carlyle
and Newman have discussions or assertions giving a fuller
and richer sense to the word 'life' (pp. 50, 199). But
besides these indications of the sage's basic task, there are
also several interesting resemblances among the detailed
methods.

In Carlyle, for example, biblical diction without direct
quotations created a certain persuasive effect (pp. 23-6).
George Eliot first uses just the same device, in writing
that Dorothea had the impressiveness of a fine quotation
from the Bible, without saying which quotation ; and then
later she explains the very process of thought upon which
this account relies, when she says that Caleb Garth was
haunted by biblical phraseology, though not any particular
biblical phrase, when he has a sense of *awe* (pp. 131, 133).
Mention of Caleb reminds one that most of these writers —
not only the novelists — introduce characters to speak for
the author's own opinions. Hardy makes Tess tell Angel
how their lives are like those of thousands of others in the
past and future ; George Eliot, besides Caleb, has Adam ;
Arnold has Arminius, Disraeli has Sidonia, Carlyle makes
use of Cromwell (p. 27 n). The novelists, and also Carlyle
as historian, have something else in common. They can
use the physical appearance of their characters to indicate
a clear moral significance, as can be seen with many of the
protagonists in *Frederick the Great*, with the description of
Dorothea referred to just now, or with Hardy's account of
Clym Yeobright's thought-drawn face.

Both Newman and Arnold take extreme care to control
the tone in which they write, and among many more
general resemblances it so happens that they both take
themselves humorously as examples of being in some
unfortunate predicament (pp. 165, 241) — though Arnold
uses his example for ironic as well as direct effect. And
there is also a close parallel between them in how each
emphasizes the mistaken tone of his opponents. Arnold

[1] TD. 216.

reproaches them for their coarse and indiscriminate method, and their failure to reconsider their views when this is urgently necessary (p. 209). Newman clinches his argument against the Pope's critics by saying that they are 'peremptory and sweeping' in their utterance (p. 175). Both authors, that is, insist that we recognize how a false tone betrays a false view.

There are also certain noticeable parallels in the use of figurative language by these authors. Both George Eliot and Hardy have apparently sentimental metaphors — Mirah like a rose, Tina like a fledgling bird, Tess like a pigeon — which in fact are not merely sentimental, but covertly show how the characters fit into the scheme of things (pp. 148-9, 269-70). Carlyle, George Eliot and Newman all use successions of metaphors to sustain the dominant atmosphere of what they are writing — the first in his menagerie of animals, or frequent passing references to flowery spaces and green landscapes (pp. 29, 32); the second in, for example, the agricultural images of *Silas Marner* or the scientific and medical images of *Middlemarch* (pp. 151, 152); and Newman in the open-air touches of the Fourth University *Discourse* (p. 187-8). And both Disraeli and George Eliot have one example of an idea that contributes once as a metaphor and once as an incident — the improving landlord's estate which Disraeli so often describes, but to which he once likens the whole body politic (p. 93), and in George Eliot the river from which, as it flows into the sea, there is at length no more jumping ashore [1] (p. 148; and compare also Carlyle, p. 67).

There is one further point of detail which is perhaps worth mentioning. It is that, when the evidence is reviewed, one can easily see how re-defining terms explicitly, and changing their senses implicitly by all the examples or

---

[1] There seems to be a difference between these two cases, where the *example* and the *illustration* are of the same point, and the incident in Hardy of pricking a wax figure with pins, which perhaps also appears elsewhere as a metaphor (p. 258). Here, if the incident contributes anything to the general picture, it is a sense of the bizarre, and if the comparison is really a significant one, of which it is hard to be sure, it hints not at the bizarre but at the vengeful in Nature.

incidents which make up a novel, are really two very
similar processes. 'Nature is *preter*natural', writes
Carlyle in one sweeping gesture (p. 50); Angel Clare
'made close acquaintance with phenomena which he had
before known but darkly . . . inanimate nature', Hardy
says quietly (p. 285). Yet the detailed accounts of inanimate
nature which he gives everywhere through his novels,
while of course they do not change our concept of nature
in the direction which Carlyle wishes to take, change it
nevertheless, and change it at least as effectively. Hardy
might perhaps have made something like his main points
by attempting to re-define words like 'strange' (just as
Carlyle re-defined 'miraculous') or 'natural' or 'idealistic'
and so on. Newman shows both methods clearly: he
argues formally about the meaning of the word 'life'
when used of the Catholic Church, and he also makes use
of a mass of vivid detail which realizes this life for his
readers in concrete and particular form. More cursorily,
Disraeli does the same. When he writes 'life . . . is
monotonous only to the monotonous', or 'life . . . is the
great wonder' (p. 102), he employs brief re-defining
formulas. But they are illustrated by nothing less than
the sequence of events practically throughout all his
novels.

This affinity between the verbal argument and the
collection of descriptions is extremely significant. Though
apparently a mere technical detail, it reveals the essence
of what these writers are doing, and it shows why their
work is always likely to contain at least an element of
genuineness, however much it may look at first sight like
extravagance or sleight of hand. The sage's abstractions,
his formal and verbal arguments, his logic-chopping,
always can and often do lead on to something realler and
richer. His aim is to make his readers see life and the
world over again, see it with a more searching, or perhaps
a more subtle and sensitive gaze. His essential equipment
is some insight that is abnormally keen. He utilizes what
Pater called 'that sort of philosophical expression, in which
. . . the language itself is inseparable from, or essentially

a part of, the thought'.[1] And this kind of expression, we must recognize, can take many unexpected forms, can conceal insight within seeming nonsense, can work through obscurity or through suggestive hints cryptically worded. One cannot reasonably demand of the sage that he should not only have an insight to convey, but should also train himself to convey it in the simplest and directest form; and more important than this, there is no assurance whatever that simplicity and directness will be his most telling form of expression, or even that they may not cause his perhaps elusive message somehow to evanesce. But, time and time again, it becomes clear that however oblique and confusing the sage's language, his message finds part of its sanction, and maybe the only solid part, in what we actually see or feel: in our environment or our emotions. Certainly all the six authors this book has been concerned with have something to say, not simply about abstractions or theories, but about ordinary experience of the ordinary world. They may say that it is not ordinary, and this, or what they say beyond this, may be confused or even false (though it is open to question whether the sense of 'true' or 'false' relevant in this field of thought is something we fully understand); and of course readers may find that some of the sages discussed in this book are of much more interest to them than others. But the point of really general significance which emerges from considering them all, is that if they do have an interest as sages, it is largely or entirely this impingement upon ordinary life which gives it to them.

[1] Essay on Coleridge, *Appreciations*, p. 93.

APPENDIX

KEY TO EDITIONS AND ABBREVIATIONS

CHAPTERS II AND III

References are to the Standard Edition of Carlyle's Works (18 vols.), Chapman and Hall, London, 1903–4. The following abbreviations have been used in footnotes to the text:

CL *Cromwell's Letters and Speeches* (1845)
FG *Frederick the Great* (1858–65, 6 vols.)
FR *The French Revolution* (1837)
HH *Heroes and Hero-Worship* (1841)
JS *The Life of John Sterling* (1851)
LDP *Latter-Day Pamphlets* (1850)
Niagara *Shooting Niagara — and After?* (1867)
PP *Past and Present* (1843)
— *Portraits of John Knox* (1875)
SR *Sartor Resartus* (first book publication, 1836)
TN *Two Notebooks of Thomas Carlyle*, ed. C. E. Norton, New York (The Grolier Club), 1898

CHAPTER IV

References to Disraeli's Novels are to the Collected Edition, Longmans Green, 1878; those to Disraeli's other works to the volume *Whigs and Whiggism*, ed. W. Hutcheon, Murray, 1913. The following abbreviations are used:

C *Coningsby* (1844)
CF *Contarini Fleming* (1832)
HT *Henrietta Temple* (1837)
— *Endymion* (1880)
L *Lothair* (1870)
S *Sybil* (1845)
T *Tancred* (1847)
V *Venetia* (1837)
VG *Vivian Gray* (1826–7)

YD *The Young Duke* (1831)
WW *Whigs and Whiggism*

CHAPTER V

References are to the standard uniform edition of George Eliot's works, published (n.d.) by Blackwood and Sons, Edinburgh and London. The following abbreviations are used :

    AB *Adam Bede* (1859)
    DD *Daniel Deronda* (1874–6)
    FH *Felix Holt* (1866)
    MF *The Mill on the Floss* (1860)
    Mid. *Middlemarch* (1871–2)
    R *Romola* (1863)
    SCL *Scenes of Clerical Life* (1858)
    SM *Silas Marner* (1861)
    TS *Impressions of Theophrastus Such* (1879)

CHAPTER VI

The editions to which references have been made are given in the list of abbreviations below :

AVS *Apologia pro Vita sua* (1864) ; references to Everyman Library edition.

DA. i   *The Difficulties of Anglicans.* Volume i contains the *Lectures*
DA. ii   originally delivered under this title in 1850 (references to the 4th edition). Volume ii contains *A Letter to Dr. Pusey* (1866), and *A Letter to the Duke of Norfolk* (1875), abbreviated here to LDN. References are to the 1876 edition.

DCD *The Development of Christian Doctrine* (1845) ; references to 1878 edition.

GA *An Essay in Aid of a Grammar of Assent* (1870) ; references to 5th edition, 1881.

— *Loss and Gain* (1848) ; references to 1st edition.

PPC *The Present Position of Catholics in England* (1851) ; references to 5th edition.

— *Sermons Preached on Various Occasions* ; references to 1857 edition.

UE *On the Scope and Nature of University Education* (1852) ; references to Everyman Library edition.

CHAPTER VII

References quote the volume and page of the de Luxe Edition of Arnold's Works (15 vols.), Macmillans, London, 1903. The following abbreviations are used :

CA   *Culture and Anarchy* (1869)
DA   *Discourses in America* (1885)
EC. i   *Essays in Criticism, First Series* (1865)
FE   *A French Eton* (1864)
FG   *Friendship's Garland* (1871)
LD   *Literature and Dogma* (1873)
ME   *Mixed Essays* (1879)
St. P.   *St. Paul and Protestantism* (1870)

CHAPTER VIII

References are to the Wessex Edition of Hardy's Works (22 vols.), Macmillans, London, 1920–26. The following abbreviations are used :

—   *A Changed Man and other Tales* (collected 1913)
DR   *Desperate Remedies* (1871)
FMC   *Far from the Madding Crowd* (1874)
HE   *The Hand of Ethelberta* (1876)
JO   *Jude the Obscure* (1896)
L   *A Laodicean* (1881)
MC   *The Mayor of Casterbridge* (1886)
PBE   *A Pair of Blue Eyes* (1873)
RN   *The Return of the Native* (1878)
TD   *Tess of the D'Urbervilles* (1891)
TM   *The Trumpet Major* (1880)
TT   *Two on a Tower* (1882)
UGT   *Under the Greenwood Tree* (1872)
W   *The Woodlanders* (1887)
WB   *The Well-Beloved* (1897 : serial publication 1892)
—   *Wessex Tales* (1888)

INDEX

This index refers only to the more extended discussions of individual books, parts of books, or general points. The reader should in the first instance consult the Table of Contents.

LITERATURE IN THE NORTON LIBRARY